THE
EVERYTHING
CROSSWORD
AND
PUZZLE BOOK

THE EVERYTHING®

CROSSWORD

AND PUZZLE BOOK

Hours of brain-teasing fun—crossword puzzles, acrostics, hidden words and more, for puzzlers at all levels

Harold Cordry

Adams Media Corporation
AVON, MASSACHUSETTS

An Everything® Series Book.
Everything® and everything.com® are registered trademarks
of F+W Publications, Inc.

Published by Adams Media, an F+W Publications Company
57 Littlefield Street, Avon MA 02322. U.S.A.
www.adamsmedia.com
ISBN 13: 978-1-55850-764-7
ISBN 10: 1-55850-764-7

Printed in the United States of America.

T S R Q P O

Thanks are due to the following for the permission to use the material indicated:
    Crossword Puzzles, Copyright© Tribune Media Services. All rights reserved.
Reprinted with permission.
    Acrostics, reprinted from *Official's Variety Puzzles,* are used by kind permission of Official Publications. If you are interested in subscribing to *Official's Variety Puzzles,* please write to Official Publications, Dept. 5, P.O. Box 2021, Marion, OH 43302. Copyright© 1994.

This book is available at quantity discounts for bulk purchases.
For information, call 1-800-289-0963.

Visit the entire Everything® series at everything.com.

CONTENTS

INTRODUCTION

Words, proverbially, are wind. They pay no debts, butter no parsnips, cook no rice, build no walls. As Shakespeare put it, summing up, "Words, words, words."

But proverbs, being shifty things, fit every occasion. So words, occasionally, are said to be tools, and though not deeds themselves, are means to an end, the wings of action, even the foundation upon which nations are built. And they are, too, occasionally, weapons, causing pain, offense, provoking a snit, perhaps, or a world war.

Proverbs don't speak of words as playthings. Many proverbs, though, some of them thousands of years old, are themselves pieces of wordplay, and especially of punning, that lowest form of humor.

Words are playthings, of course (among other things). Just as blocks and miniature space aliens entertain us in childhood, so do words, as words, entertain us in our adult years. To take a delight in reading a novel or a short story in a magazine, and especially a poem, is to take delight not only in its content but in its form as well, in the choice of words and in their arrangement. But the idea of wordplay goes beyond this. For example:

- The quotation from Shakespeare in the first paragraph— "Words, words, words." You might observe that he managed to say a lot in three words (three words, each of which is words).
- When a national magazine announced it would trim its circulation by eliminating low-income subscribers and thereby increase profits, the headline over the story in one newspaper was Weed 'em and Reap (punning with cardplaying's Read 'em and Weep).
- A sign on the door of a watch repair shop: "Out to unwind. Back in 15 minutes."
- A Dear Abby response to a woman who wanted to know what to do about knobby knees: "As long as they get you where you're going—don't knock 'em."
- From a church bulletin: "If you realize that you aren't as wise today as you thought you were yesterday, then you're wiser today."

- One of the classic headlines of all time: T***, Inc., Makes Offer to Screw Co. Stockholders (that is, to the stockholders of a company that manufactures screws).
- And another: Jerk Injures Neck.

Of course, you've probably heard about the crossword puzzle addict who died and was buried six feet down and three across. But you get the idea. Any of the foregoing examples, expressed in different words, would cease to be funny (or witty, or whatever they happen to be).

The possibilities for wordplay are seemingly limitless, and we exploit them with abandon. We play with language the way we played with our food, pushing the bland and squishy aside, isolating the unfamiliar, poking at it, testing its consistency between thumb and forefinger, trying it on the tip of the tongue. Perhaps, by way of research, inquiring of the cook precisely what it is, where it came from, why it's here (as opposed to being still there, where it might better have remained).

And what makes you go even further, those of you who beguile the hours by writing letters inside little boxes? Why the delight in putting words together so that they form other words? Why this manic obsession with reading DOWN a language that was intended to be read ACROSS? "Always left to right, please. No pointing. No moving the lips." (By the way, what, precisely, is wrong with pointing at words and moving the lips?)

What about our forebears? Not bears that preceded us but fore-be-'ers—it's a Middle English word—people who were, who existed, before us. (Unless of course you happen to be thinking about the antecedents of a bear, in which case they would be, quite literally, fore-bears.) But bears or not, did our forefathers (and foremothers, too, of course) have this same fascination with words and letters? Did they pass the time by chewing on pencils and playing word games when they ought to have been out besieging some castle or otherwise promoting the advance of civilization?

The short answer is no. (It has only two letters). The longer answer is yes (which has three). The fascination existed, to be sure, but it manifested itself differently, and relatively few people were held in its grip.

Archaeologists have found no prehistoric petroglyphs (Greek petra, rock + glyphe, carving) of crossword puzzles. (Alas, just think how much more impressive that would have been than merely doing them in ink.) Nor has excavation of the pyramids yielded a single fill-in or mixer. No connect-the-dots, no rebus. Not even a vanity license plate.

But acrostics date at least to the Erythraean sibyl (mentioned by Plato), to whose prophecies the term was first applied. She wrote them on loose leaves, in Greek hexameters, and when they were correctly sorted the initial letter of each line combined to spell a word. Hence, acrostic (Greek akros, outermost, etc. + stichos, line).

The same technique was used in the Old Testament. In the 119th Psalm, for example, the stanzas begin with sequential letters of the Hebrew alphabet. It's known, by the way, as the Abecedarian Psalm, abecedarian meaning like or relating to the alphabet. Notice, too, that the word abecedarian is similar to the word alphabet, each containing the alphabet's beginning letters: A-Be-Ce-Darian and Alpha-Bet(a).

Palindromes were popular in ancient Rome. Lawyers liked this one: "Si nummi immunis," which carries the same message right to left as it does from left to right—If you pay you will go free.

Also traceable to ancient times is the word square, the most famous being the so-called SATOR square.

```
R O T A S
O P E R A
T E N E T
A R E P O
S A T O R
```

The square was discovered in England in 1868, in a church in Cirencester built by the Romans in about 300 A.D. Arepo, the only non-Latin word in the square, is Celtic for a plough, but it is presumed to be a name. (The same square was found in 1936 inscribed on plaster in the ruins of Pompeii, which was destroyed in an eruption of Vesuvius in 79 A.D.)

The square has been translated variously as "Arepo, the sower, watches over his works," "The sower Arepo holds the wheels at work," "Arepo the sower holds the wheels with force," etc.

Notice that ROTAS and SATOR are palindromes—each, spelled backward, becomes the other—and that the square may be read in four directions. It's also been pointed out that if one starts reading at the S's

there are four ways of reaching SATOR OPERA TENET ("The Creator maintains his works"), and that SATOR OPERA TENET is an anagram of PATER NOSTER A (ET) O—Our Father, Alpha and Omega (beginning and end), and that the letters could be arranged in the shape of a cross:

```
             A
             P
             A
             T
             E
             R
   APATERNOSTERO
             O
             S
             T
             E
             R
             O
```

It was also suggested that the square was intended to be used as a cure for toothaches. For the magic to work, the sufferer had to eat the words—literally. So they were to be written on pieces of bread and butter, which would be the vehicles of their consumption. This theory draws support from the fact that the only examples of the word square so far discovered by archaeologists have been engraved or written on walls, all the edible examples having perhaps been eaten.

Riddles, too, have roots deep in the past. As Kevin Crossley-Holland puts it, "The business of naming began with the Creation; the business of deceiving followed soon after, in the Garden of Eden."

Among the best known is the riddle posed by Samson to the Philistines: "Out of the eater came forth meat and out of the strong came forth sweetness," based on his having seen a swarm of bees making honey in the carcass of a lion. They answered it correctly, with the help of Delilah, and Samson's wrath resulted in the deaths of thousands of Philistines.

In the Greek legend of Oedipus, you may recall, a less than good-natured Sphinx confronted Oedipus on his way to Thebes and posed the following riddle: "What walks on four legs in the morning, two legs in the afternoon, and three legs in the evening?" He answered it correctly. "It is man," he said, "who crawls as a child, walks upright in his prime, and uses a cane in old age." Whereupon the Sphinx committed suicide, and Oedipus, who had already killed the King of Thebes, not knowing that he was his father, then married the queen, Jocasta, who he later found to be his mother. When the truth came to light, Jocasta hanged herself and Oedipus tore out his own eyes.

Such dismal experiences aside, the Greeks delighted in riddles. They were primarily entertainment, to be sure—riddles were standard fare at banquets. But to the Greek they were more than mere entertainment. The Greeks placed high value on skill in riddling, which they regarded as a measure of intelligence and of the quality of one's education.

Riddles were common elements in the life and legend of virtually every other culture. The Egyptians liked them, and they are found in important early Persian writings, for example, and in sacred works of Hinduism.

The Victorians are said to have been especially fond of wordplay. It was they, according to Roger Millington (Crossword Puzzles: Their History and Their Cult), who introduced acrostic puzzles. The following "Acrostic Charade" by Rev. J. Bradley appeared in 1856 in The Illustrated London News.

The Words

> A mighty centre of woe and wealth;
> A world in little, a kingdom small.
> A tainted scenter, a foe to health;
> A quiet way for a wooden wall.
> Find out these words as soon as you can, sir,
> And then you'll have found the Acrostic's answer.

The Letters

> Untax'd I brighten the poor man's home—
> My wings wave over the beauty's brow—
> I steal by St. Petersburgh's gilded dome—
> While Bomba's subjects below me bow.
> A Cook has reason to dread my name,
> Though I carry the tidings of pride and shame.

Bradley precedes the solution with a third verse explaining his clues:

The Words

London's the 'world in little'; make a
note on't, Thames is its —cesspool;
that's the long and short on't

The Answer

The Letters

At State receptions in day's untaxed
    Light,
Are Ostrich plumes a fair and goodly
    sight.
The Neva with old Thames will ne-ver
    cope,
Though Despotism dwell in Naples
    soap.
As for poor Cook? O-why-hee must
    excuse
The tale of his sad fate; 'tis now no
    News.

The crossword puzzle was attributed indirectly to the English by its inventor, Arthur Wynne of the New York World, who said that as a child in Liverpool he'd seen something similar. In any event, his own version was an immediate hit. If you'd like to try your hand at the first crossword—or "word-cross," as it was called—here it is.

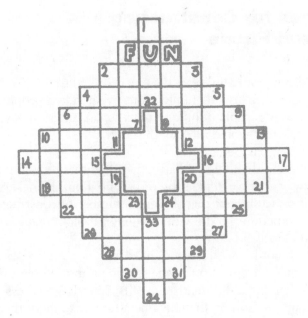

Clues:

2-3   What bargain hunters enjoy

4-5   A written acknowledgment

6-7   Such and nothing more

10-11   A bird

14-15   Opposed to less

18-19   What this puzzle is

22-23   An animal of prey

26-27   The close of day

28-29   To elude

30-31   The plural of is

8-9   To cultivate

12-13   A bar of wood or iron

16-17   What artists learn to do

20-21   Fastened

24-25   Found on the seashore

10-18   The fiber of the gomuti palm

6-22   What we all should be

4-26   A day dream

2-11   A talon

19-28   A pigeon

F-7   Part of your head

23-30   A river in Russia

1-32   To govern

33-34   An aromatic plant

N-8   A fist

24-31   To agree with

3-12   Part of a ship

20-29   One

5-27   Exchanging

9-25   To sink in mud

13-21   A boy

Answer on page 268.

Guidelines for Constructing a Crossword Puzzle

Eugene T. Maleska, for many years the crossword editor of The New York Times, once estimated that only about five hundred people in the entire country were capable of putting together an American-style crossword puzzle that would meet all the criteria.

That's not very encouraging.

But having said that, and perhaps concerned that he might be frightening away a whole generation of potential puzzle-makers, Maleska went on to suggest that the small number of constructors probably had something to do with how few people actually were aware of all the do's and don'ts.

On which point he was clearly right. After all, most constructors are simply former solvers who for one reason or another have decided to try their hand at a different stage of the puzzling process—the production stage. As solvers they became aware of some of the rules by which puzzles are created but not necessarily all of them. So if you fall into this category, the best first step is to familiarize yourself with the criteria by which crosswords are judged.

The Basics

Will Shortz, the puzzle editor of *The New York Times,* offers these basic rules:

- The pattern of black and white squares must be symmetrical. Generally this rule means that if you turn the grid upside-down, the pattern will look the same as it does right-side-up.
- Do not use too many black squares. In the old days of puzzles, black squares were not allowed to occupy more than 16 percent of a grid. Nowadays there is no strict limit, in order to allow maximum flexibility for the placement of theme entries. Still, "cheater" black squares (ones that do not affect the number of words in the puzzle, but are added to make constructing

easier) should be kept to a minimum, and large clumps of black squares anywhere in a grid are strongly discouraged.

- Do not use unkeyed letters (letters that appear in only one word across or down). In fairness to solvers, every letter has to appear in both an Across and a Down word.
- Do not use two-letter words. The minimum word length is three letters.
- The grid must have all-over interlock. In other words, the black squares may not cut the grid up into separate pieces. A solver, theoretically, should be able to proceed from any section of the grid to any other without having to stop and start over.
- Long theme entries must be symmetrically placed. If there is a major theme entry three rows down from the top of the grid, for instance, then there must be another theme entry in the same position three rows up from the bottom. Also, as a general rule, no non-theme entry should be longer than any theme entry.
- Do not repeat words in the grid.
- Do not make up words and phrases. Every answer must have a reference or else be in common use in everyday speech or writing.

Additional Guidelines

The preceding list of rules, which is sent out to persons who inquire about guidelines for contributors, is accompanied by a style sheet of "special rules" applying only to The Times. But with one or two exceptions this second set of rules simply establishes more discriminating criteria by which a puzzle is to be judged, no matter where it is submitted.

With regard to themed puzzles (which Shortz likes), the specifications call for themes that are "fresh, interesting, narrowly defined and consistently applied throughout the puzzle." Moreover, the themes should be "accessible to everyone."

Puzzles "should emphasize lively words and names and fresh phrases," and The Times encourages use of "phrases from everyday writing and speech, whether or not they're in the dictionary," as well as a scattering of lesser-used letters—"J, Q, X, Z, K, W, etc."

Brand names are acceptable if they're "well-known nationally" and used "in moderation." (But some more traditional puzzle editors won't accept them, so check before you begin construction.)

In an ideal puzzle the clues should "provide a well-balanced test of vocabulary and knowledge," ranging from such subjects as classical music and mythology to "movies, TV, popular music, sports and names in the news." Further, "clues should be precise, accurate, colorful and imaginative," with puns and humor "welcome."

But "partial phrases longer than five letters (ONE TO A, A STITCH IN, etc.)" are not welcome, nor is "uninteresting obscurity," uncommon abbreviations or uncommon foreign words. "Crosswordese" must be kept to a minimum.

If difficult words are used they must be interesting or useful additions to one's vocabulary. But obscure words should never cross each other. Difficult crossings, "blind crossings," are considered unfair to solvers.

The maximum word count for The Times, by the way, is 78 for a themed 15x15 (72 if unthemed), 140 for a 21x21, and 168 for a 23x23.

Magazine Editorial Services, which provides crosswords to a number of puzzle magazines, has the same specifications for 15x15 puzzles but accepts a maximum of 150 entries for a 21x21. MES also takes 19x19's, with a maximum of 130 entries. Themed puzzles are more likely to be accepted, provided the theme is more imaginative than dogs, colors, trees, etc.

(Send submissions to Magazine Editorial Services, 7002 W. Butler Pike #100, Ambler, PA 19002.)

Another "don't"—perhaps it's really a "don't-unless-you-have-to"—comes from the Random House Puzzle Maker's Handbook, whose authors caution against excessive use of plurals, third-person singular forms (ending in -s), verbs in past tense (ending in -ed), and words beginning with re- or in-.

Finally, as Maleska points out, constructors have always adhered to an unwritten rule prohibiting words related to disease, bodily functions, drug addiction, violence, and vulgarity. The point, he says, is that most solvers do puzzles partly to escape from such matters.

CHAPTER 1

ACROSTICS

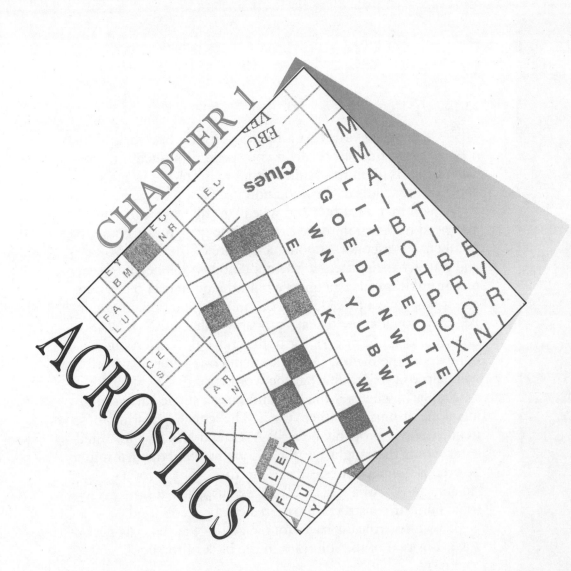

I f these are your first acrostics you may find them difficult at first, especially if you spend too much time trying to fill in the blanks without also trying to guess some of the words in the quotation itself.

As you may already know, when you fill in a word you'll also need to pencil in those letters in the grid, making sure the numbers correspond. As you guess more of the clued words and transfer their letters to the quotation, you'll begin to see recognizable words emerging within the quotation. For example, if you have a three-letter word in the quotation ending in AS, then you'll know that it's probably either HAS or WAS. So pencil in an H or a W (or both) above the corresponding numbers in the blanks. Often, knowing one letter of a word will help you to decide what the word is.

Similarly, wherever the quotation has a single letter standing alone, it must be either A or I. The letters appearing most frequently will probably be E, T, A, O, and N. Look for three-letter words that might be "the." Look for patterns that might be prepositional phrases, such as "to the _____," "for a _____," "in an _____," "of a _____." You'll be surprised at how easily some familiar construction patterns can be recognized.

If you nevertheless have trouble getting started, just peek at a word or two of the solutions in the back of the book.

Enjoy.

Answers begin on page 268.

1

A. Diamond judges, for short . . . .
124 76 4 80

B. Lucy's best friend . . . .
25 117 91 45 5

C. Coaxed, using flattery . . . .
36 38 114 32 44 57 54

D. Show deference . . . .
43 88 83 35 82 18

E. Stress . . . .
13 58 1 60 34 116 85 99

F. "Portnoy's Complaint" author . . . .
103 74 90 111

G. Easy victory, informally . . . .
42 79 70 23 28 19 95 121

H. Desire for food . . . .
16 102 125 71 59 107 27 10

I. Told the teacher . . . .
100 47 86 66 106 112 11

J. Sleeve ends . . . .
120 115 87 73 20

K. Bird of prey . . . .
64 61 78 9

L. Impede, legally . . . .
2 26 31 104 118

M. Scull's kin . . . .
75 3 67 93 98 65 81

N. Feature of olden desks . . . .
122 108 39 63 6 53 48

O. Zilch . . . .
40 101 17 37 119 113 109

P. Small pastries . . . .
123 84 69 21 8

Q. Nun's wear . . . .
15 94 24 50 97

R. Beset by conflict . . . .
77 12 46 29 110 51 96 92 72

S. Observe . . . .
14 7 55 33 22

T. Bagel, e.g.
89 68 105 49

U. Adolescence . . . .
30 52 41 62 56

1 E	2 L	3 M	4 A	5 B	6 N		7 S	8 P	9 K	10 H	11 I		12 R	13 E		14 S	15 Q	16 H	17 O		18 D	19 G
20 J		21 P	22 S	23 G		24 Q	25 B	26 L	27 H		28 G	29 R	30 U		31 L	32 C		33 S	34 E	35 D	36 C	37 O
	38 C		39 N	40 O	41 U	42 G	43 D	44 C	45 B		46 R	47 I	48 N	49 J		50 Q		51 R	52 U	53 N	54 C
55 S	56 U	57 C	58 E		59 H	60 E	61 K	62 U		63 N	64 K	65 M	66 I		67 M	68 T	69 P	70 G	71 H	72 R		73 J
74 F	75 M		76 A	77 R		78 K	79 G	80 A		81 M	82 D		83 D	84 P	85 E	86 I		87 J	88 D	89 T		90 F
91 B	92 R		93 M	94 Q	95 G	96 R		97 Q	98 M		99 E	100 I	101 O	102 H		103 F	104 L	105 T	106 I	107 H	108 N	109 O
	110 R	111 F	112 I	113 O		114 C	115 J	116 E	117 B		118 L	119 O	120 J	121 G		122 N	123 P		124 A	125 H

2

A. Most yielding . . . .
　2　9　77　145　105　55　43

B. May horse race: 2 wds. . . . .
　24　61　74　50　20　101　16　11　33　32　49　123　122

C. 1960 film about the Scopes trial: 3 wds. . . . .
　127　152　67　48　139　96　114　8　51　65　107　25　103　113

D. Rocky and Bullwinkle's foe . . . .
　69　85　144　45　27　136　71

E. Hula wear: 2 wds. . . . .
　47　80　147　26　72　13　23　54　35　66

F. Tact: hyph. . . . .
　7　34　126　4　88　38　76　111　68　82　120

G. State claimed by India and Pakistan . . . . .
　95　18　106　3　40　138　121

H. Cause a blush . . . .
　137　133　92　78　87　5　83　42　100

I. Circus performer: 2 wds. . . . .
　14　150　131　29　110　75　64　116　10

J. January 1994 event in L.A. . . . .
　125　1　118　30　60　19　93　41　36　109

K. Unstated . . . .
　53　73　148　117　58

L. Surveillance . . . .
　151　104　62　99　124　119　102　135　28　81　56

M. Polaris: 2 wds. . . . .
　142　57　86　94　115　98　59　52　132

N. Issue in Word C . . . .
　22　44　17　63　149　79　140　112　12　97　84

O. Turn on an axis . . . .
　146　39　128　89　6　108

P. Crude representation of an enemy . . . . . .
　91　130　37　21　70　129

Q. Doing the dishes . . . .
　141　143　134　31　15　46　90

1 J		2 A	3 G	4 F	5 H	6 O		7 F	8 C	9 A	10 I	11 B		12 N	13 E		14 I	15 Q	16 B	17 N		18 G
	19 J	20 B	21 P	22 N	23 E		24 B	25 C	26 E	27 D		28 L	29 I		30 J	31 Q	32 B		33 B	34 F	35 E	36 J
	37 P	38 F	39 O	40 G		41 J		42 H	43 A	44 N	45 D	46 Q	47 E	48 C	49 B		50 B	51 C	52 M	53 K		54 E
55 A		56 L	57 M	58 K		59 M	60 J	61 B		62 L	63 N	64 I	65 C		66 E	67 C	68 F	69 D	70 P		71 D	72 E
	73 K	74 B		75 I	76 F	77 A	78 H	79 N	80 E		81 L	82 F		83 H		84 N	85 D	86 M	87 H	88 F	89 O	90 Q
91 P		92 H	93 J	94 M		95 G	96 C	97 N	98 M	99 L	100 H		101 B	102 L	103 C		104 L	105 A		106 G	107 C	108 O
109 J	110 I		111 F	112 N	113 C		114 C	115 M	116 I	117 K	118 J		119 L	120 F	121 G	122 B		123 B	124 L	125 J	126 F	127 C
128 O	129 P		130 P	131 I	132 M	133 H	134 Q		135 L	136 D	137 H	138 G	139 C		140 N	141 Q	142 M		143 Q	144 D	145 A	146 O
147 E	148 K	149 N	150 I	151 L	152 C																

3

A. Writes quickly . . . .
$\overline{69}$ $\overline{9}$ $\overline{19}$ $\overline{108}$

B. Shakespearean play . . . .
$\overline{36}$ $\overline{135}$ $\overline{2}$ $\overline{111}$ $\overline{95}$ $\overline{158}$ $\overline{47}$

C. 50th U.S. state . . . .
$\overline{27}$ $\overline{133}$ $\overline{1}$ $\overline{87}$ $\overline{91}$ $\overline{53}$

D. Cuddled . . . .
$\overline{127}$ $\overline{70}$ $\overline{17}$ $\overline{54}$ $\overline{10}$ $\overline{116}$ $\overline{149}$

E. Rural burg, slangily: 2 wds. . . . .
$\overline{93}$ $\overline{89}$ $\overline{12}$ $\overline{75}$ $\overline{85}$ $\overline{155}$ $\overline{37}$

F. Knocked . . . .
$\overline{154}$ $\overline{16}$ $\overline{103}$ $\overline{45}$ $\overline{161}$ $\overline{119}$

G. Left out . . . .
$\overline{141}$ $\overline{7}$ $\overline{105}$ $\overline{61}$ $\overline{99}$ $\overline{24}$ $\overline{48}$

H. Breaks to bits . . . .
$\overline{56}$ $\overline{125}$ $\overline{63}$ $\overline{123}$ $\overline{132}$ $\overline{92}$ $\overline{52}$ $\overline{30}$

I. Recoil . . . .
$\overline{110}$ $\overline{29}$ $\overline{40}$ $\overline{128}$ $\overline{163}$ $\overline{18}$ $\overline{78}$ $\overline{65}$

J. 1990 Lawrence Kasdan film: 5 wds. . . . . . .
$\overline{120}$ $\overline{162}$ $\overline{153}$ $\overline{90}$ $\overline{51}$ $\overline{13}$ $\overline{156}$ $\overline{142}$ $\overline{34}$ $\overline{136}$ $\overline{60}$ $\overline{77}$ $\overline{113}$ $\overline{124}$
$\overline{20}$

K. Calls forth . . . .
$\overline{44}$ $\overline{96}$ $\overline{126}$ $\overline{112}$ $\overline{21}$ $\overline{143}$ $\overline{5}$

L. Cereal grass . . . .
$\overline{160}$ $\overline{150}$ $\overline{86}$ $\overline{8}$ $\overline{23}$ $\overline{114}$ $\overline{88}$

M. Submarine bomb: 2 wds. . . . .
$\overline{98}$ $\overline{118}$ $\overline{38}$ $\overline{83}$ $\overline{100}$ $\overline{71}$ $\overline{76}$ $\overline{144}$ $\overline{137}$ $\overline{26}$ $\overline{66}$

N. Began . . . .
$\overline{81}$ $\overline{14}$ $\overline{25}$ $\overline{104}$ $\overline{55}$ $\overline{58}$ $\overline{152}$ $\overline{101}$ $\overline{121}$

O. Scolded . . . .
$\overline{50}$ $\overline{130}$ $\overline{39}$ $\overline{11}$ $\overline{148}$ $\overline{159}$

P. Stormy . . . .
$\overline{64}$ $\overline{3}$ $\overline{32}$ $\overline{82}$ $\overline{146}$ $\overline{57}$ $\overline{72}$ $\overline{49}$ $\overline{102}$ $\overline{157}$ $\overline{22}$

Q. Spain's peninsula . . . .
$\overline{107}$ $\overline{140}$ $\overline{68}$ $\overline{43}$ $\overline{59}$ $\overline{94}$ $\overline{145}$

R. "_ Christian Soldiers" . . . .
$\overline{33}$ $\overline{4}$ $\overline{15}$ $\overline{131}$ $\overline{80}$ $\overline{74}$

S. Least ingratiating . . . .
$\overline{122}$ $\overline{139}$ $\overline{115}$ $\overline{109}$ $\overline{35}$ $\overline{97}$ $\overline{134}$ $\overline{129}$

T. Following . . . .
$\overline{6}$ $\overline{84}$ $\overline{41}$ $\overline{73}$ $\overline{46}$

U. "I Got _" . . . .
$\overline{67}$ $\overline{62}$ $\overline{138}$ $\overline{28}$ $\overline{117}$ $\overline{106}$

V. Desert plant . . . .
$\overline{147}$ $\overline{42}$ $\overline{151}$ $\overline{79}$ $\overline{31}$

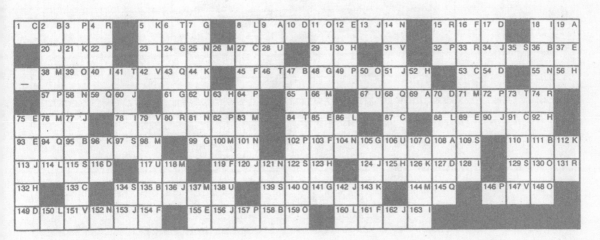

1 C	2 B	3 P	4 R		5 K	6 T	7 G		8 L	9 A	10 D	11 O	12 E	13 J	14 N		15 R	16 F	17 D		18 I	19 A
	20 J	21 K	22 P		23 L	24 G	25 N	26 M	27 C	28 U		29 I	30 H		31 V		32 P	33 R	34 J	35 S	36 B	37 E
—	38 M	39 O	40 I	41 T	42 V	43 Q	44 K		45 F	46 T	47 B	48 G	49 P	50 O	51 J	52 H		53 C	54 D		55 N	56 H
	57 P	58 N	59 Q	60 J		61 G	62 U	63 H	64 P		65 I	66 M		67 U	68 Q	69 A	70 D	71 M	72 P	73 T	74 R	
75 E	76 M	77 J		78 I	79 V	80 R	81 N	82 P	83 M		84 T	85 E	86 L		87 C		88 L	89 E	90 J	91 C	92 H
93 E	94 Q	95 B	96 K	97 S	98 M		99 G	100 M	101 N	102 P	103 F	104 N	105 G	106 U	107 Q	108 A	109 S		110 I	111 B	112 K
113 J	114 L	115 S	116 D		117 U	118 M		119 F	120 J	121 N	122 S	123 H		124 J	125 H	126 K	127 D	128 I		129 S	130 O	131 R
132 H		133 C		134 S	135 B	136 J	137 M	138 U		139 S	140 Q	141 G	142 J	143 K		144 M	145 Q		146 P	147 V	148 O
149 D	150 L	151 V	152 N	153 J	154 F		155 E	156 J	157 P	158 B	159 O		160 L	161 F	162 J	163 I					

4

A. Crouched fearfully . . . .

B. Sobber's sound . . . .
103 27 137 94 142 18 57

C. Atlanta University . . . .
132 179 161 75 81 65

D. SoHo home . . . .
15 144 168 135 83

E. Harbor noisemakers . . . .
184 127 147 82

F. Emulated Siskel and Ebert . . . .
177 182 129 96 52 134 24 10

G. Trojan War hero . . . .
36 130 115 44 63 186 30 74

H. Best Picture of 1939: 4 wds. . . . .
105 106 62 99 183 77 6 69

4 35 139 120 92 146 152 164 26 45 40 162 171 51

189

I. Love and hate, e.g. . . . .
50 180 37 11 56 87 14 155

J. Diverse collection . . . .
9 19 118 133 7 21 34 90 124 163

K. Chablis and Meursault, e.g. . . . .
153 29 5 54 148 8 23 160 49 39

L. Causes immense distress . . . .
46 3 31 85 138 101 111 176 173

M. Coward's color . . . .
185 117 145 80 72 86

N. There are no atheists there, they say . . . .
60 136 66 104 84 126 159 48

O. Settles down in the chicken coop . . . .
121 169 59 79 20 108

P. Best Picture of 1954: 3 wds. . . . .
187 128 172 22 109 67 123 61 112 178 158 150 114 100

28

Q. "Love Takes Time" singer: 2 wds. . . . . . .
113 33 98 157 41 181 174 154 91 122 125

R. 1967 Gaye-Weston duet: 3 wds. . . . .
116 70 1 107 170 97 55 43 119 149

S. Major roads . . . .
110 93 188 17 143 175 25 12 64 165 131 58 42

T. Simply terrible . . . .
2 71 141 102 156

U. Line parallel to the equator . . . .
78 16 167 151 166 38 89 68

V. Pole-to-pole line . . . .
32 73 88 140 76 95 53 47 13

1 R	2 T	3 L	4 H	5 K	6 G	7 J		8 K	9 J	10 E		11 I	12 S	13 V		14 I	15 C	16 U	17 S	18 A	19 J	20 O
	21 J	22 P	23 K	24 E	25 S		26 H	27 A		28 P	29 K	30 F		31 L	32 V	33 Q	34 J	35 H	36 F	37 I	38 U	39 K
	40 H	41 Q	42 S	43 R		44 F		45 H	46 L	47 V		48 N	49 K	50 I	51 H		52 E	53 V	54 K	55 R	56 I	57 A
58 S		59 O	60 N		61 P	62 G	63 F		64 S	65 B	66 N		67 P	68 U	69 G	70 R	71 T	72 M	73 V	74 F		75 B
76 V	77 G	78 U	79 O		80 M	81 B	82 D		83 C	84 N	85 L		86 M	87 I	88 V	89 U	90 J	91 Q		92 H	93 S	94 A
95 V	96 E	97 Q	98 Q		99 G	100 P		101 L	102 T	103 A	104 N		105 G		106 G	107 R	108 O	109 P		110 S	111 P	112 P
	113 Q	114 P	115 F	116 R	117 M	118 J		119 R	120 H	121 O	122 Q		123 P	124 J	125 Q		126 N	127 D	128 P	129 E	130 P	131 S
	132 B	133 J	134 E	135 C	136 N	137 A	138 L	139 H	140 V		141 T	142 A	143 S	144 C		145 M	146 H	147 D	148 K		149 R	150 P
	151 U	152 H		153 K	154 Q	155 I		156 T	157 Q	158 P	159 N		160 K	161 B	162 H		163 J	164 H	165 S	166 U		167 U
168 C	169 O	170 R		171 H	172 P	173 L		174 O	175 S	176 L		177 E	178 P	179 B	180 I		181 Q	182 E	183 G	184 D	185 M	186 F
187 P	188 S	189 H																			

5

A. Unforgettable . . . .
24 3 128 86 153 118 120 179 183

B. Snow slide . . . .
39 167 83 148 51 10 108 117 124

C. Affinity . . . .
184 155 8 141 57 34 126

D. "And __ hangs a tale" . . . .
136 170 100 188 121 161 89

E. Repeated . . . .
178 164 122 38 33 97 71 111

F. Needful . . . .
113 166 156 143 181 80 65 87 50

G. Figures of speech . . . .
52 63 152 160 7 134 47 174 125

H. Green light: hyph. . . . .
11 162 103 2 158 112 32

I. Get more singles . . . .
109 23 133 151 61 74

J. Lots . . . .
49 129 106 44 77 14 150 165

K. Sure . . . .
144 131 147 41 27 115 88 168

L. __ boy (scapegoat) . . . .
76 185 149 84 182 145 110 15

M. Tads and lads . . . .
96 186 171 62 79 75 90 107 31 36

N. Bedside stand: 2 wds. . . . .
123 73 28 157 138 116 135 67 60 35

O. Detach . . . .
187 172 92 6 139 55 180 78

P. Confined . . . .
40 154 169 46

Q. Made level with wedges . . . .
119 22 9 177 99 142 173

R. Establishes . . . .
26 66 140 95 137 1 58 19 68 69

S. With skill . . . .
176 102 18 59 5 56

T. Productive . . . .
70 94 81 53 64 13 21 146 130

U. Insists upon . . . .
42 175 25 45 48 114 101

V. Meddlesome . . . .
37 4 85 98 104 93 17 163 16

W. Keeps back . . . .
12 30 43 105 20 91 82 132 54

X. Pen points . . . .
72 127 29 159

1 R	2 H	3 A		4 V	5 S	6 O	7 G	8 C	9 Q	10 B	11 H		12 W	13 T	14 J	15 L	16 V		17 V	18 S		19 R
20 W	21 T		22 Q	23 I	24 A	25 U	26 R	27 K	28 N	29 X	30 W	31 M	32 H		33 E	34 C	35 N		36 M	37 V		38 E
39 B	40 P	41 K	42 U		43 W	44 J	45 U	46 P		47 G	48 U	49 J	50 F		51 B		52 G	53 T	54 W	55 O	56 S
57 C	58 R	59 S	60 N	61 I	62 M	63 G		64 T	65 F	66 R		67 N	68 R		69 R	70 T	71 E	72 X		73 N	74 I	75 M
	76 L	77 J	78 O	79 M	80 F		81 T	82 W	83 B	84 L		85 V	86 A	87 F	88 K	89 D		90 M	91 W		92 O	93 V
94 T	95 R	96 M		97 E	98 V	99 Q	100 D	101 U		102 S	103 H	104 V	105 W		106 J	107 M	108 B	109 I	110 L	111 E		112 H
113 F	114 U		115 K	116 N		117 B	118 A	119 Q		120 A	121 D	122 E	123 N		124 B	125 G	126 C	127 X	128 A	129 J	130 T	131 K
132 W		133 I	134 G	135 N	136 D		137 R	138 N	139 O		140 R	141 C	142 Q	143 F	144 K		145 L	146 T		147 K	148 B	149 L
150 J	151 I	152 G		153 A	154 P	155 C	156 F	157 N	158 H	159 X		160 G	161 D	162 H	163 V	164 E		165 J	166 F	167 B	168 K	169 P
	170 D	171 M	172 O	173 Q	174 G	175 U	176 S		177 Q	178 E	179 A	180 O	181 F		182 L	183 A	184 C		185 L	186 M	187 O	188 D

6

A. Oshkosh, Wisconsin's lake . . . .
19 98 24 31 169 118 164 79 86

B. Clear utterance . . . .
18 121 48 156 191 179 142 74 131 148 133

C. "Imagine" singer . . . .
145 55 46 165 12 35

D. Lettuce's characteristic . . . .
83 192 96 125 182 16 181 140 88

E. Lord Peter Wimsey's creator . . . .
67 117 84 139 105 126

F. Person of no importance . . . .
6 32 56 137 13 162 78 38 157

G. Fortuitous . . . .
159 111 47 52 143 135 29 87 3

H. "The Bare __" ("Jungle Book" song) . . . . .
128 154 64 58 14 108 114 82 20 8 42

I. Immediacy . . . .
132 100 69 40 107 51 11 161 7 30

J. Good assistant's characteristic . . . .
50 94 10 184 180 41 89 81 122 37

K. President Mandela . . . .
170 75 22 183 65 152

L. Disco decade . . . .
188 92 95 44 73 62 144 28 4

M. Bubbly . . . .
103 59 187 27 36 72 127 53 33

N. Ends the meeting . . . .
155 102 186 134 60 49 66 129

O. Dreamy musical pieces . . . .
185 9 138 178 112 160 149 15 91

P. Disturbs . . . .
1 113 124 176 26 77 123 168

Q. 1932 Marx Brothers film: 2 wds. . . . . . .
163 39 71 119 106 174 130 166 61 2 5 45 101

R. What the defense attorney raises . . . . . .
93 167 175 120 43 115 68 63 136 153

S. Laxity . . . .
21 99 109 54 151 85 70 17 177

T. Of smell . . . .
34 76 110 25 171 189 173 97 146

U. Metamorphic rock . . . .
104 90 23 190 150 57

V. Toadies: hyph . . . .
116 80 141 158 172 147

1 P	2 Q	3 G		4 L	5 Q	6 F	7 I	8 H		9 O	10 J		11 I	12 C	13 F	14 H	15 O	16 D	17 S	18 B		19 A
20 H	21 S	22 K		23 U	24 A	25 T	26 P	27 M	28 L		29 G	30 I		31 A	32 F	33 M		34 T	35 C	36 M	37 J	
38 F	39 Q		40 I	41 J	42 H	43 R	44 L	45 Q	46 C		47 G	48 B	49 N	50 J		51 I	52 G	53 M	54 S	55 C	56 F	57 U
58 H		59 M	60 N	61 Q		62 L	63 R		64 H	65 K	66 N	67 E	68 R	69 I	70 S	71 Q		72 M	73 L	74 B	75 K	76 T
77 P	78 F	79 A	80 V	81 J	82 H	83 D	84 E		85 S	86 A	87 G	88 D	89 J	90 U	91 O	92 L		93 R	94 J		95 L	96 D
97 T	98 A	99 S	100 I	101 Q		102 N	103 M	104 U	105 E	106 Q	107 I	108 H		109 S	110 T		111 G	112 O	113 P	114 H	115 V	116 V
117 E	118 A	119 Q	120 R	121 B	122 J	123 P		124 P	125 D		126 E	127 M	128 H	129 N	130 Q		131 B	132 I		133 B	134 N
135 G		136 R	137 F	138 O	139 E	140 D	141 V	142 B	143 G	144 L	145 C	146 T		147 V	148 B	149 O	150 U	151 S	152 K	153 R	154 H
155 N	156 B	157 F		158 V	159 G	160 O	161 I		162 F	163 Q	164 A	165 C		166 Q	167 R	168 P	169 A	170 K	171 T	172 V	173 T
174 Q		175 R	176 P	177 S	178 O	179 B	180 J	181 D		182 D	183 K		184 J	185 O	186 N	187 M	188 L	189 T	190 U	191 B	192 D

7

A. Anti-fly weapons . . . .
20 43 7 191 125 116 161 62

B. "Little Rascals" character . . . .
143 173 89 112 21 38 29 1 78

C. Quiver fillers . . . .
26 4 124 80 127 54

D. Friction-reducing substances . . . .
102 142 167 165 186 6 65 111 137 42

E. Near the bottom . . . .
113 164 58 170 63 153

F. Goes to . . . .
36 160 55 105 139 32 82

G. Rating anew . . . .
56 12 98 148 92 22 37 194 123 108 14

H. Insane . . . .
70 114 11 87 132 163 185 109

I. "Goldilocks" character . . . .
180 66 162 117 96 27 74 181 184 145 19

J. Barry Bonds and Willie Mays, e.g. . . . . . .
40 168 152 17 192 72 156 53 31 91 141

K. Trivial . . . .
115 178 73 68 94 97 52 189 140 59 183

L. Pets . . . .
149 135 188 10 48 39 79 93 159

M. Admonitory, to a lawyer . . . .
44 104 144 77 41 190 64 138 86 3

N. "NBC __ News" . . . .
179 103 118 134 147 71 34

O. Bullets and BBs . . . .
110 51 193 158 81 175 101 5 90 13

P. British stables . . . .
50 154 9 100

Q. Anarchist's target . . . .
128 88 119 176 47 157 99 126 25 2 24 136 169

R. Rebounds . . . .
30 49 146 182 67 120 85 177 166

S. Minds someone else's business . . . .
155 171 61 84 187 35 130 151 18 121

T. Workplace recesses: 2 wds. . . . .
133 15 172 75 46 95 33 23 69 107 122 106

U. PGA star with an "army" of fans: 2 wds. . . . .
57 174 8 150 83 45 28 60 16 76 131 129

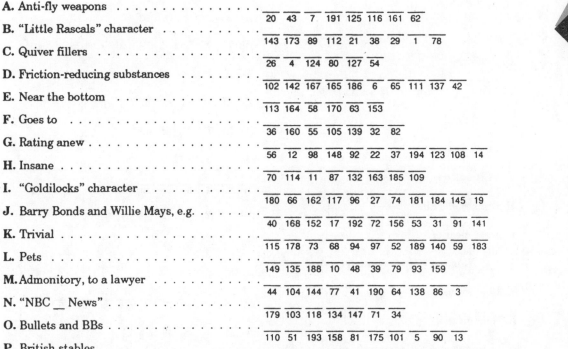

1 B	2 Q	3 M	4 C	5 O	6 D	7 A	8 U		9 P	10 L	11 H	12 G	13 O		14 G	15 T	16 U	17 J	18 S	19 I	20 A
21 B	22 G	23 T	24 Q		25 Q	26 C	27 I	28 U	29 B	30 R	31 J	32 F		33 T	34 N		35 S	36 F	37 G	38 B	39 L	40 J
41 M	42 D		43 A	44 M	45 U	46 T		47 Q	48 L	49 R	50 P	51 O	52 K	53 J		54 C	55 F	56 G	57 U	58 E		59 K
60 U	61 S	62 A		63 E	64 M	65 D	66 I	67 R	68 K	69 T	70 H		71 N	72 J	73 K		74 I	75 T		76 U	77 M	78 B
79 L	80 C	81 O		82 F	83 U	84 S	85 R	86 M	87 H	88 Q		89 B	90 O	91 J	92 G	93 L	94 K	95 T	96 I		97 K	98 G
99 Q	100 P	101 O	102 D	103 N	104 M	105 F	106 T		107 T	108 G	109 H		110 O	111 D	112 B	113 E	114 H		115 K	116 A	117 I	118 N
119 Q	120 R		121 S	122 T	123 G	124 C	125 A	126 Q		127 C	128 Q	129 U	130 S		131 U	132 H	133 T	134 N	135 L	136 Q	137 D	138 M
139 F	140 K		141 J	142 D	143 B	144 M	145 I	146 R	147 N	148 S		149 L	150 U	151 S		152 J	153 E	154 P		155 S	156 J	157 O
158 O	159 L	160 F	161 A	162 I	163 H	164 E	165 D	166 R		167 D	168 J	169 Q		170 E	171 S	172 T	173 B	174 U	175 O	176 Q	177 R	178 K
179 N	180 I		181 I	182 R		183 K	184 I	185 H	186 D	187 S		188 L	189 K	190 M	191 A	192 J	193 O	194 G			

8

A. In the wake . . . .
7   83   24   75   6   93

B. Hurry . . . .
130   64   78   59

C. Give way . . . .
47   113   60   79   68

D. "The ___ Strain" (1971 sci-fi thriller) . . . .
80   51   55   61   8   37   19   32   15

E. Eat daintily . . . .
114   33   43   117   97   105

F. Light-fingered one . . . .
120   49   124   13   73

G. VCR button . . . .
35   67   2   69   31   18

H. Blackmail's kin . . . .
129   95   111   36   46   103   17   21   90

I. Steer clear of . . . .
116   123   88   99   84

J. "___ Yankees" (Gwen Verdon musical) . . .
87   91   81   28

K. Ubiquitous . . . .
62   16   50   44   77   12   128   40   106   25

L. Hold on to . . . .
9   52   70   45   85   109

M. Mount Rushmore's locale: 2 wds. . . . . . .
125   20   72   23   104   102   30   26   3   86   1

N. "___ Right Thing" (Spike Lee film): 2 wds. .
14   118   63   112   101

O. April payment: 2 wds. . . . .
126   66   96   110   4   121   48   56   53

P. Hearty laugh . . . .
115   119   74   22   5   89

Q. Sinclair Lewis novel: 2 wds. . . . .
107   76   82   131   65   29   98   127   38   10   57

R. Shrimp or lobster . . . .
58   71   94   41   122   34   27   108   39

S. "___ of Athens" (Shakespeare) . . . .
54   42   100   11   92

1 M		2 G	3 M	4 O	5 P	6 A		7 A	8 D	9 L	10 Q	11 S	12 K	13 F	14 N		15 D		16 K	17 H	18 G	19 D
20 M		21 H	22 P		23 M	24 A	25 K		26 M	27 R	28 J	29 Q		30 M	31 G	32 D		33 E		34 R	35 G	36 H
37 D		38 Q	39 R	40 K		41 R	42 S	43 E	44 K	45 L	46 H	47 C		48 O	49 F	50 K		51 D	52 L	53 O	54 S
55 D	56 O	57 Q		58 R	59 B	60 C		61 D	62 K	63 N	64 B	65 Q	66 O	67 G	68 C		69 G	70 L		71 R	72 M	73 F
74 P	75 A	76 Q	77 K		78 B	79 C	80 D	81 J	82 Q	83 A	84 I		85 L	86 M		87 J	88 I	89 P	90 H		91 J	92 S
93 A		94 R	95 H	96 O	97 E	98 Q	99 I	100 S	101 N	102 M		103 H	104 M	105 E	106 K	107 Q	108 R		109 L	110 O	111 H	112 N
113 C	114 E	115 P		116 I	117 E	118 N	119 P	120 F		121 O	122 R	123 I	124 F	125 M		126 O	127 Q		128 K	129 H	130 B	131 Q

9

A. Purchaser's guarantee . . . .
<u>121</u> <u>147</u> <u>67</u> <u>11</u> <u>166</u> <u>114</u> <u>137</u> <u>156</u>

B. Rococo . . . .
<u>103</u> <u>29</u> <u>100</u> <u>132</u> <u>66</u> <u>153</u>

C. Desert pit stop . . . .
<u>24</u> <u>95</u> <u>112</u> <u>31</u> <u>96</u>

D. Yom Kippur, in English: 3 wds. . . . . . .
<u>155</u> <u>44</u> <u>38</u> <u>48</u> <u>102</u> <u>136</u> <u>140</u> <u>158</u> <u>148</u> <u>97</u> <u>71</u> <u>163</u> <u>165</u> <u>21</u>

E. Day care denizens . . . .
<u>63</u> <u>130</u> <u>19</u> <u>79</u> <u>53</u> <u>65</u> <u>157</u> <u>160</u> <u>36</u> <u>124</u>

F. Bustling . . . .
<u>35</u> <u>73</u> <u>105</u> <u>20</u> <u>162</u> <u>110</u>

G. Talkative . . . .
<u>23</u> <u>139</u> <u>18</u> <u>43</u> <u>122</u> <u>6</u> <u>72</u> <u>2</u> <u>3</u> <u>76</u>

H. Lower back complaint . . . .
<u>159</u> <u>58</u> <u>16</u> <u>150</u> <u>119</u> <u>26</u> <u>138</u>

I. English king, 976-1016: 3 wds. . . . .
<u>22</u> <u>61</u> <u>146</u> <u>126</u> <u>120</u> <u>109</u> <u>91</u> <u>101</u> <u>1</u> <u>47</u> <u>46</u> <u>10</u> <u>25</u> <u>152</u>
<u>151</u> <u>54</u> <u>149</u> <u>41</u>

J. Like Gomer Pyle's voice . . . .
<u>174</u> <u>154</u> <u>145</u> <u>107</u> <u>49</u>

K. Flatterer . . . .
<u>77</u> <u>164</u> <u>161</u> <u>50</u> <u>135</u>

L. With high principles . . . .
<u>141</u> <u>168</u> <u>8</u> <u>57</u> <u>45</u> <u>111</u> <u>59</u> <u>37</u> <u>123</u>

M. Notable periods . . . .
<u>179</u> <u>104</u> <u>78</u> <u>173</u>

N. Prepares to remove a shirt . . . .
<u>33</u> <u>69</u> <u>62</u> <u>144</u> <u>172</u> <u>86</u> <u>89</u> <u>52</u> <u>4</u>

O. ___ off (cheated through substitution) . . . .
<u>40</u> <u>99</u> <u>142</u> <u>125</u> <u>170</u> <u>80</u>

P. Rosy . . . .
<u>113</u> <u>27</u> <u>176</u> <u>51</u> <u>169</u> <u>117</u> <u>88</u> <u>108</u> <u>39</u> <u>131</u>

Q. Pestles' pals . . . .
<u>167</u> <u>68</u> <u>143</u> <u>30</u> <u>81</u> <u>92</u> <u>118</u>

R. Like a worm-catching bird . . . .
<u>15</u> <u>64</u> <u>134</u> <u>34</u> <u>12</u>

S. Spread rumors . . . .
<u>55</u> <u>175</u> <u>87</u> <u>127</u> <u>14</u> <u>83</u>

T. Unselfish . . . .
<u>28</u> <u>75</u> <u>129</u> <u>82</u> <u>60</u> <u>56</u> <u>17</u> <u>116</u> <u>85</u> <u>178</u>

U. Baptists and Catholics, e.g. . . . .
<u>98</u> <u>106</u> <u>133</u> <u>177</u> <u>84</u> <u>9</u> <u>93</u> <u>74</u> <u>171</u> <u>13</u>

V. Summoning . . . .
<u>7</u> <u>90</u> <u>70</u> <u>32</u> <u>5</u> <u>128</u> <u>115</u> <u>42</u> <u>94</u>

1 I	2 G		3 G	4 N		5 V		6 G	7 V	8 L	9 U	10 I	11 A	12 R		13 U	14 S	15 R	16 H	17 T		18 G
19 E	20 F	21 D	22 I		23 G	24 C	25 I	26 H		27 P	28 T	29 B	30 Q	31 C	32 V	33 N	34 R	35 F	36 E	37 L	38 D
39 P	40 O		41 I	42 V	43 G		44 D	45 L	46 I		47 I	48 D	49 J	50 K	51 P	52 N	53 E		54 I	55 S		56 T
57 L	58 H		59 L	60 T	61 I		62 N	63 E		64 R	65 E	66 B	67 A	68 Q	69 N	70 V	71 D	72 G	73 F	74 U	75 T
76 G	77 K	78 M	79 E	80 O	81 Q	82 T	83 S	84 U		85 T	86 N		87 S	88 P		89 N	90 V	91 I	92 Q		93 U	94 V
	95 C		96 C	97 D	98 U	99 O	100 B	101 I		102 D	103 B	104 M		105 F	106 U	107 J	108 P		109 I	110 F	111 L	112 C
113 P	114 A		115 V	116 T		117 P	118 Q		119 H	120 I	121 A	122 G	123 L	124 E		125 O	126 I	127 S	128 V		129 T	130 E
	131 P	132 B	133 U	134 R	135 K		136 D		137 A	138 H	139 G	140 D	141 L	142 O	143 Q	144 N	145 J	146 I		147 A	148 D	149 I
	150 H	151 I		152 I	153 B	154 J	155 D	156 A		157 E	158 D		159 H	160 E	161 K	162 F	163 D		164 K	165 D		166 A
	167 Q	168 L	169 P	170 O	171 U	172 N	173 M		174 J	175 S	176 P	177 U	178 T	179 M								

10

A. Australian marsupial . . . .
59 86 74 137 94 69

B. Very dark . . . .
124 100 140 81

C. European airline . . . .
172 131 127 77 63 165 126 103 25

D. Con game decoy . . . .
141 111 168 153 80

E. Deed holders . . . .
106 70 26 31 117 154

F. Digit . . . .
68 151 35 161 97 129

G. Sickly . . . .
75 143 98 122 5 164

H. Parsimonious . . . .
7 47 167 21 72 133 96 66 91

I. Prates . . . .
85 19 152 123 174 34 23 45

J. Different . . . .
128 144 41 57 109

K. Puritan clergyman Cotton . . . .
24 108 120 28 148 90

L. Ancient autocrat . . . .
113 56 163 43 84 125 33

M. Agile . . . .
147 112 95 51 22

N. Weaken . . . .
38 169 20 136 30 48 159 71

O. Made a crude roof . . . .
134 105 170 18 149 93 162 79

P. Removes from danger . . . .
101 37 138 8 87 114 150 13 62

Q. Hemmed and hawed . . . .
42 130 121 142 53 173 104 11 89 78 67

R. Judges . . . .
73 145 6 17 110

S. Not wholesome . . . .
65 157 15 36 52 146 76 60 116 44 107

T. American car, for short . . . .
139 2 54 12 61

U. National song . . . .
29 88 40 9 156 58

V. 27th U.S. President . . . .
14 132 4 1

W. Wouldn't take no for an answer . . . .
99 49 27 82 115 32 119 158

X. Playful water mammals . . . .
160 92 55 135 166 50

Y. However . . . .
39 64 83 118 155 10 16 171 3 46 102

1 V	2 T	3 Y		4 V	5 G	6 R	7 H	8 P	9 U		10 Y	11 Q	12 T	13 P		14 V	15 S	16 Y	17 R		18 O	19 I
20 N		21 H	22 M	23 I	24 K	25 C	26 E	27 W		28 K	29 U	30 N	31 E		32 W	33 L	34 I	35 F		36 S	37 P	38 N
39 Y		40 U	41 J	42 Q		43 L	44 S	45 I	46 Y	47 H	48 N	49 W	50 X		51 M	52 S	53 Q	54 T		55 X	56 L	57 J
58 U		59 A	60 S	61 T		62 P	63 C	64 Y	65 S	66 H	67 Q	68 F	69 A		70 E	71 N		72 H	73 R	74 A	75 G	76 S
77 C	78 Q	79 O	80 D	81 B		82 W	83 Y		84 L		85 I	86 A	87 P	88 U	89 Q	90 K	91 H		92 X	93 O	94 A	95 M
	96 H	97 F	98 G	99 W	100 B	101 P	102 Y		103 C	104 Q	105 O	106 E	107 S	108 K	109 J	110 R	111 P	112 M	113 L		114 P	115 W
116 S	117 E	118 Y	119 W		120 K	121 Q	122 G	123 I	124 B	125 L	126 C		127 C	128 J	129 F		130 Q	131 C	132 V	133 H	134 O
135 X	136 N	137 A	138 P	139 T	140 B	141 D		142 Q	143 G	144 J	145 R	146 S	147 M	148 K	149 O	150 P	151 F	152 I	153 D	154 E		155 Y
156 U	157 S	158 W		159 N	160 X		161 F	162 O		163 L		164 G	165 C	166 X	167 H	168 D	169 N	170 O	171 Y		172 C	173 Q
174 I																					

11

A. Bill Haley and His Comets hit: 4 wds. . . . . . $\overline{175}$ $\overline{28}$ $\overline{141}$ $\overline{129}$ $\overline{88}$ $\overline{21}$ $\overline{52}$ $\overline{108}$ $\overline{110}$ $\overline{124}$ $\overline{62}$ $\overline{6}$ $\overline{78}$ $\overline{184}$
$\overline{16}$ $\overline{81}$ $\overline{85}$ $\overline{38}$

B. 1968 hit for the Beatles . . . . $\overline{11}$ $\overline{74}$ $\overline{19}$ $\overline{181}$ $\overline{36}$ $\overline{3}$ $\overline{138}$ $\overline{54}$ $\overline{127}$ $\overline{162}$

C. "Picnic" playwright . . . . $\overline{139}$ $\overline{70}$ $\overline{159}$ $\overline{178}$

D. Author of "The Rebel" . . . . $\overline{98}$ $\overline{136}$ $\overline{61}$ $\overline{33}$ $\overline{75}$

E. Photographer's unit . . . . $\overline{25}$ $\overline{172}$ $\overline{135}$ $\overline{158}$ $\overline{125}$ $\overline{31}$ $\overline{73}$ $\overline{183}$

F. Carpenters' gear . . . . $\overline{157}$ $\overline{128}$ $\overline{95}$ $\overline{58}$ $\overline{67}$ $\overline{164}$ $\overline{156}$ $\overline{72}$ $\overline{121}$

G. 1991 "Top Gun" takeoff: 2 wds. . . . . . . $\overline{173}$ $\overline{57}$ $\overline{76}$ $\overline{147}$ $\overline{43}$ $\overline{168}$ $\overline{27}$ $\overline{130}$

H. Encouraged: 2 wds. . . . . $\overline{177}$ $\overline{180}$ $\overline{87}$ $\overline{44}$ $\overline{163}$ $\overline{9}$ $\overline{55}$

I. Least stale . . . . $\overline{103}$ $\overline{182}$ $\overline{170}$ $\overline{140}$ $\overline{152}$ $\overline{122}$ $\overline{14}$ $\overline{120}$

J. Narrow strips of land . . . . $\overline{84}$ $\overline{32}$ $\overline{151}$ $\overline{118}$ $\overline{46}$ $\overline{104}$ $\overline{8}$ $\overline{148}$ $\overline{169}$

K. Nolan Ryan specialty: hyph. . . . . . . $\overline{142}$ $\overline{18}$ $\overline{93}$ $\overline{150}$ $\overline{117}$ $\overline{89}$ $\overline{45}$ $\overline{165}$

L. Jurisdiction . . . . $\overline{109}$ $\overline{82}$ $\overline{48}$ $\overline{167}$ $\overline{101}$ $\overline{132}$ $\overline{69}$ $\overline{24}$ $\overline{30}$

M. "Let's kill all the ___" (Shakespeare) . . . . $\overline{35}$ $\overline{15}$ $\overline{166}$ $\overline{80}$ $\overline{29}$ $\overline{5}$ $\overline{143}$

N. Make impure . . . . $\overline{92}$ $\overline{133}$ $\overline{63}$ $\overline{71}$ $\overline{171}$ $\overline{94}$ $\overline{49}$ $\overline{115}$ $\overline{153}$ $\overline{144}$ $\overline{20}$

O. D-Day beach . . . . $\overline{50}$ $\overline{90}$ $\overline{107}$ $\overline{145}$ $\overline{174}$

P. Without legal force: 3 wds. . . . . $\overline{179}$ $\overline{10}$ $\overline{100}$ $\overline{7}$ $\overline{39}$ $\overline{51}$ $\overline{116}$ $\overline{59}$ $\overline{66}$ $\overline{161}$ $\overline{106}$

Q. Prescience . . . . $\overline{131}$ $\overline{146}$ $\overline{96}$ $\overline{60}$ $\overline{41}$ $\overline{154}$ $\overline{47}$ $\overline{83}$ $\overline{105}$ $\overline{68}$ $\overline{26}$ $\overline{79}$ $\overline{2}$

R. Give a false estimate . . . . . . $\overline{123}$ $\overline{99}$ $\overline{149}$ $\overline{176}$ $\overline{23}$ $\overline{53}$ $\overline{86}$

S. Spineless critter . . . . $\overline{114}$ $\overline{1}$ $\overline{56}$ $\overline{13}$ $\overline{102}$ $\overline{42}$ $\overline{97}$ $\overline{126}$ $\overline{160}$ $\overline{119}$ $\overline{65}$ $\overline{17}$

T. Of color . . . . $\overline{12}$ $\overline{111}$ $\overline{22}$ $\overline{155}$ $\overline{134}$ $\overline{34}$ $\overline{4}$ $\overline{77}$ $\overline{40}$

U. Country on the Black Sea . . . . $\overline{64}$ $\overline{91}$ $\overline{137}$ $\overline{113}$ $\overline{112}$ $\overline{37}$

1 S	2 Q	3 B	4 T	5 M	6 A	7 P		8 J	9 H	10 P	11 B	12 T	13 S	14 I		15 M	16 A	17 S		18 K	19 B	20 N
21 A	22 T	23 R	24 L	25 E	26 Q		27 G	28 A	29 M	30 L		31 E	32 J	33 D	34 T	35 M	36 B	37 U		38 A	39 P	40 T
41 Q		42 S	43 G	44 H		45 K	46 J	47 Q	48 L	49 N	50 O	51 P	52 A	53 R		54 B	55 H	56 S	57 G	58 F	59 P	60 Q
61 D	62 A	63 N	64 U		65 S	66 P		67 F	68 Q		69 L	70 C	71 N	72 F	73 E	74 B	75 D	76 G	77 T	78 A	79 Q
80 M	81 A	82 L		83 Q	84 J	85 A	86 R		87 H	88 A	89 K		90 O	91 U	92 N	93 K		94 N	95 F	96 Q	97 S
98 D	99 R	100 P	101 L	102 S	103 I	104 J	105 Q		106 P	107 O	108 A	109 L		110 A	111 T	112 U		113 U	114 S	115 N	116 P
117 K	118 J	119 S	120 I		121 F	122 I	123 R	124 A	125 E		126 S	127 B	128 F	129 A	130 G		131 Q	132 L	133 N	134 T		135 E
136 D	137 U	138 B	139 C	140 I	141 A	142 K	143 M		144 N	145 O	146 Q	147 G	148 J		149 R	150 K	151 J	152 I		153 N	154 Q
155 T	156 F		157 F	158 E		159 C	160 S	161 P	162 B	163 H		164 F	165 K		166 M	167 L	168 G	169 J	170 I		171 N	172 E
	173 G	174 O	175 A		176 R	177 H	178 C	179 P		180 H	181 B	182 I	183 E	184 A							

12

A. Depleted . . . .
154 170 124 70 179 115 122 111 10

B. Dark-sounding bestseller of 1989: 3 wds. . . .
84 4 21 49 155 29 126 174 8 11 5 47 148 180
59 41 17 142

C. Scandalous 19th-century financier James . . .
131 14 28 135

D. Getting the better of . . . .
76 36 1 164 107 16 163 45 140 181

E. Omar Khayyam opus, with "The" . . . .
13 77 67 56 64 113 42 35

F. Author of Word B: 2 wds. . . . .
27 138 81 105 114 183 48 152 97 66 44 130 57

G. Huge comedy hit of 1987: 5 wds. . . . .
94 178 9 167 128 157 125 176 18 108 139 26 101 79
161 136

H. Rock star known as "Slow Hand": 2 wds. . . .
24 95 150 145 134 32 116 85 119 99 37

I. California spokesfruit . . . .
147 175 171 78 22 38 129

J. Cowboy's greeting . . . .
91 146 25 74 6

K. In a safe spot: 4 wds. . . . .
62 55 15 12 69 153 143 166 30 156 63 121 52

L. In a disorganized manner: hyph. . . . .
149 73 86 23 100 169 158 65 51 53

M. Outlooks on life . . . .
2 72 93 39 46 162 118 165 20

N. Ecstatic . . . .
182 160 98 172 75 144 88 117 103

O. John Forsythe's TV show . . . .
58 33 43 133 106 151 127

P. Native of Riyadh . . . .
34 87 173 137 104

Q. Humor fad of the '60s: 2 wds. . . . .
102 159 112 31 61 92 80 109 132 83 3 68 71

R. Popular bird-feeder visitor . . . .
50 96 19 120 168 123 82 110

S. Petula Clark hit of 1964 . . . .
177 141 7 89 90 54 60 40

1 D	2 M	3 Q	4 B		5 B	6 J		7 S	8 B	9 G	10 A		11 B	12 K	13 E		14 C	15 K		16 D	17 B	18 G
19 R		20 M	21 B	22 I	23 L	24 H		25 J	26 G	27 F		28 C	29 B	30 K	31 Q	32 H	33 O		34 P	35 E	36 D	37 H
38 I	39 M	40 S	41 B		42 E	43 O	44 F		45 D	46 M		47 B	48 F		49 B	50 R	51 L	52 K		53 L	54 S	55 K
	56 E	57 F	58 O		59 B		60 S	61 Q	62 K		63 K	64 E	65 L	66 F		67 E	68 O		69 K	70 A	71 Q	72 M
73 L	74 J	75 N	76 D	77 E	78 I		79 G	80 Q	81 F		82 R	83 Q	84 B	85 H	86 L	87 P	88 N	89 S		90 S	91 J	92 Q
93 M		94 G	95 H	96 R	97 F		98 N	99 H	100 L		101 G	102 Q	103 N	104 P	105 F	106 O		107 D	108 G		109 Q	110 R
111 A		112 Q	113 E	114 F	115 A		116 H	117 N	118 M	119 H	120 R	121 K	122 A		123 R	124 A	125 G		126 B	127 O	128 G
129 I		130 F	131 C		132 Q	133 O	134 H	135 C	136 G		137 P	138 F	139 G		140 D	141 S	142 B		143 K	144 N	145 H	146 J
147 I	148 B		149 L	150 H	151 O	152 F		153 K	154 A	155 B		156 K	157 G	158 L	159 Q	160 N		161 G	162 M	163 D	164 D
165 M	166 K	167 G		168 R	169 L	170 A	171 I	172 N	173 P	174 B		175 I	176 G	177 S		178 G	179 A	180 B	181 D	182 N	183 F

13

A. Printer's proofs . . . .

$\overline{53}\ \overline{79}\ \overline{68}\ \overline{65}\ \overline{10}\ \overline{70}\ \overline{43}$

B. Rich or Chicken . . . .

$\overline{38}\ \overline{139}\ \overline{95}\ \overline{151}\ \overline{66}\ \overline{75}$

C. Michael Jackson's pre-"Thriller"
album: 3 wds. . . . .

$\overline{5}\ \overline{121}\ \overline{31}\ \overline{62}\ \overline{154}\ \overline{3}\ \overline{93}\ \overline{135}\ \overline{116}\ \overline{105}$

D. "The Desert Fox" . . . .

$\overline{150}\ \overline{132}\ \overline{59}\ \overline{49}\ \overline{108}\ \overline{134}$

E. Reckless . . . .

$\overline{52}\ \overline{40}\ \overline{104}\ \overline{141}\ \overline{77}\ \overline{2}\ \overline{149}\ \overline{110}\ \overline{130}$

F. Signed . . . .

$\overline{86}\ \overline{72}\ \overline{125}\ \overline{54}\ \overline{33}\ \overline{50}\ \overline{44}\ \overline{63}\ \overline{99}\ \overline{13}\ \overline{124}$

G. Field trip meal: 2 wds. . . . .

$\overline{109}\ \overline{28}\ \overline{11}\ \overline{115}\ \overline{8}\ \overline{123}\ \overline{87}\ \overline{152}$

H. Leisurely . . . .

$\overline{55}\ \overline{29}\ \overline{90}\ \overline{60}\ \overline{73}\ \overline{9}\ \overline{16}\ \overline{164}\ \overline{1}$

I. Cable junkie: 2 wds. . . . .

$\overline{12}\ \overline{113}\ \overline{23}\ \overline{98}\ \overline{96}\ \overline{84}\ \overline{119}\ \overline{74}\ \overline{97}\ \overline{89}\ \overline{71}$

J. Religious order dating from the Crusades:
3 wds. . . . .

$\overline{140}\ \overline{21}\ \overline{94}\ \overline{34}\ \overline{78}\ \overline{136}\ \overline{15}\ \overline{101}\ \overline{148}\ \overline{92}\ \overline{158}\ \overline{85}\ \overline{107}\ \overline{35}$

K. Subtle difference . . . .

$\overline{159}\ \overline{114}\ \overline{67}\ \overline{42}\ \overline{19}\ \overline{83}$

L. Abode of the blessed, in mythology . . . . .

$\overline{129}\ \overline{157}\ \overline{112}\ \overline{14}\ \overline{27}\ \overline{64}\ \overline{102}$

M. Get ready for the big show . . . .

$\overline{144}\ \overline{88}\ \overline{126}\ \overline{47}\ \overline{106}\ \overline{100}\ \overline{163}\ \overline{76}$

N. "Wheel of Fortune" purchase . . . .

$\overline{17}\ \overline{20}\ \overline{57}\ \overline{147}\ \overline{156}$

O. "___ man with seven wives...": 3 wds. . . . .

$\overline{122}\ \overline{146}\ \overline{127}\ \overline{56}\ \overline{161}$

P. Complaint of Father Damien's flock . . . . .

$\overline{69}\ \overline{58}\ \overline{133}\ \overline{82}\ \overline{155}\ \overline{22}\ \overline{6}$

Q. ___ of Nantes . . . .

$\overline{103}\ \overline{37}\ \overline{162}\ \overline{46}\ \overline{26}$

R. Fundamental unit of speech . . . .

$\overline{51}\ \overline{143}\ \overline{7}\ \overline{120}\ \overline{39}\ \overline{24}\ \overline{32}$

S. Not hated . . . .

$\overline{45}\ \overline{36}\ \overline{61}\ \overline{142}\ \overline{118}\ \overline{128}\ \overline{131}\ \overline{18}\ \overline{81}$

T. Tease . . . .

$\overline{80}\ \overline{137}\ \overline{91}\ \overline{160}\ \overline{138}\ \overline{153}$

U. "She ___ Conquer" (Congreve): 2 wds. . . . . .

$\overline{117}\ \overline{4}\ \overline{145}\ \overline{41}\ \overline{25}\ \overline{48}\ \overline{111}\ \overline{30}$

1 H	2 E	3 C		4 U	5 C		6 P	7 R	8 G	9 H		10 A	11 G	12 I	13 F	14 L	15 J	16 H	17 N	18 S			19 K
20 N	21 J	22 P	23 I	24 R	25 U	26 Q	27 L	28 G	29 H		30 U	31 C		32 R	33 F	34 J		35 J	36 S	37 Q		38 B
39 R	40 E	41 U	42 K		43 A	44 F	45 S	46 Q	47 M	48 U		49 D	50 F		51 R	52 E	53 A	54 F	55 H	56 O		57 N
58 P		59 D	60 H	61 S	62 C		63 F	64 L	65 A	66 B		67 K	68 A	69 P		70 A	71 I	72 F	73 H		74 I	75 B
76 M	77 E	78 J		79 A	80 T	81 S		82 P	83 K	84 I	85 J	86 F	87 G	88 M		89 I	90 H	91 T	92 J		93 C	94 J
95 B	96 I		97 I		98 I	99 F	100 M	101 J	102 L	103 Q		104 E	105 C	106 M	107 J	108 D		109 G	110 E	111 U		112 L
113 I	114 K	115 G	116 C		117 U	118 S	119 I	120 R		121 C	122 O	123 G	124 F		125 F	126 M	127 O	128 S	129 L	130 E		131 S
132 D		133 P	134 D	135 C	136 J	137 T		138 T	139 B	140 J	141 E		142 S	143 R	144 M	145 U	146 O	147 N		148 J	149 E	150 D
	151 B	152 G	153 T		154 C	155 P	156 N	157 L	158 J	159 K	160 T	161 O	162 Q	163 M	164 H						

14

A. Swiss river . . . .
124 86 131 3 169

B. Right away: 3 wds. . . . .
171 48 118 17 186 180 163 6

C. Ready money . . . .
105 182 25 98

D. The First Lady of the American
   Theater: 2 wds. . . . .
165 102 28 99 174 153 179 161 36 136

E. Rob Lowe movie based on a
   David Mamet play: 3 wds. . . . .
59 125 95 67 164 46 173 137 84 151 41 192 73 97

F. Take away . . . .
76 121 101 82 177 154

G. "Star Trek: ___": 3 wds. . . . .
37 147 133 9 119 134 23 172 27 191 92 120 166

H. '60s comedy classic: hyph. . . . .
40 190 30 49 113 77 148

I. Beatles hit of 1966: 2 wds. . . . .
123 189 114 167 110 145 64 160 104 94 71 70

J. Relaxing of international tensions . . . . . .
4 143 149 53 15 85 43

K. Desire to equal another . . . .
63 108 55 11 194 152 156 139 42

L. Go from A to Z: 3 wds. . . . .
115 2 93 158 188 61 52 135 13 83 26

M. 1987 Steven Spielberg film: 4 wds. . . . . . .
74 21 10 109 184 38 90 33 60 155 126 31 50 107

N. Eighth Old Testament book . . . .
103 193 16 58

O. Desisted: 2 wds. . . . .
89 18 181 142 176 96 45

P. Obnoxious . . . .
69 54 132 129 1 138 62 14

Q. Winner of three gymnastics golds in
   1976: 2 wds. . . . .
78 106 111 22 51 88 32 144 80 128 12 39 150

R. High-frequency nuclear emissions: 2 wds. . . .
79 100 146 68 47 19 5 65 7

S. To the nth degree . . . .
8 56 168 44 91 34

T. 1988 Steven Segal film: 3 wds. . . . .
141 81 66 122 20 187 117 72 29 75 57

U. Six-time NHL MVP: 2 wds. . . . .
195 159 170 24 183 116 35 162 185 178

V. Basic components . . . .
127 175 196 130 87 140 112 157

Grid

1 P	2 L	3 A	4 J	5 R	6 B	▪	7 R	8 S	9 G	10 M	11 K	12 Q	13 L	14 P	15 J	16 N	▪	17 B	18 O	19 R	20 T	21 M
22 Q	23 G	24 U	25 C	▪	26 L	27 G	28 D	29 T	▪	30 H	31 M	▪	32 Q	33 M	▪	34 S	35 U	36 D	▪	37 G	38 M	39 Q
40 H	41 E	42 K	43 J	▪	44 S	45 O	▪	46 E	47 R	48 B	49 H	50 M	51 Q	52 L	53 J	▪	54 P	55 K	56 S	▪	57 T	58 N
59 E	60 M	61 L	62 P	63 K	64 I	▪	65 R	66 T	67 E	▪	68 R	69 P	70 I	▪	71 I	72 T	▪	73 E	74 M	75 T	76 F	77 H
78 Q	79 R	▪	80 Q	81 T	82 F	83 L	84 E	▪	85 J	86 A	87 V	▪	88 Q	89 O	90 M	91 S	92 G	93 L	94 I	▪	95 E	96 O
▪	97 E	98 C	99 D	▪	100 R	101 F	102 D	103 N	104 I	105 C	106 Q	107 M	▪	108 K	109 M	110 I	111 Q	▪	112 V	113 H	114 I	115 L
116 U	▪	117 T	118 B	119 G	▪	120 G	121 F	122 T	123 I	124 A	▪	125 E	126 M	127 V	128 Q	▪	129 P	▪	130 V	131 A	132 P	133 G
▪	134 G	135 L	136 D	137 E	138 P	139 K	140 V	141 T	142 O	143 J	▪	144 Q	145 I	146 R	147 G	148 H	149 J	▪	150 Q	151 E	▪	152 K
153 D	154 F	▪	155 M	156 K	157 V	158 L	159 U	160 I	161 D	▪	162 U	163 B	▪	164 E	165 D	166 G	▪	167 I	168 S	169 A	170 U	171 B
172 G	173 E	174 D	▪	175 V	176 O	177 F	178 U	▪	179 D	180 B	181 O	182 C	183 U	184 M	▪	185 U	186 B	187 T	188 L	▪	189 I	190 H
191 G	192 E	193 N	194 K	195 U	196 V																	

15

A. Frustrated another's efforts . . . . $\overline{25}$ $\overline{149}$ $\overline{168}$ $\overline{134}$ $\overline{34}$ $\overline{96}$ $\overline{195}$ $\overline{84}$

B. Used . . . . $\overline{160}$ $\overline{118}$ $\overline{188}$ $\overline{3}$ $\overline{27}$ $\overline{39}$ $\overline{185}$ $\overline{127}$

C. Abhorrent . . . . $\overline{2}$ $\overline{139}$ $\overline{100}$ $\overline{44}$ $\overline{159}$ $\overline{60}$ $\overline{189}$ $\overline{37}$ $\overline{18}$

D. Public brawl . . . . . $\overline{153}$ $\overline{89}$ $\overline{145}$ $\overline{69}$ $\overline{128}$ $\overline{86}$

E. "Byzantium" poet: 3 wds. . . . . $\overline{99}$ $\overline{38}$ $\overline{129}$ $\overline{58}$ $\overline{95}$ $\overline{106}$ $\overline{191}$

F. Tough and elastic . . . . $\overline{162}$ $\overline{51}$ $\overline{108}$ $\overline{12}$ $\overline{67}$ $\overline{120}$ $\overline{177}$

G. Hollywood costume designer: 2 wds. . . . . $\overline{119}$ $\overline{163}$ $\overline{45}$ $\overline{87}$ $\overline{26}$ $\overline{82}$ $\overline{9}$ $\overline{183}$ $\overline{33}$

H. French astrologer of note . . . . $\overline{104}$ $\overline{63}$ $\overline{141}$ $\overline{98}$ $\overline{115}$ $\overline{76}$ $\overline{50}$ $\overline{155}$ $\overline{182}$ $\overline{20}$ $\overline{190}$

I. Sonny and Cher's daughter . . . . $\overline{57}$ $\overline{43}$ $\overline{166}$ $\overline{74}$ $\overline{111}$ $\overline{79}$ $\overline{180}$ $\overline{154}$

J. Composure . . . . . . $\overline{165}$ $\overline{19}$ $\overline{109}$ $\overline{117}$ $\overline{46}$ $\overline{192}$ $\overline{70}$ $\overline{161}$ $\overline{187}$ $\overline{54}$

K. Dieter's downfall: 2 wds. . . . . . . $\overline{62}$ $\overline{30}$ $\overline{174}$ $\overline{5}$ $\overline{148}$ $\overline{17}$ $\overline{122}$ $\overline{88}$ $\overline{14}$ $\overline{112}$

L. Represent . . . . . . $\overline{49}$ $\overline{11}$ $\overline{193}$ $\overline{16}$ $\overline{92}$ $\overline{107}$

M. Respect highly . . . . $\overline{102}$ $\overline{78}$ $\overline{80}$ $\overline{143}$ $\overline{55}$ $\overline{10}$ $\overline{47}$ $\overline{83}$

N. "Green" holiday: 2 wds. . . . . $\overline{150}$ $\overline{103}$ $\overline{164}$ $\overline{81}$ $\overline{48}$ $\overline{73}$ $\overline{36}$ $\overline{24}$

O. In spite of . . . . . . $\overline{144}$ $\overline{172}$ $\overline{157}$ $\overline{75}$ $\overline{186}$ $\overline{124}$ $\overline{66}$ $\overline{179}$ $\overline{110}$ $\overline{21}$ $\overline{15}$ $\overline{114}$ $\overline{97}$ $\overline{6}$ $\overline{42}$

P. Abrasive object: 2 wds. . . . . . $\overline{173}$ $\overline{140}$ $\overline{4}$ $\overline{105}$ $\overline{156}$ $\overline{126}$ $\overline{121}$ $\overline{93}$ $\overline{181}$ $\overline{91}$ $\overline{113}$

Q. Hugely . . . . $\overline{90}$ $\overline{167}$ $\overline{142}$ $\overline{137}$ $\overline{40}$ $\overline{59}$ $\overline{116}$ $\overline{23}$ $\overline{151}$

R. Famous Norse explorer: 2 wds. . . . $\overline{194}$ $\overline{178}$ $\overline{41}$ $\overline{64}$ $\overline{132}$ $\overline{138}$ $\overline{169}$ $\overline{184}$ $\overline{101}$ $\overline{32}$ $\overline{175}$

S. Made plywood . . . . . $\overline{22}$ $\overline{130}$ $\overline{152}$ $\overline{68}$ $\overline{135}$ $\overline{85}$ $\overline{53}$ $\overline{29}$ $\overline{7}$

T. P.S., e.g. . . . . . . $\overline{1}$ $\overline{123}$ $\overline{158}$ $\overline{56}$ $\overline{131}$ $\overline{65}$ $\overline{94}$ $\overline{146}$ $\overline{13}$ $\overline{136}$ $\overline{31}$ $\overline{170}$

U. Clarifies butter . . . . $\overline{8}$ $\overline{35}$ $\overline{72}$ $\overline{133}$ $\overline{176}$ $\overline{147}$ $\overline{28}$

V. Arab patriarch: var. . . . . $\overline{52}$ $\overline{171}$ $\overline{61}$ $\overline{71}$ $\overline{77}$ $\overline{125}$

1 T	2 C	3 B		4 P	5 K	6 O		7 S	8 U	9 G	10 M	11 L		12 F	13 T	14 K		15 O	16 L	17 K		18 C
19 J	20 H	21 O	22 S	23 Q	24 N		25 A	26 G	27 B	28 U	29 S		30 K	31 T	32 R		33 G	34 A	35 U	36 N	37 C
38 E	39 B		40 Q	41 R	42 O	43 I	44 C		45 G	46 J		47 M	48 N	49 L		50 H	51 F	52 V	53 S	54 J		55 M
56 T	57 I	58 E	59 Q	60 C	61 V	62 K		63 H	64 R		65 T	66 O	67 F	68 S	69 D		70 J	71 V	72 U	73 N	74 I
75 O	76 H	77 V	78 M		79 I	80 M		81 N	82 G	83 M		84 A	85 V	86 D		87 G	88 K		89 D	90 Q	91 P	92 L
	93 P	94 T	95 E	96 A		97 O	98 H		99 E	100 C	101 R		102 M	103 N	104 H	105 P	106 E	107 L		108 F	109 J	110 O
	111 I	112 K	113 P		114 O	115 H	116 Q	117 J	118 B	119 G	120 F	121 P		122 K	123 T		124 O	125 V	126 P		127 B	128 D
129 E		130 S	131 T	132 R		133 U	134 A	135 S	136 T	137 Q	138 R	139 C	140 P	141 H		142 Q	143 M	144 O		145 D	146 T	147 U
	148 K	149 A	150 N	151 Q		152 S	153 D	154 I		155 H	156 P	157 O		158 T	159 C	160 B	161 J	162 F		163 G	164 N	165 J
166 I	167 Q		168 A	169 R	170 T	171 V		172 O	173 P	174 K	175 R		176 U	177 F	178 R	179 O		180 I	181 P		182 H	183 G
184 R	185 B		186 O	187 J		188 B	189 C	190 H	191 E	192 J	193 L	194 R	195 A								

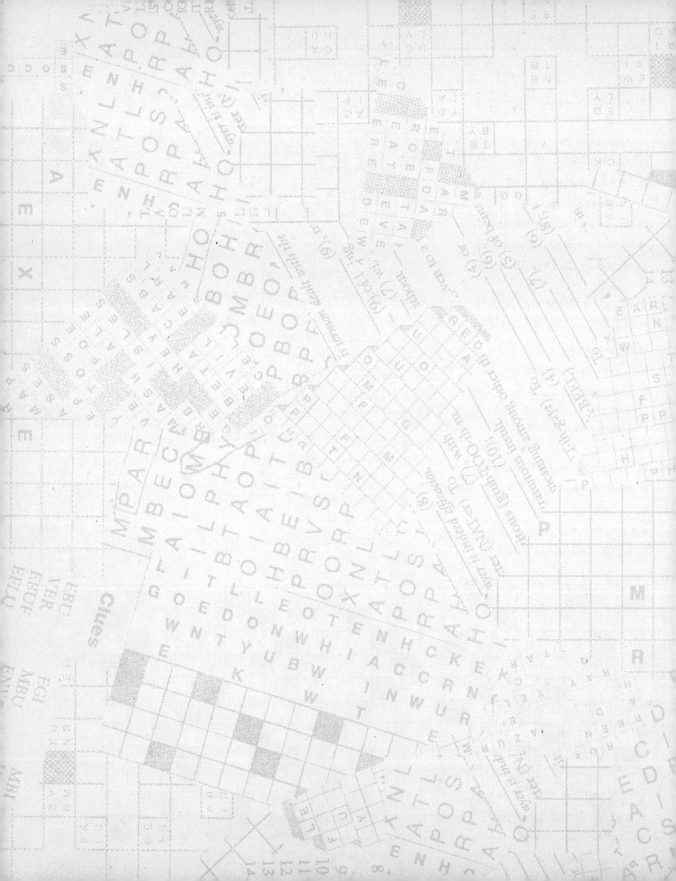

CHAPTER 2

CONNECTORS

Fill in your answers from left to right. Each word begins in a numbered square but overlaps by at least one letter the word that comes next, providing at least one clue for every word.

Answers begin on page 272.

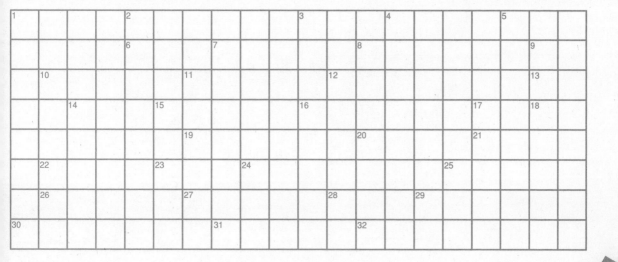

Clues

1 Dull-witted
2 Nautically sound
3 Herb
4 Wander
5 Vagrant
6 Go off on a _____; digress
7 Anyone not a Jew
8 Sluggishness; apathy
9 Revolve; whirl
10 Studio or workshop
11 Uproot
12 Religious Q and A
13 Bring in or take out in secret
14 To collect gradually
15 Something that is analogous
16 Irregular soldier
17 South American beast of burden

18 Secretary, jocularly
19 "Bridge" of land
20 Calm; composed
21 Dull and drawn-out
22 One who lends money at an exorbitant rate of interest
23 Wandering, esp. in search of adventure
24 Aversion; strong dislike
25 Of a wedding or marriage
26 Outdoors
27 Whip or flog
28 Icy; extremely cold
29 Ideological exponent
30 Breed of dairy cow
31 Jewish school
32 Condition of being dull; flavorlessness

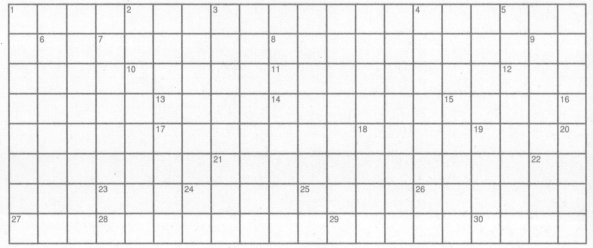

Clues

1 Israelites' departure
2 Legal right to enjoy the benefits of something belonging to another
3 Make fruitful
4 Small two-masted sailing vessel
5 Clear
6 Censure
7 Enigmatic
8 Concealed; in secret
9 Novice
10 Defensible; sustainable
11 Dominant theme
12 Artificially produced
13 Wrongly appropriate power or authority
14 One who knows several languages
15 Indolent; ineffective
16 Angelic
17 Enemy of sacred cows
18 Starry
19 Unsympathetic
20 Meddlesome
21 Haughtily contemptuous
22 Satisfy
23 Yield rights to something
24 Belch
25 Thing of little significance
26 Merciful
27 Swollen; inflated
28 Characteristically expressed
29 Decanter
30 Wild; untamed

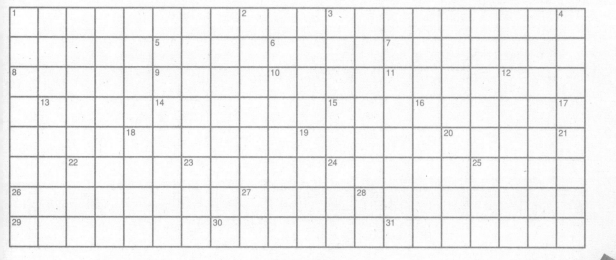

Clues

1 Ridged
2 Bring out; elicit
3 Tending toward the center or axis
4 Amulet
5 Nullify
6 Close relationship
7 Grandiloquent
8 Harsh; grating
9 Impose as an obligation
10 Unlawful
11 Fortress
12 Mislead
13 Debase
14 Diametrically opposed
15 Spanish artist
16 Burst inward

17 Striking incidental scene
18 Self-rule
19 Faithful, unquestioning follower
20 Dungeon
21 Burden
22 Trace amount
23 Cultivation of land
24 Friendly; cordial
25 Textual gap
26 Excessive admiration of oneself
27 Stain
28 Trickery; subterfuge
29 Jewish skullcap
30 Prevalent in a particular area
31 Solicit votes; conduct a survey

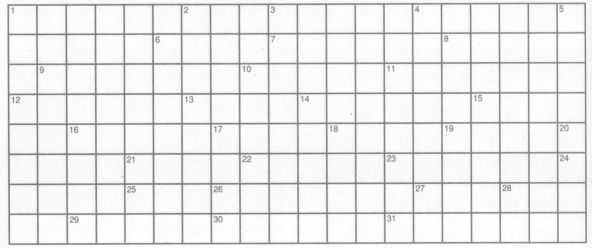

Clues

1 Repentant
2 Concise
3 Close together in rows
4 Building
5 Swiftness; speed
6 Magnate
7 Branch of philosophy
8 Government by women
9 Assertion subject to verification
10 Mythological stone-roller
11 Place for political speechmaking
12 Carried out speedily, without ceremony
13 Desire deeply
14 Golf club
15 Israeli collective
16 West wind

17 Ludicrous; laughable
18 Flinch; shy away from
19 Tease good-naturedly
20 Compliment excessively or insincerely
21 Pertaining to controversy or discord
22 Revolutionary War fort
23 Belittle; deprecate
24 Dark and gloomy
25 Stirring; exciting
26 Rare; extraordinary
27 Brief rule or direction
28 Fragile; shaky
29 Resembling a drum
30 Saint widely honored in America
31 Road surface

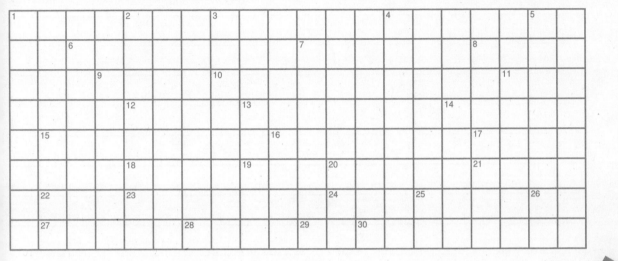

Clues

1 Falling piece of celestial debris
2 Projecting bay window
3 Qualified
4 Lightness and frivolity
5 Pleasure boat
6 Person likened to a caveman
7 Pertaining to worldly affairs
8 Opposite of egoism
9 Gloomy
10 Given to pompous moralizing
11 Timely
12 Sanctify
13 Diligent; painstaking
14 Set apart
15 Explain
16 Facilitate for greater speed

17 Atonement
18 Beginner
19 Mythological being, half horse, half man
20 Second sign of the Zodiac
21 Endure or bear
22 List of names
23 Third
24 Yin and _____
25 Nazi security police
26 One who forsakes his faith
27 Dignified; majestic
28 Lecture hall
29 The cone of shadow from a planet or satellite on the side opposite the sun
30 Exhibit in a menacing way

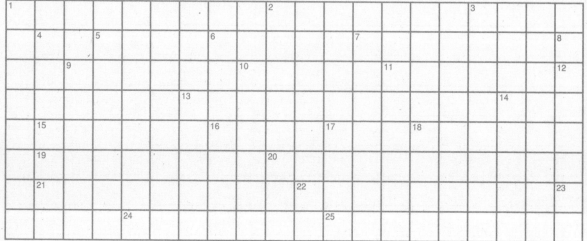

Clues

1 Having extraordinary talent or energy
2 Irregular
3 Interpret
4 Regret
5 Bring out
6 Say repeatedly
7 Foolhardiness
8 Something that unites or connects
9 Open to interpretation
10 Inexperienced; immature
11 Event marking a new phase
12 Doctrine defining pleasure as the principal good
13 Having many parts

14 Relevant
15 Retinue
16 List of things to be done
17 Speaker's platform
18 Summary
19 Phrase or practice identified with a particular group
20 Precise and painstaking
21 Unnecessary; uncalled for
22 Easily affected
23 Like a lion
24 Vague
25 One who is aggressively antisocial

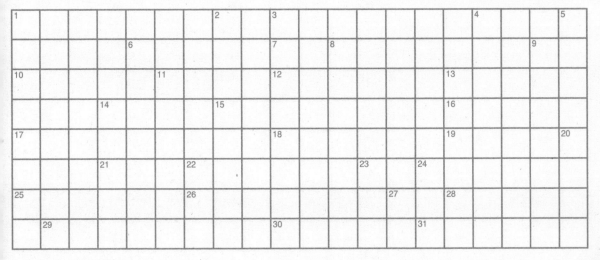

Clues

1 Arousing sympathy or pity
2 Point or pointed end
3 Plausible but not genuine
4 Causing sleep
5 Opening or cavity
6 Mythological three-headed dog guarding the gate of Hades
7 Stratagem or trick
8 Tending to be a follower; accepting the ideas of others
9 Expel or eject
10 Rule or limiting condition
11 Dish for serving soup
12 Deprive of strength; debilitate
13 Stubborn and determined
14 Mark of disgrace; something that detracts from character or reputation

15 Clumsy
16 Having equal effect
17 Charlatan
18 Central, topmost stone in an arch
19 Connection or link
20 Excess or overabundance
21 One or the other of two
22 Abstruse
23 Image or representation
24 Burdensome
25 Confident; optimistic
26 New word
27 Fashionable; stylish
28 Ingenuous; without guile
29 Sleepwalk
30 Hidden or undeveloped
31 Dormant; sluggish; dull

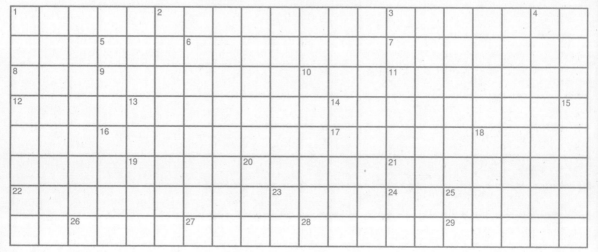

Clues

1 Refute charges
2 Absolute; explicit; without qualification
3 Gourd from which some pipes are made
4 Hindu place
5 One of two more or less equal parts
6 Study of the origin and development of words
7 Fear of women
8 Prejudice
9 Conjecture
10 Boundary
11 Minute
12 Envoy
13 Experimental or provisional
14 Habitually truthful
15 Satisfy or assuage

16 Writing desk
17 Rise again; be resurrected
18 Kneel reverently
19 Long, vehement speech
20 Without; destitute of
21 Condition of being divided into two sharply distinct parts
22 Abnormal tendency to lie or exaggerate
23 Divination based on the interpretation of omens
24 Kind of whiskey
25 Lessen the seriousness of a fault
26 Lukewarm
27 Salivate
28 Grieve
29 Delay; linger

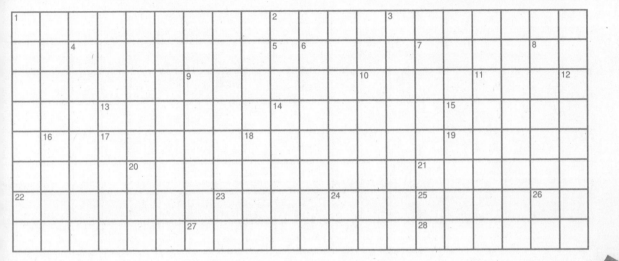

Clues

1 Approval
2 Continuing
3 Ignominious
4 Make one dull or torpid
5 Sweet potato
6 Combination of diverse parts
7 Opening step designed to elicit a response
8 Travel schedule
9 Veil worn by Moslem women
10 Arouse or inflame
11 Agent or influence that works subtly to modify the whole of which it is a part
12 Façade
13 Irregular
14 Run counter to established rules

15 Revere
16 Abound; swarm with
17 Identification with the feelings of another
18 Excessive, uncontrollable emotion
19 Promising; favorable
20 More than necessary
21 Cessation
22 Liking to be apart from others
23 Easily excused or forgiven
24 Dissimilar in nature
25 Direct or impose authoritatively
26 Deep-rooted; long-established
27 Postpone; act evasively in order to gain time
28 Rub off or erase

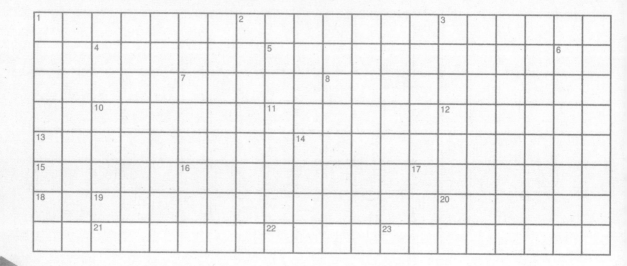

10

Clues

1 Lewd
2 Touchable
3 Exonerate
4 Requiring immediate action
5 God-centered
6 Blameworthy
7 Entangle
8 Exaggeration for effect
9 Show clearly
10 Monument or tomb honoring a deceased person whose body is somewhere else
11 Roman counterpart of the Greek sun god Apollo
12 Job in which little work is required

13 Hindsight
14 Beyond normal experience or understanding
15 Basic text of Orthodox Judaism
16 Fundamentally dissimilar
17 Speculate on the basis of known facts or observations
18 Tardy
19 Equivocation; evasion; subterfuge
20 Having to do with a certain branch of philosophy
21 Hard and unfeeling
22 Lit., to lead apart
23 Unmarried

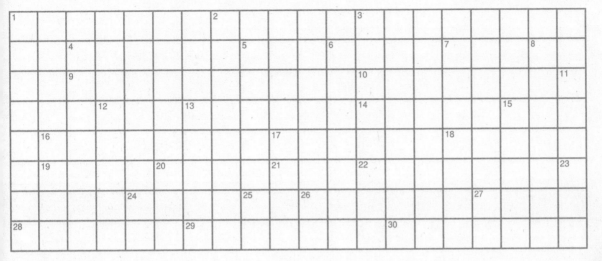

Clues

1 Omission of a word or words
2 Underlying
3 A person at least 100 years old
4 Belief that life has no purpose or meaning
5 Annoyingly self-satisfied
6 Stare sullenly; scowl
7 Given to sophistical argument and specious reasoning
8 Object or haggle, esp. about trifles
9 Abnormal, persistent impulse to steal
10 Curved like an eagle's beak
11 Dutch scholar
12 Collect or summon up
13 Having to do with dancing
14 Small, routine task
15 Strengthen and temper (the will, for example)
16 Occur by turns

17 The surface area directly above the origin or focus of an earthquake
18 A boisterous, quarrelsome woman
19 Daughter of Oedipus
20 Daughter of King Lear
21 Rivulet
22 Becoming liquid or like liquid; melting or appearing to melt
23 Messanine
24 A "slash" or slanting line
25 Twilight
26 Jumpy; easily frightened
27 Bundle of papers
28 Supporting point on which a lever pivots
29 Fundamental change
30 Coming into existence; emerging

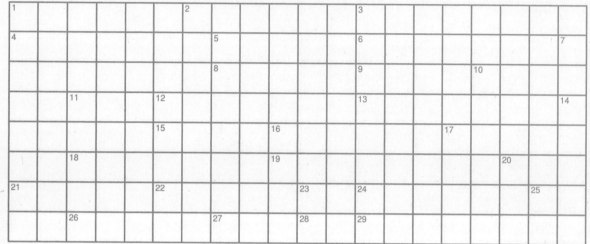

Clues

1 Injurious; morally harmful
2 Playful; vivacious
3 Irritating; annoying
4 Counterfeit
5 Phlegmatic; impassive
6 Assign authority to
7 Fair and impartial
8 The action or right of going out
9 Pertaining to sacred rites
10 Estrange; make hostile or indifferent
11 General sense; purport
12 Religious composition for voices and orchestra
13 Hard and unyielding
14 Issue from
15 Endow with a quality or trait
16 Explain or discuss in detail

17 Tyrannize; exercise arbitrary or overbearing control over
18 Evocative or suggestive of
19 Easily led or managed
20 Try to equal or surpass
21 At or on the side
22 Even though
23 Large, weighty book
24 Wander aimlessly
25 Consider something abstract as being material or concrete
26 Language originating among Jews of Central and Eastern Europe
27 Not genuine
28 One's bearing or aspect
29 Formal tribute; expression of praise

13

Clues

1 Trite; commonplace; worn out
2 Amusement providing relief from more serious pursuits
3 Lacking distinctive qualities
4 In title only; nominal
5 Involving great labor and hardship
6 Vulgar; grossly offensive
7 Superficial similarity
8 Knight of Arthurian legend
9 Pass across or through
10 Coming one after another
11 Set apart for a specific purpose
12 Earthquake
13 Opera glasses attached to a handle
14 Decorated with small mosaic squares
15 Frustrate or disconcert

16 Pertaining to the sense of touch
17 Capable of causing death
18 Prosperous; golden; conducing to happiness
19 Invalid
20 Using few words
21 A pause or interruption in conversation
22 Seventh planet from the sun
23 One who acts in the place of another
24 Decree or formal command
25 Not spoken; implicit
26 Quote as an authority
27 Moderate or adjust

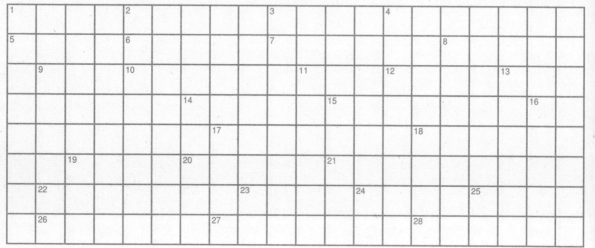

Clues

1 Highly skilled
2 Proposition to be argued
3 Simple and austere
4 Tempt teasingly
5 Acme
6 Block or frustrate
7 Three-paneled work of art
8 Of long duration; continuing
9 Of the same time period
10 Substantiate
11 Group of four
12 Primary source
13 Fear or hatred of what is strange or foreign
14 Slander
15 Winding and twisting

16 Not to be moved or prevailed upon
17 Scanty; meager; inadequate
18 Below the threshold of conscious awareness
19 Refer to indirectly
20 Pass on to a successor
21 Tending to produce dizziness
22 Specify in an agreement
23 Period during which something is held
24 Keep
25 Appeal to
26 Insulting word or phrase
27 Permeate; instill
28 Withdraw from

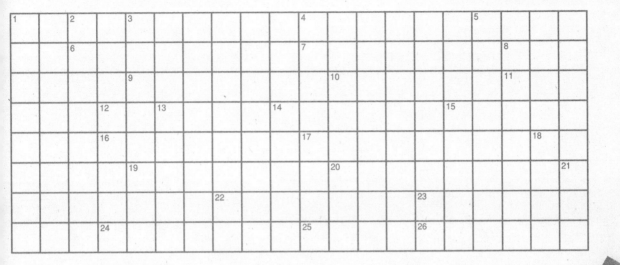

15

Clues

1 Withered and dry
2 Ward off
3 Very clear
4 Popular or common
5 Pertaining to the body
6 Lighten or ease
7 Something that flows out
8 Winding and twisting
9 Profanation
10 Pertinent and appropriate
11 Put into code
12 Therefore
13 Glutton; one who delights in good food
14 Authoritative command or go-ahead

15 Rambling and digressive
16 Curse or denounce
17 Outgoing
18 Strenuous work; tribulation
19 Carry out a lawsuit
20 State in a clear and methodical way
21 Clarify
22 Captivate
23 Exaggeratedly mournful or morose
24 Bitter; scornful
25 Lenient; merciful
26 Something that has particular and independent existence

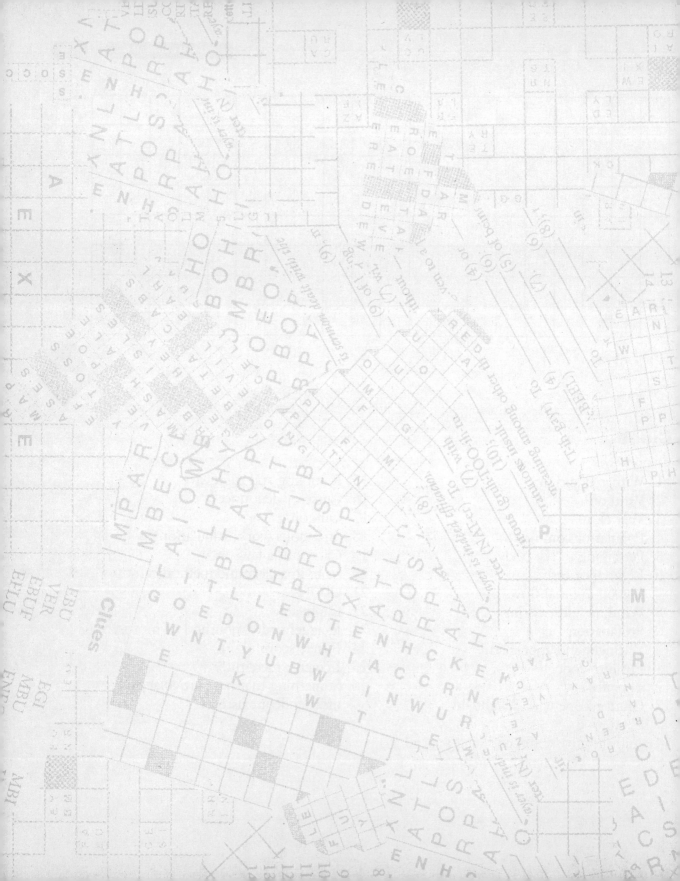

CHAPTER 3

DIRECTIONAL PUZZLES

No, this puzzle is *not* sponsored by an eraser manufacturer. It simply involves a little trial and error. Or maybe a lot. So if you're feeling cranky today we suggest that you go watch TV instead.

Down to business…The N, S, E, and W after the number of the clue indicates the direction in which the answer is to be written. N indicates the top of the page, S the bottom; W signifies left and E signifies right—unless you're lying face-up next to the puzzle, in which case W signifies right and E signifies left. (We suggest keeping things simple by not lying face-up next to the puzzle.)

The next complication is that after you fill in one square in the specified direction, the word may turn at the first available open square. So you'll have to begin by filling in a couple of answers and determining whether they may cross or overlap by one or more letters. If they do, work from there—but later answers may necessitate some rearranging of your early ones.

It will help to know that the numbers following the clues tell you how many letters are in the answers.

If you need help, you have our permission to peek at enough of the filled-out puzzle to provide a starting point.

1

Clues

1E	Was judged to be (6)
2E	Hypocritical (5)
3W	In imitation of (5)
4S	Home-wrecker (7)
5E	Some degrees (10)
6E	Seduce (6)
7W	Avenger (7)
8W	Terminus (5)
9E	Brought out (8)
10W	Hanger-on in cold weather (6)
11N	Senseless (8)
11W	Frustrate (10)
12N	Break (7)
13S	Impenetrable (6)
14W	Follow (5)
15E	Separate (5)
16E	Powder source (4)
17W	Setting (6)
18S	Scholarly community (8)
19N	One of the chewies (7)

Clues

1S   Austen novel (4)
2S   Assignation (5)
3W   Puzzle specification (6)
4N   Rope (5)
5W   Saxophonic pipe (8)
6W   Friendly (8)
7N   Prelude to splashdown (7)
8W   Feeling guilt, unworthiness, etc. (7)
9E   Stroke (4)
10W   Llama wool (6)
11E   Serenade for newlyweds (8)

11E   Aegis (6)
12S   Hang around (5)
13N   Sensation (6)
14W   To react, interact
14W   Norse dining hall (8)
15N   Superfluous (9)
16S   Winding (9)
17E   Respectable (6)
18W   Guaranteed (9)
19W   Natural ability (6)
20W   Rounded out (6)
21W   Unskilled or transient laborer (10)

3

Clues

1S   Cattle panic (8)
2S   Had a yen for (6)
3W   Officially withdraw from a body (6)
4W   Gay and playful (4)
5S   To be relied upon (10)
5S   Reliance (10)
6E   Priority (10)
7N   Diminish (6)
8S   Risk-taker (9)

9N   Whiten (6)
10W   Having a ridged roof (6)
11S   Strip (6)
12E   Hesitate (5)
13E   Rescue (7)
14E   Delete (6)
15S   Manners and customs (5)
16N   Foreknowledge (9)
17W   Satisfied (5)
18N   Timely (9)

Clues

1W   Cigar type (7)
2W   Mix (9)
2W   Mull (8)
3S   Ragged (8)
4N   Wetland (5)
5E   Minty seasoning (7)
6E   Polish up, so to speak (7)
7S   Worldly (7)
8E   Abnormality (7)
9E   Temporary relief (8)
9W   Aromatic (8)
9S   Return to (6)

10N   Alienate (8)
11W   "Dirty money" (5)
12W   Strand (6)
13W   Partyer (7)
14S   Burdensome (7)
15E   Lag (8)
16E   Turncoat (7)
17S   Ill will (6)
18W   According to title (7)
19W   Woman graduate (6)

Clues

1S	In the interior (6)	9W	Loosen (7)
1S	Flat or tasteless (7)	9S	Underwater passer-by (9)
2W	Skilled (5)	10N	Norse god (4)
2E	Warning (5)	11N	Licit (5)
3N	"Double-chinned" water bird (7)	12S	Nut's soft center (6)
4W	Omen (4)	13N	Musket essential (6)
4E	Locate (7)	14W	Execrate (6)
5W	Mexican staple (6)	15W	Guard, for example (7)
6E	More viscous (7)	16W	Dependent (7)
7W	Threaten (6)	17S	Witches' group (5)
7S	Reposition troops (8)	17S	Fashion business (7)
8W	Pertinent (7)	18W	Rock-bottom (5)
9N	One of the Seven Deadly Sins (5)		

Clues

1W	Resent (8)
1W	Scold (6)
1E	Reveler (9)
2E	Tradition (6)
3W	Remorse (6)
3N	Partial refund (6)
4E	Property (6)
5W	Art of riding and training horses (6)
5W	Supervise (6)
6W	Pardon (7)
7W	Interfere with (6)
8W	Security measure (9)
9W	Sluggish (6)

9E	Glowing (8)
10W	A Catholic, for example (6)
10W	Worn (10)
11E	Poison (7)
12S	Loving (7)
13S	Fathered (5)
14S	Local (7)
15W	Imaginary flower that never fades (8)
16W	Pollen producer (6)
16W	Alternate or overlap (7)
17E	Mercenary (5)
18S	Great mental or physical pain (5)
19N	Sundered (5)

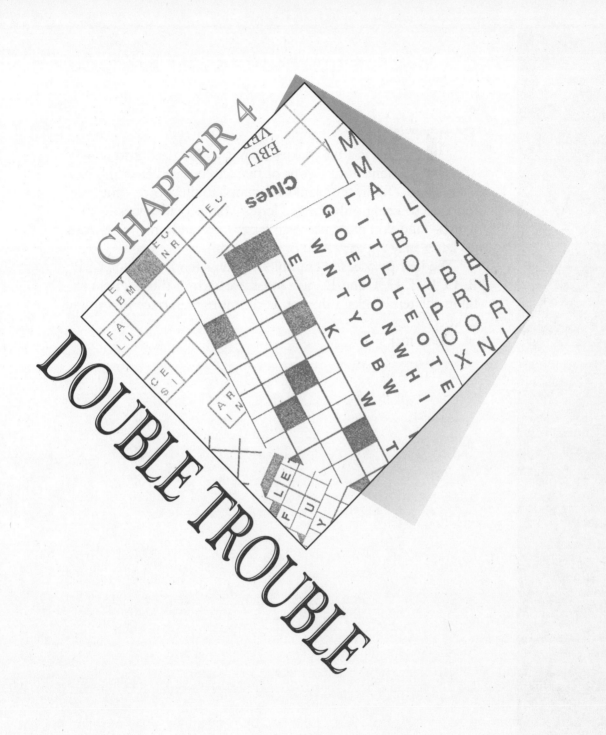

CHAPTER 4

DOUBLE TROUBLE

This is a bit trickier than it looks. Each grid contains four words of five letters each. Your job is to fill in the blanks to complete the words. But you must do so using only the ten letters that provide clues to the words—and you must use each letter once and only once. And no letter may appear twice in any word.

The first puzzle, for example, contains ten letters—V, C, P, R, O, E, T, U, I, and D. You must use each of those letters to fill in the ten blanks, using no letter more than once in a single word.

Good luck!

Answers begin on page 277.

1

	V		C	
P	R	O		
		E		T
	U		I	D

2

	O		I	
B		A		
P		V		T
	R		C	E

3

	R			E
M			T	Y
B	U		P	
S		O		

4

		G		O
	P	U		N
B				S
	R	I		T

5

			O	N
S			M	
	F	T	E	
P		A	L	

6

	U		L	
S		A		T
M		G		
	I		E	R

B	O		
I		E	
S	T	L	
	R	A	D

7

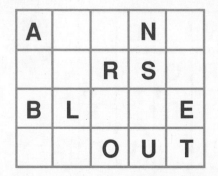

A		N	
	R	S	
B	L		E
	O	U	T

8

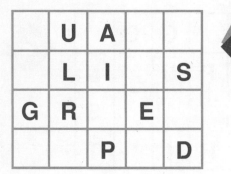

	U	A	
	L	I	S
G	R	E	
		P	D

9

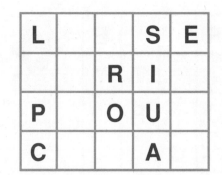

L		S	E
	R	I	
P	O	U	
C		A	

10

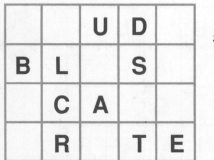

	U	D	
B	L	S	
	C	A	
	R	T	E

11

P	A		E
		I	R	T
C		S	
L		H	

12

CHAPTER 5

DROPOUTS

Select letters from the vertical columns to fill the spaces directly below them. After a little tinkering—and maybe a little erasing—you'll begin to see words taking shape.

Answers begin on page 278.

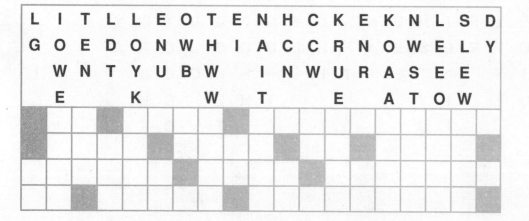

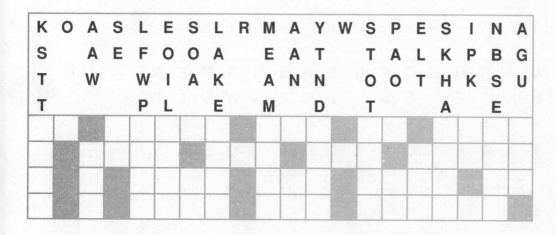

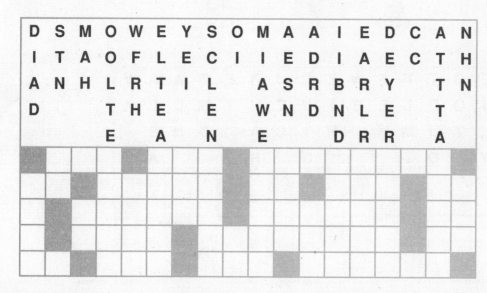

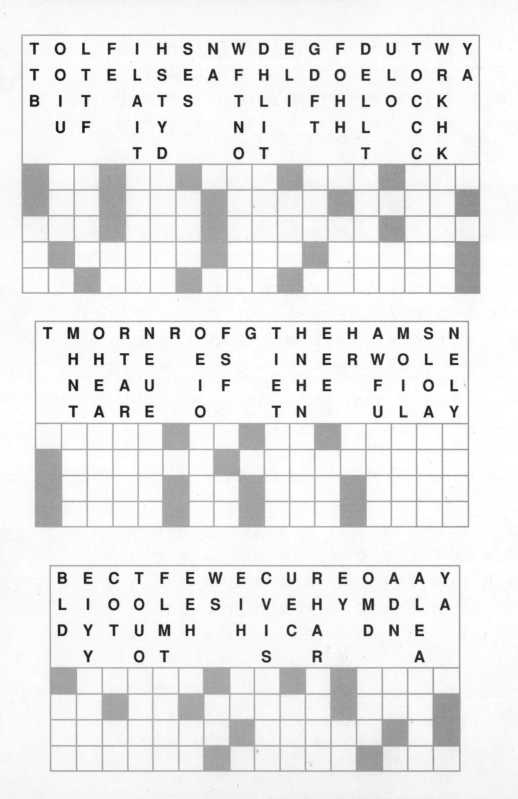

7

```
T S O L E     E H E L M V R D E H Y A E E
L H E S E     T H S Y A A R S   L R P E L
  E I O V Y   W R E   F O E E   T O E N
  N S N E     A N O   A L E     F H   B
```

8

```
B S F W H H N E T C O R P S I N S I N E L
Y I B E E E H S H O R O E K E B T T N M A
E E T T T T E R E W R T E O T D L S A E
        E       A     O     O     O   C
```

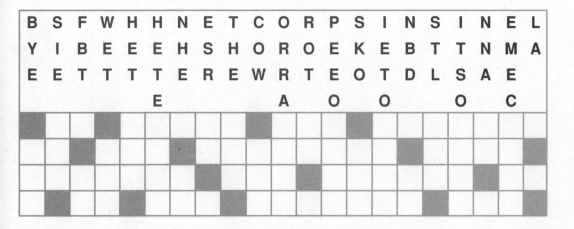

9

```
T I F T C O N S I H F E T H V E G I T E E R
I H E   L O O E T O E R S O E O T H B H T
G H Y   W H V   L O V   L   N I R   V U U
  T E   O F     D E   S   W   T   P R
```

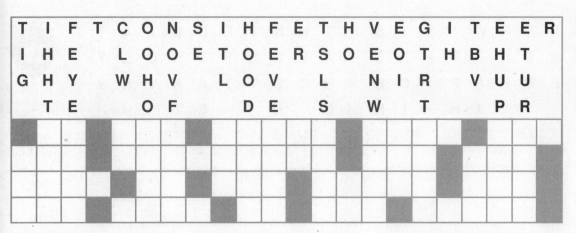

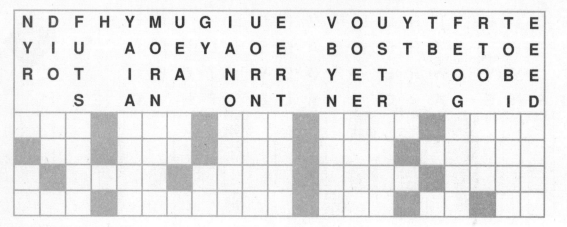

10

```
N D F H Y M U G I U E     V O U Y T F R T E
Y I U   A O E Y A O E     B O S T B E T O E
R O T   I R A   N R R     Y E T   O O B E
    S     A N     O N T   N E R     G   I D
```

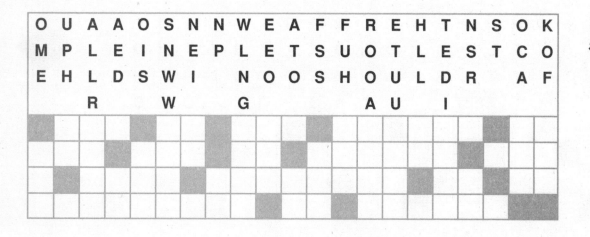

11

```
O U A A O S N N W E A F F R E H T N S O K
M P L E I N E P L E T S U O T L E S T C O
E H L D S W I   N O O S H O U L D R   A F
    R     W     G         A U   I
```

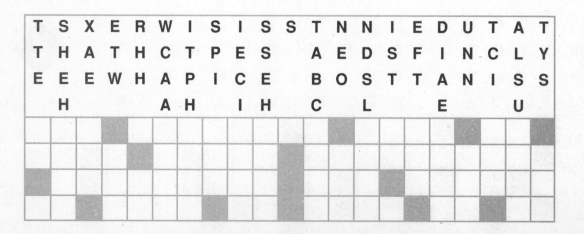

12

```
T S X E R W I S I S S T N N I E D U T A T
T H A T H C T P E S   A E D S F I N C L Y
E E E W H A P I C E   B O S T T A N I S S
  H     A H   I H   C   L     E     U
```

13

```
U L E I I O U R E M O N E Y C I S A E D O F
O L D E T T I O V Y R U O N P O C O T T   U
B T H   Y S A N   E T   R A Y E T K N O   P
  T         F     S O   W             D
```

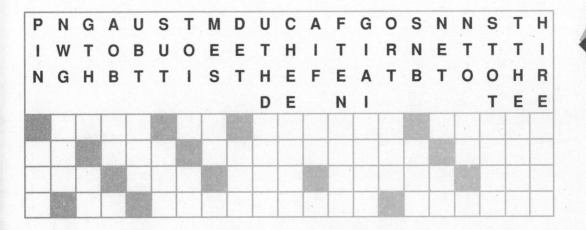

14

```
P N G A U S T M D U C A F G O S N N S T H
I W T O B U O E E T H I T I R N E T T T I
N G H B T T I S T H E F E A T B T O O H R
          D E   N I           T E E
```

15

```
E D O U I A L C A T S C O S E I D S B A N
Y R K A O W I E S U E I O M E L T O E E F
O H E N G T T N M N   T T B E   T I V L F
T       G H   D G       F       I D
```

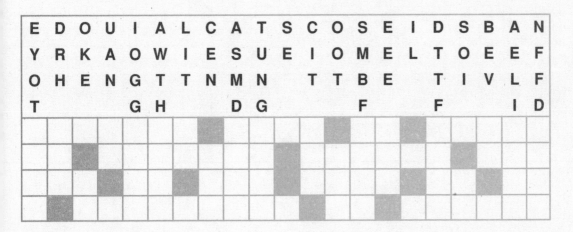

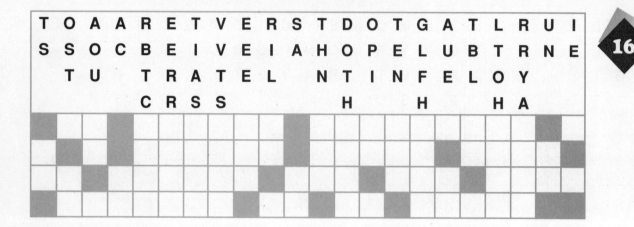

16

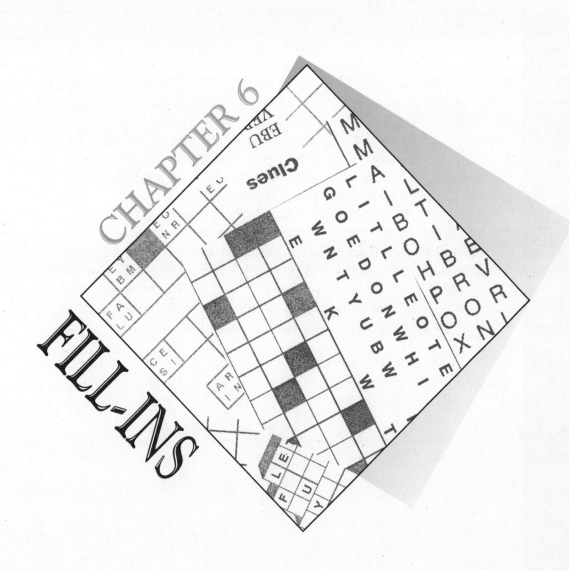

CHAPTER 6

FILL-INS

Every boldface letter is either the first or last letter in a five- or six-letter word. But as you see, all the letters between them are missing. Your job is to select the three- and four-letter pieces from the list and put them where they belong. (Words read both across and down.)

An added complication is that some of them may fit in more than one place. (In the first puzzle, for example, there is a horizontal P _ _ _ _ T and a vertical P _ _ _ _ T.) If you choose the wrong place, you'll find it impossible—that is, we *think* you'll find it impossible—to make all the other pieces fit.

Answers begin on page 281.

1

												R		
			I		A				S					
										A				T
	N					E								
							P					T		
			E											
	D				B					M		A		
														D
			I		R					R				
							T							
	R					F		T				T		
		A					Y							
			E		X					E				

Clues

EBU
VER
EBUF
EFLU

EGI
MBU
ENEG

MBI
UBIL
ANCO

ENE
EDAN
MBRU

EMU
EDLA
ORPI

XIO
UGUR
PLOM

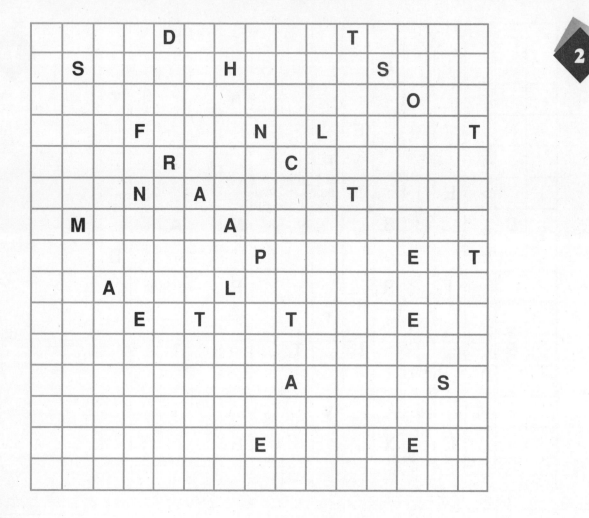

Clues

ERS	ENE	EFE	AIV	DUC	MBI
EIG	VAI	CHIS	UMUL	AVEA	EGIR
EUVR	IATU	UCEN	RRAN	IASM	NIMU
FFET	ERUS				

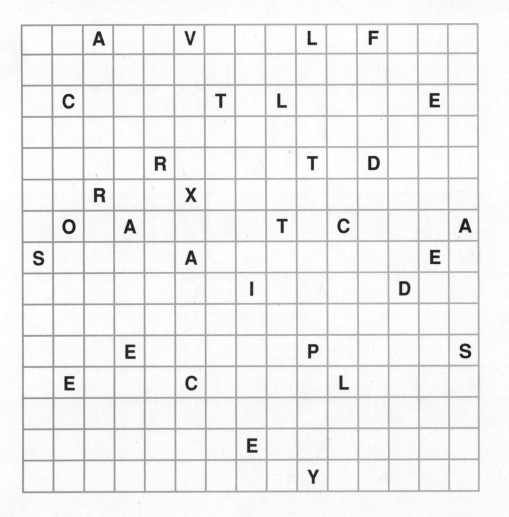

Clues

ARR	GAP	NTI	IRC	ETI	ENA
ICI	TIOS	TIGM	ATOI	AUSA	MPEN
MMUR	ELIC	OEVA	VINC	OATH	VATA
AVOR	ORTE				

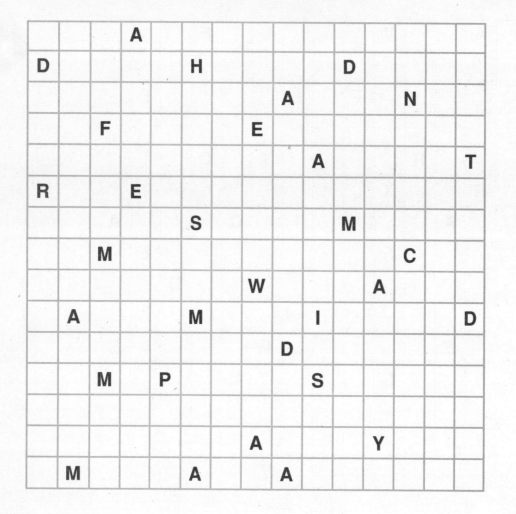

4

Clues

AXI	ANI	EFE	XIO	OGM	MIT
VIA	SCHE	IASM	ATHO	PATH	MPEN
ORPI	TTES	OETI	ICTU	CHIS	IATU
ACAD	EART	RCAN			

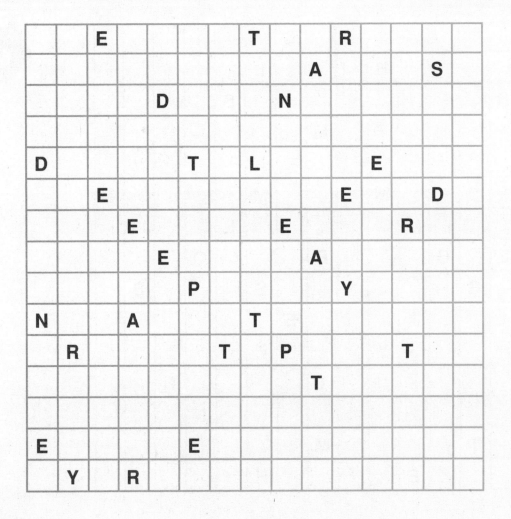

Clues

API	OSI	RGO	EGI	EIG	APS
EIF	EBU	XHOR	VOLV	EMEA	IVER
ERIV	VINC	UCEN	EVER	ENUR	ERUS
VATA	FFAC	EPOS			

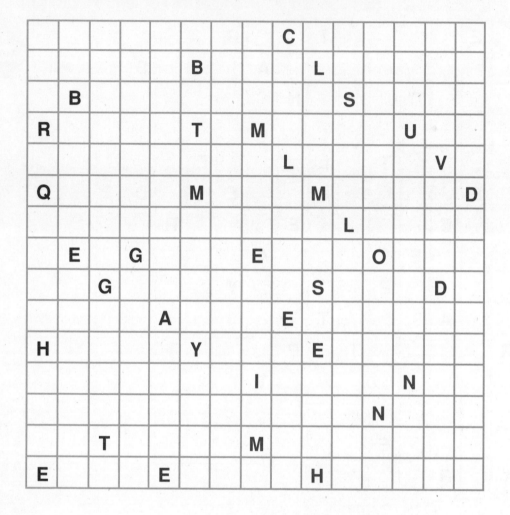

6

Clues

ENC	TON	NNU	UIL	POC	API
API	IBY	AVI	ANA	OIET	OMIL
AMBI	LLUD	EDIU	MPUG	UORU	ELIC
PPUG	YRIA	ILIE	EMUS		

7

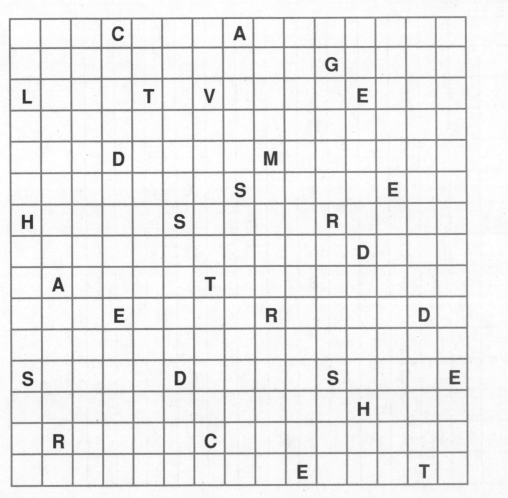

Clues

OAT	ICI	TAV	IRC	VER	UBRI
TOLI	DVER	UBRI	ECED	ICTU	NIMU
ENTO	ERIV	VATA	ORDI	EMAN	IVES
IABL	LOWE	EART			

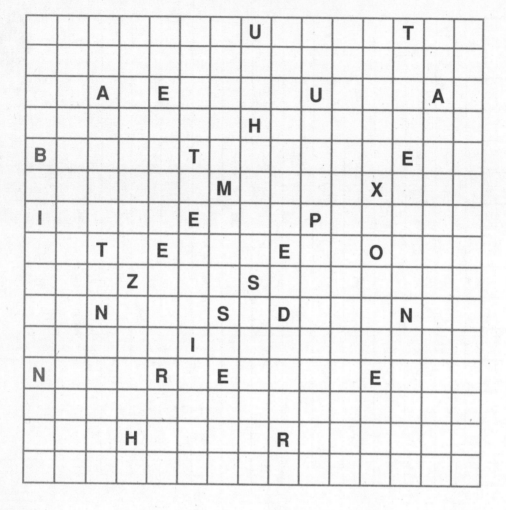

Clues

NNU	EFE	SUR	BES	ERS	MBR
NDU	EXU	OYE	ADI	ATRI	MPUT
FFAC	ECTO	MLAU	MPUG	BRUP	ENIT
FFET	IATU	EREF			

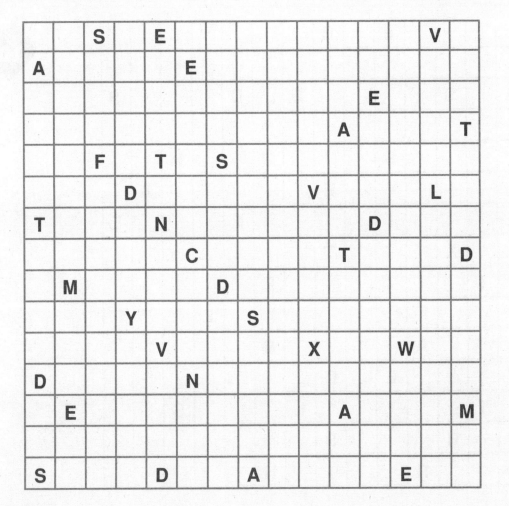

9

Clues

API	API	OKE	ELE	XIO	ENA
MBI	MEN	AIV	RUC	HEA	ANO
ECR	TEA	DHER	RRAN	ENIA	ERTE
ORTE	ICTU	DDUC	TIGM	EMEA	YRIA
AVOR					

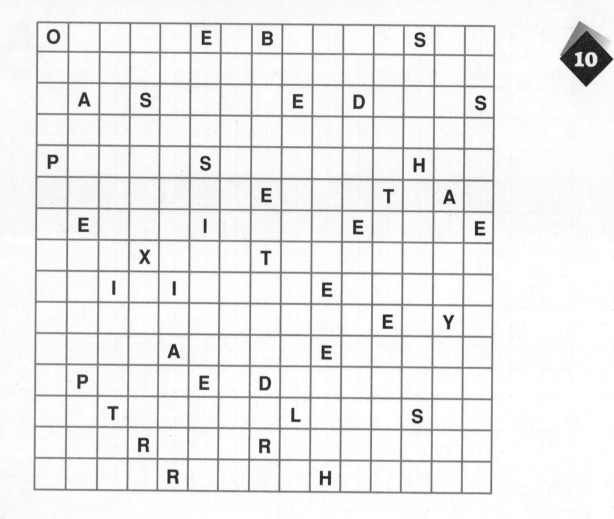

10

Clues

RAS	ROS	OCU	IGO	SSA	LOT
RIT	RON	POC	UMI	ROS	VEN
NNU	THO	STI	NER	BAS	EUVR
ATHO	PHER	ATHO	NDUC	TTIR	ERAT
NNAT	PHIN				

CHAPTER 7

FOUR CORNERS

U se the clues above each small square to arrive at eight words—four horizontal, four vertical.

Then transfer each of the four-by-four squares to one of the quarter sections of the larger square so that you have eight-letter words or phrases across the top and bottom and down both sides.

Answers begin on page 283.

NW	NE	SW	SE
Volcano product	Light source	Hinder	Hodgepodge
Novelist Wister	Moneychanger's	"_____ and	Margarine
Memo	fee	hounds"	Baseball's Musial
Shine brightly	Pub staple	Track	Story
Extended	Dispatched	Impart	Entertainer
Over the hill	Chemists' work-	Expended, so to	_____ Vista
(abbr.)	shops	speak	Imprint
Reject	Author of *Letters to*	Wash	Sharpen
Again	*Father Flye*	Of the mouth	
	Bearing	Healthy	
	Wine type		

NW NE SW SE

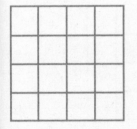
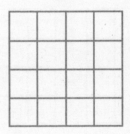

NW

Merriment
Mountain strong-
hold
Eldest of the
Pleiades
Makes out
Amusement; com-
petition
Disclosure
Great lake
Nestling hawk

NE

Ball team
Civil rights figure
Parks
Matures
Nothing more
than
Study
Theater box
Consumer
Mean; corrupt

SW

Strikebreaker
Tramp
Poems of praise
Ambulate
Win, place, and
_____
Musically, at the
"tail" end
Cain's brother
Small wooded area

SE

Check counterfoil
Zhivago's love
Kind of exam
Unusual height
Casino machine
Literary plantation
Russian range
Pitching essential

NW

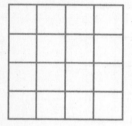

NE

SW

SE

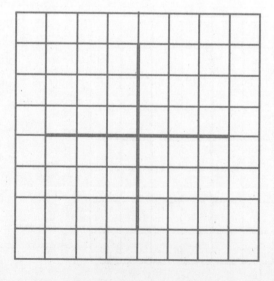

NW

Impervious
Lamb's pseudo-
  nym
Irreducible con-
  stituent
Love fatuously
Beer feature
Sax genus
Public disturbance
Agatha Christie,
  for example

NE

A latrine, nautical-
  ly
Musical notation
Fled
One coming of age
Handle
Women's magazine
On the downwind
  side
Quiescent

SW

Inclined passage
Jacob's brother
Door base
Difficult, as in a
  _____ order
Leftover part
European neigh-
  bor
Teen hangout
Influence

SE

Interlock harmo-
  niously
Sandwich spread
Thailand's former
  name
False account
Superlative of
  many
Famous pen name
Mark of authenticity
Abode

NW

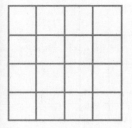

NE

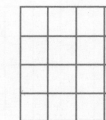

SW

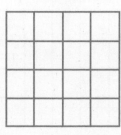

SE

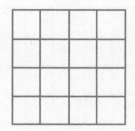

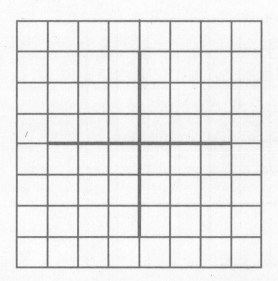

NW

Hobbled
Certain goat
Dole out by measure
Expression of regret
Bean type
Biblical brother
Changed, as in _____*morphosis*
Former mates

NE

Amphibious truck
Comic Young
Hamlet, for example
Pot content
Artistic and literary movement of early twentieth century _____ Bator
Set at an oblique angle
Athletes' Achilles heel, so to speak

SW

Polish
_____ Stanley Gardner
Deteriorates
Sequent
Noggin
Exhort
Bend
An occasion for much or many

SE

Handled
Entertainer _____ Adams
Frost
Cease
Belonging to a woman
Emend
Classy transportation
Abstruse

NW

NE

SW

SE

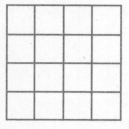

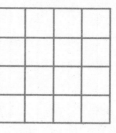

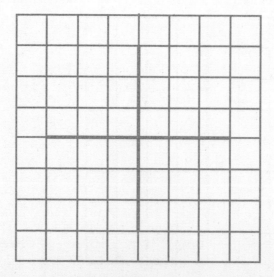

CHAPTER 8
GROUPIES

G roupies have lots of blanks and no clues. Actually, there is one clue, the one word supplied for you in each puzzle. This word not only provides a couple of letters in adjoining words but also is a clue to the group from which the other words are to be drawn.

For example, if the word is CAR, then the other words are probably all vehicles, perhaps limited to those having internal-combustion engines.

Or perhaps not. But after all, it's the perhapses that make life interesting.

Answers begin on page 284.

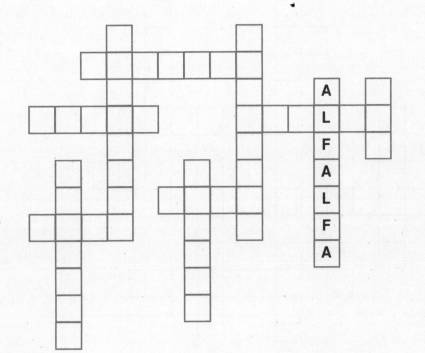

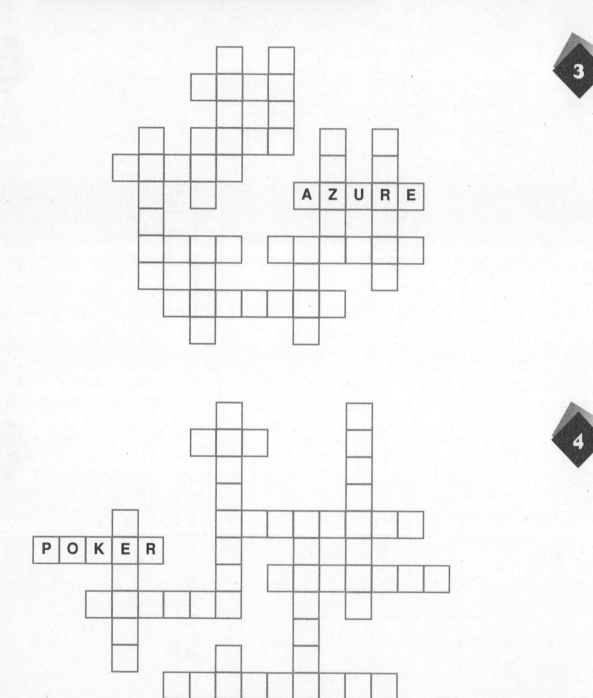

3

4

Z I N N I A

5

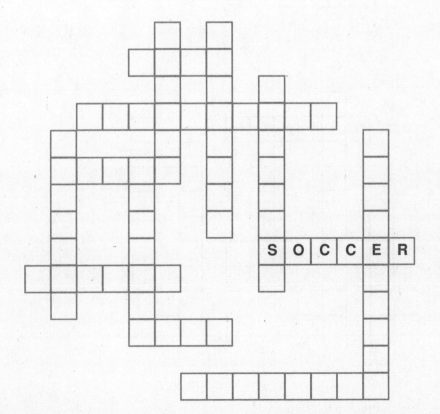

S O C C E R

6

7

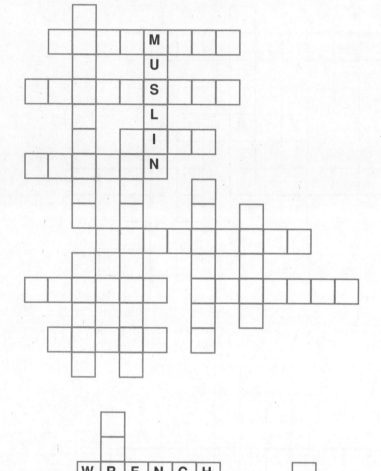

8

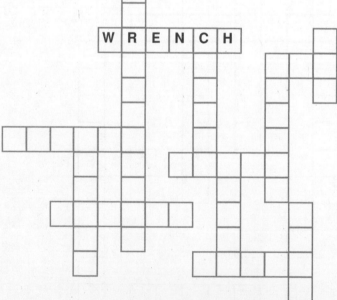

MEXICO

MONTANA

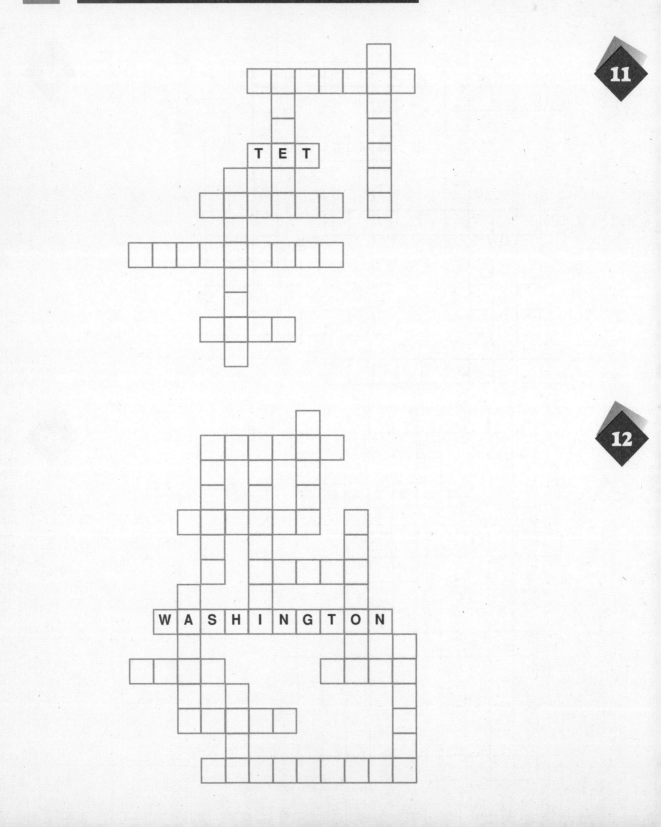

11

12

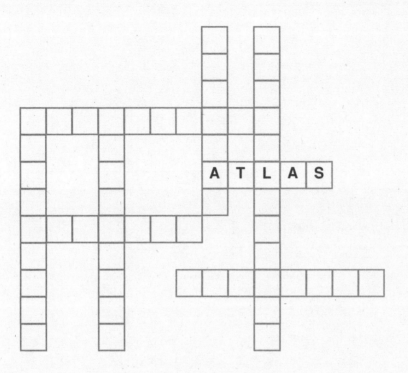

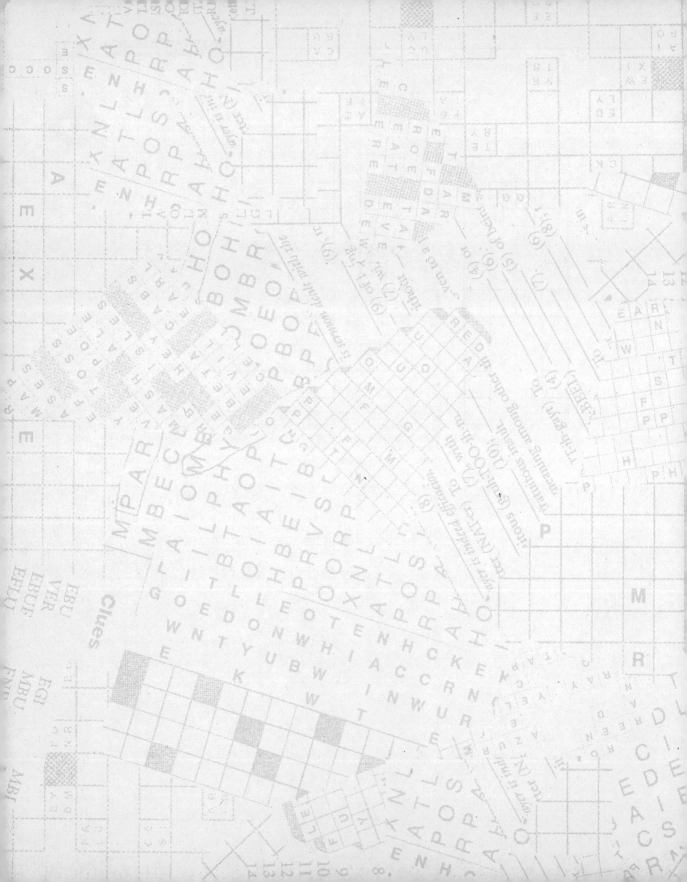

CHAPTER 9

HIDDEN MEANINGS

Here's a little exercise in vocabulary-building. You may find it less puzzling if you already know what some of the words mean, but you'll still have to fill in the blanks in the definitions using words from the list at the bottom of the page. The number after each blank tells you the number of letters in the word that precedes it.

Some words may seem to fit in more than one definition, but each word may be used only once, so you may have to go back and change an answer here and there.

Answers begin on page 288.

1. **peruse** (peh-ROOZ) To _____ (4) or _____ (7), esp. with _____ (5) _____ (4).

2. **obfuscate** (OB-fus-kayt) To _____ (4) _____ (7): *His explanation obfuscated the issue*; to _____ (7).

3. **peremptory** (peh-REMP-ter-ee) _____ (9); _____ (11); _____ (9) so _____ (10) and _____ (12) as to _____ (5) of no _____ (7) _____ (5), _____ (10), or _____ (13).

4. **nominal** (NAH-mih-nul) In _____ (4) _____ (4); so _____ (5) as to be _____ (11) or _____ (13). A related word is *titular*, meaning in title only.

5. **propinquity** (proh-PIN-kwih-tee) _____ (8) in _____ (4) or _____ (5); _____ (9) of _____ (12); _____ (7).

6. **recidivism** (rih-SID-ih-viz-'m) _____ (8) or _____ (7) _____ (7) into a _____ (6) _____ (7) of _____ (8), esp. _____ (8).

7. **extrapolate** (ek-STRAP-uh-layt) To _____ (5) or _____ (8) by _____ (10) _____ (5) _____ (5) or _____ (7).

8. **misprision** (mis-PRIH-zhun) _____ (10) in _____ (6) _____ (6); _____ (7) to _____ (7) or _____ (6) a _____ (5).

9. **sciamachy** (sy-AM-uh-kee) A _____ (8) with _____ (7) or _____ (9) _____ (7).

10. **umbrage** (UM-brij) _____ (7) or _____ (10): *to take umbrage at a remark.*

Word List

4 Letters
ONLY
MAKE
NAME
CARE
TIME
READ

5 Letters
KNOWN
INFER
PLACE
SMALL
CRIME
FACTS
DELAY

ADMIT
GREAT

6 Letters
PUBLIC
REPORT
FORMER
OFFICE

7 Letters
FIGURES
PREVENT
ENEMIES
OFFENSE
SHADOWS
FAILURE

OBSCURE
FURTHER
CHRONIC
PATTERN
RELAPSE
KINSHIP
CONFUSE
EXAMINE

8 Letters
ESTIMATE
FIGHTING
NEARNESS
HABITUAL
CRIMINAL
BEHAVIOR

9 Letters
CLOSENESS
IMPERIOUS
IMAGINARY
EXPRESSED

10 Letters
PROJECTING
DISCUSSION
DECISIVELY
MISCONDUCT
RESENTMENT

11 Letters
UNIMPORTANT
DICTATORIAL

12 Letters
CONCLUSIVELY
RELATIONSHIP

13 Letters
INSIGNIFICANT
CONTRADICTION

1

2

1. **efficacious** (ef-ih-KAY-shus) Being _____ (7) of _____ (9) the _____ (8) _____ (6): *His sermon dealt with the question of whether prayer is indeed efficacious.*

2. **natter** (NAT-er) To _____ (4) _____ (9), mostly to _____ (7), with the _____ (9) of being _____ (9).

3. **gratuitous** (gruh-TOO-ih-tus) _____ (7) without _____ (6) or _____ (10); _____ (5) without _____ (5) or _____ (13): a gratuitous insult.
    Gratuity, meaning among other things a tip given to a porter, comes from the same Greek root.

4. **mitigate** (MIT-ih-gayt) To _____ (4) or _____ (6) _____ (6) or _____ (4) _____ (6).

5. **dishabille** (dis-uh-BEEL) _____ (5) of being _____ (4) _____ (6) _____ (7).

6. **asperse** (uh-SPURSS) To _____ (6) _____ (5) or _____ (8) _____ (7) or _____ (8); to _____ (8) (one's) _____ (10).
    Most people use the noun form, *aspersion*, as in *cast aspersions*. But *cast aspersions* is only a longer way of saying *asperse*.

7. **expatiate** (eks-PAY-shee-ayt) To _____ (7) at _____ (5) _____ (6) or in _____ (6).

8. **heuristic** (hyoo-RIS-tik) Applied to a _____ (6) of _____ (8) by which _____ (8) _____ (5) through _____ (13) and _____ (9).
    Think of *Eureka!* (*I have found it!*), which Archimedes is said to have exclaimed when he discovered a method of determining the purity of gold.

9. **caveat** (KAV-ee-ut or KAY-vee-ut) A _____ (7) _____ (9) (some-one) from _____ (8) _____ (4) or _____ (9): *issued a caveat against any further incursions.*
    Caveat is most familiar, probably, in the Latin maxim *Caveat emptor* (*Let the buyer beware*).

10. **exigency** (EK-sih-jen-see) An _____ (9) or _____ (8) _____ (9) _____ (7) for _____ (9) _____ (6) or _____ (9).

Word List

4 Letters						10 Letters
TALK	STATE	SEVERE	GRANTED	BESMIRCH	SITUATION	REPUTATION
ACTS	CAUSE	MILDER	CHARGES	DAMAGING	IMMEDIATE	OBLIGATION
ONLY	GIVEN	RESULT	DRESSED	TEACHING	ENJOINING	
LESS	FALSE	BECOME	CAPABLE	INTENDED	PRACTICES	13 Letters
MAKE		PARTLY	ONESELF	INNUENDO	EMERGENCY	
	6 Letters	DETAIL	WARNING	SPECIFIC	INTENTION	JUSTIFICA-TION
5 Letters	ACTION	SPREAD	DISCUSS	STUDENTS	OVERHEARD	INVESTIGA-TION
LEARN	METHOD				DISCOVERY	
GREAT	CHARGE	7 Letters	8 Letters	9 Letters	NAGGINGLY	
	LENGTH	CALLING	CRITICAL	ATTENTION	PRODUCING	

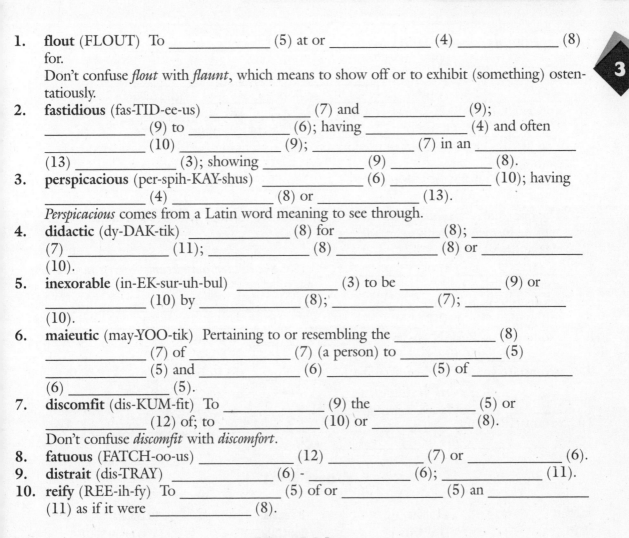

1. **flout** (FLOUT) To _____ (5) at or _____ (4) _____ (8) for.
Don't confuse *flout* with *flaunt*, which means to show off or to exhibit (something) ostentatiously.

2. **fastidious** (fas-TID-ee-us) _____ (7) and _____ (9); _____ (9) to _____ (6); having _____ (4) and often _____ (10) _____ (9); _____ (7) in an _____ (13) _____ (3); showing _____ (9) _____ (8).

3. **perspicacious** (per-spih-KAY-shus) _____ (6) _____ (10); having _____ (4) _____ (8) or _____ (13).
Perspicacious comes from a Latin word meaning to see through.

4. **didactic** (dy-DAK-tik) _____ (8) for _____ (8); _____ (7) _____ (11); _____ (8) _____ (8) or _____ (10).

5. **inexorable** (in-EK-sur-uh-bul) _____ (3) to be _____ (9) or _____ (10) by _____ (8); _____ (7); _____ (10).

6. **maieutic** (may-YOO-tik) Pertaining to or resembling the _____ (8) _____ (7) of _____ (7) (a person) to _____ (5) _____ (5) and _____ (6) _____ (5) of _____ (6) _____ (5).

7. **discomfit** (dis-KUM-fit) To _____ (9) the _____ (5) or _____ (12) of; to _____ (10) or _____ (8).
Don't confuse *discomfit* with *discomfort*.

8. **fatuous** (FATCH-oo-us) _____ (12) _____ (7) or _____ (6).

9. **distrait** (dis-TRAY) _____ (6) - _____ (6); _____ (11).

10. **reify** (REE-ih-fy) To _____ (5) of or _____ (5) an _____ (11) as if it were _____ (8).

Word List

3 Letters
WAY
NOT

4 Letters
KEEN
HIGH
SHOW

5 Letters
AWARE
BRING
PLANS
IDEAS
SCOFF

FORTH
THINK
TREAT

6 Letters
BECOME
STUPID
ABSENT
HIGHLY
LATENT
PLEASE
MINDED

7 Letters
PROCESS
ADAMANT

REFINED
FOOLISH
HELPING
CAREFUL
MORALLY

8 Letters
TEACHING
DISTRESS
ENTREATY
INTENDED
CONCRETE
PEDANTIC
DELICACY
JUDGMENT
SOCRATIC

BORINGLY
CONTEMPT

9 Letters
STANDARDS
DIFFICULT
PERSUADED
EXCESSIVE
EXACTING
FRUSTRATE

10 Letters
INFLUENCED
MORALISTIC
PERCEPTIVE
CAPRICIOUS

DISCONCERT
RELENTLESS

11 Letters
ABSTRACTION
INATTENTIVE
INSTRUCTIVE

12 Letters
COMPLACENTLY
EXPECTATIONS

13 Letters
UNDERSTANDING
OVERSENSITIVE

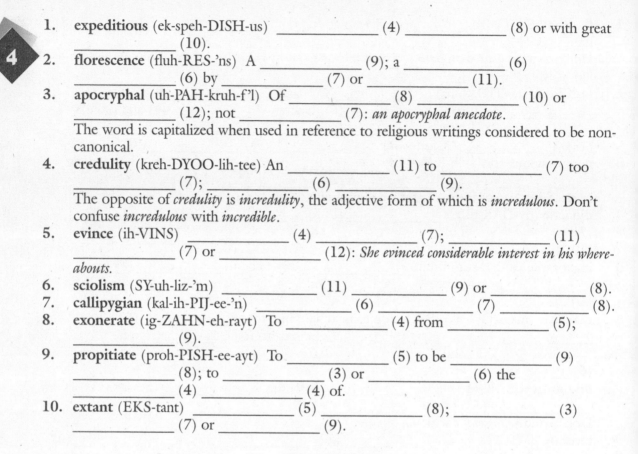

1.   **expeditious** (ek-speh-DISH-us) _____ (4) _____ (8) or with great _____ (10).

2.   **florescence** (fluh-RES-'ns) A _____ (9); a _____ (6) _____ (6) by _____ (7) or _____ (11).

3.   **apocryphal** (uh-PAH-kruh-f'l) Of _____ (8) _____ (10) or _____ (12); not _____ (7): *an apocryphal anecdote.*
     The word is capitalized when used in reference to religious writings considered to be non-canonical.

4.   **credulity** (kreh-DYOO-lih-tee) An _____ (11) to _____ (7) too _____ (7); _____ (6) _____ (9).
     The opposite of *credulity* is *incredulity*, the adjective form of which is *incredulous*. Don't confuse *incredulous* with *incredible*.

5.   **evince** (ih-VINS) _____ (4) _____ (7); _____ (11) _____ (7) or _____ (12): *She evinced considerable interest in his where-abouts.*

6.   **sciolism** (SY-uh-liz-'m) _____ (11) _____ (9) or _____ (8).

7.   **callipygian** (kal-ih-PIJ-ee-'n) _____ (6) _____ (7) _____ (8).

8.   **exonerate** (ig-ZAHN-eh-rayt) To _____ (4) from _____ (5); _____ (9).

9.   **propitiate** (proh-PISH-ee-ayt) To _____ (5) to be _____ (9) _____ (8); to _____ (3) or _____ (6) the _____ (4) _____ (4) of.

10. **extant** (EKS-tant) _____ (5) _____ (8); _____ (3) _____ (7) or _____ (9).

Word List

3 Letters
NOT
WIN

4 Letters
GOOD
FREE
SHOW
DONE
WILL

5 Letters
CAUSE
BLAME
STILL

6 Letters
HAVING
REGAIN
MARKED
PERIOD
EASILY

7 Letters
BELIEVE
SHAPELY
GENUINE
PLAINLY
SUCCESS
DEFUNCT
CLEARLY
READILY

8 Letters
INCLINED
EXISTING
LEARNING
SPEEDILY
BUTTOCKS
DOUBTFUL

9 Letters
DESTROYED
KNOWLEDGE
EXCULPATE
PERSUADED
FLOWERING
FAVORABLY

10 Letters
AUTHORSHIP
EFFICIENCY

11 Letters
SUPERFICIAL
DEMONSTRATE
INCLINATION
ACHIEVEMENT

12 Letters
CONVINCINGLY
AUTHENTICITY

5

1. **meticulous** (meh-TIK-yuh-lus) _____ (9) or _____ (11) _____ (7).

2. **inveterate** (in-VET-ur-it) _____ (6) _____ (11) over an _____ (8) _____ (8) as a _____ (5); _____ (10) in _____ (8) _____ (9) of _____ (4) _____ (8).

3. **inure** (in-YOOR) To _____ (4) (one) _____ (10) to _____ (9) _____ (11); to _____ (9).

4. **extenuate** (ek-STEN-yoo-ayt) To _____ (6) or _____ (8) the _____ (11) of an _____ (7), _____ (5), etc., by _____ (6) an _____ (6).
   More and more, it seems, errors are attributed to *extenuating circumstances*.

5. **vitiate** (VISH-ee-ayt) To _____ (8) the _____ (5) of; to _____ (7); to _____ (6) _____ (7) _____ (11).

6. **fulsome** (FUL-sum) _____ (11) _____ (9) or _____ (9): *fulsome praise*.

7. **Zeitgeist** (TSYT-gyst) The _____ (6) of the _____ (4); the _____ (8) and _____ (7) _____ (10) with a _____ (6).

8. **hebetude** (HEB-eh-tood) The _____ (8) or _____ (9) of being _____ (4) or _____ (9).

9. **mores** (MOR-ayz) _____ (8) and _____ (7) that are _____ (10) _____ (9) to the _____ (7) of _____ (7) and through _____ (10) have become _____ (7) _____ (7).

10. **troglodyte** (TRAHG-luh-dyt) _____ (11) _____ (4) _____ (7); a _____ (6) who _____ (7) to _____ (4) in _____ (9); (anyone) having _____ (8) _____ (6) or _____ (8).

Word List

4 Letters
LIVE
LONG
TIME
CAVE
DULL
MAKE

5 Letters
ERROR
HABIT
VALUE

6 Letters
PERIOD
RENDER
LESSEN
SPIRIT
FIRMLY
PERSON
HABITS
EXCUSE
GIVING

7 Letters
CORRUPT

CUSTOMS
WELFARE
BINDING
SOCIETY
CAREFUL
FEELING
QUALITY
OFFENSE
DWELLER
CHOOSES
LEGALLY
MORALLY

8 Letters
THINKING
DIMINISH
OPINIONS
HABITUAL
FOLKWAYS
EXTENDED
OUTMODED
DOWNPLAY
STANDING
DURATION

9 Letters
INSINCERE

LETHARGIC
SOMETHING
BEHAVIOR
CONDITION
EXTREMELY
SECLUSION
EXCESSIVE
HABITUATE
CONDUCIVE

10 Letters
OBSERVANCE
IDENTIFIED
CONSIDERED

PERSISTING
ACCUSTOMED

11 Letters
INEFFECTIVE
UNDESIRABLE
PREHISTORIC
EXCESSIVELY
OFFENSIVELY
SERIOUSNESS
ESTABLISHED

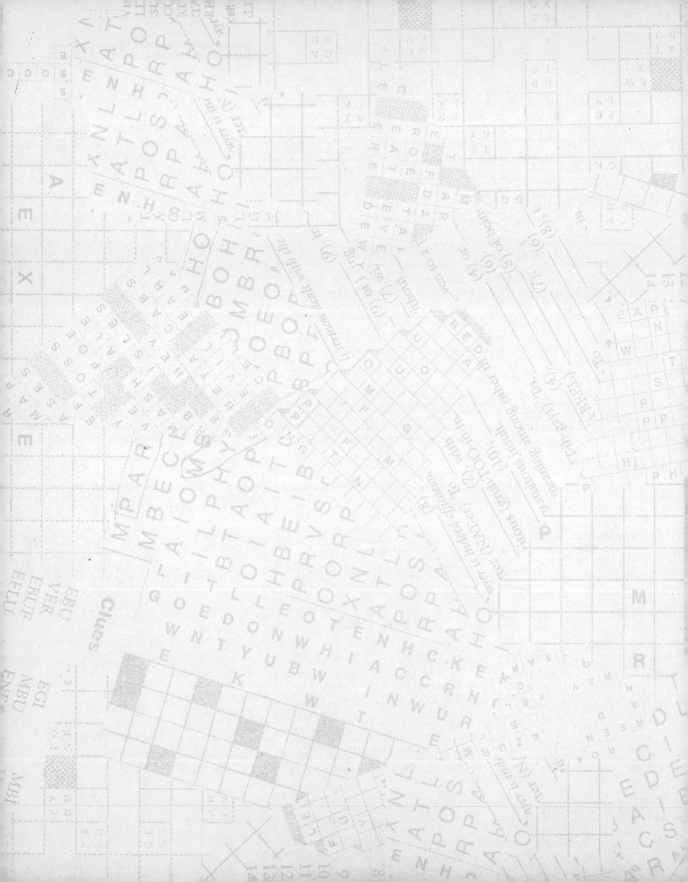

CHAPTER 10

HIDDEN NAMES

E ach of the boxes below contains the name of a famous person. Unfortunately, the boxes are too small for the entire name. See if you can identify them anyway. The first name is on top and the last name on the bottom.

Answers begin on page 290.

American Authors

1.
R	N	E
I	N	G

2.
M	I	L
K	I	N

3.
H	O	M
O	L	F

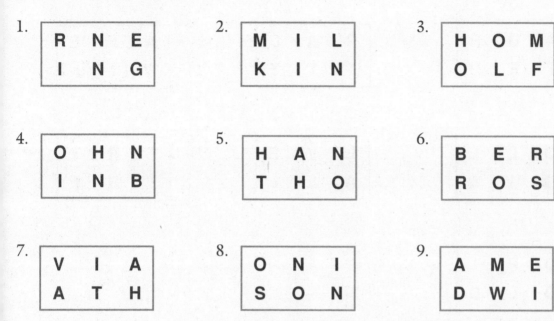

4.
O	H	N
I	N	B

5.
H	A	N
T	H	O

6.
B	E	R
R	O	S

7.
V	I	A
A	T	H

8.
O	N	I
S	O	N

9.
A	M	E
D	W	I

Rock 'n' Roll Stars

1.
H	U	C
E	R	R

2.
T	T	L
C	H	A

3.
A	T	S
M	I	N

4.
M	E	S
R	O	W

5.
K	I	E
I	L	S

6.
R	E	T
N	K	L

7.
L	O	R
S	T	E

8.
L	A	N
R	I	S

9.
U	R	T
B	A	I

Film Stars

3

1.

A	U	R
I	E	R

2.

R	A	D
I	T	T

3.

A	L	E
W	I	N

4.

O	L	L
G	W	A

5.

L	V	E
A	L	L

6.

E	R	Y
T	R	E

7.

O	P	I
O	L	D

U.S. Presidents

4

1.

F	O	R
Y	E	S

2.

V	E	R
E	V	E

3.

J	A	M
I	S	O

4.

W	I	G
O	W	E

5.

N	A	L
A	G	A

6.

A	N	D
S	O	N

U.S. Artists

1.
S	L	O
H	O	M

2.
R	I	C
R	E	M

3.
D	M	A
S	E	S

4.
M	A	N
C	K	W

5.
A	N	D
A	R	H

6.
C	K	S
L	O	C

7.
G	I	A
E	E	F

8.
C	O	B
W	R	E

Thinkers

1.
S	A	A
T	O	N

2.
E	N	E
S	C	A

3.
M	A	N
A	N	T

4.
R	A	N
A	C	O

5.
B	E	R
S	T	E

6.
M	I	L
L	I	A

7.
A	R	A
D	A	N

TV's Biggest Stars

7

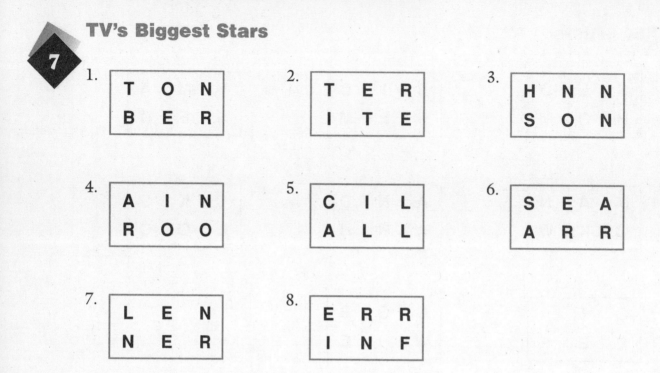

1.

T	O	N
B	E	R

2.

T	E	R
I	T	E

3.

H	N	N
S	O	N

4.

A	I	N
R	O	O

5.

C	I	L
A	L	L

6.

S	E	A
A	R	R

7.

L	E	N
N	E	R

8.

E	R	R
I	N	F

CHAPTER 11

HIDDEN WORDS

1. Common Word Searches

The words are all in there somewhere, running forward and backward, up, down, and diagonally. Happy hunting!

Answers begin on page 291.

SOME PHOBIAS

1

```
M P A R T H E N O P H O B I A O S L
M B E C E R S A I B O H P O D E P H A
A I O M B H E Z O M B R O P H O B T
I L P H Y A I G O E O M T A A L A F
B T A O P R I P B O B D L O E T I T
O I A I T O M B P R P T H N W L B A
H B E I B A P E O O O H N E A H O I
P R V S B O M P C H P O O P H T H B
O O R P S O H O I O P H D B P E P O
X N L A O O H P P H P O O I I I O H
A T L H B M N P O H A H L B D A M P
P O S I N T A B O I O H O T I H S A
R P A U D L I T O S S B E B N A A I
A H S C I A P H O C U A I O I A H N
H O E D E T N I R P E M G A S A P E
I B A I B O H P A I C S A R C N A P
U I C S A I B O H P E N O L E B U F
M A R N A H G Y M N O P H O B I A P
```

ANTLOPHOBIA	HARPAXOPHOBIA	PEDOPHOBIA
BELONEPHOBIA	HIPPOPHOBIA	PENIAPHOBIA
BLENNOPHOBIA	MUSOPHOBIA	PHASMOPHOBIA
BRONTOPHOBIA	MYRMECOPHOBIA	POTAMOPHOBIA
ERGASIOPHOBIA	OMBROPHOBIA	SCIAPHOBIA
GYMNOPHOBIA	PARTHENOPHOBIA	ZOOPHOBIA

SOME MANIAS

```
A A N A I N A M O L E M N I T C H R
M T I T S H S E M O N O M A N W E R
N A S N P C N I A A A Y O E E G D O
A A N I A L H T N I N O O L M E O I
N B Y I E M F R N A I D E C A E N A
N F N H A O O A E N M U D A T M O I
N I U O E M M C O M T O B A E E M N
G E N P S O A M A H A L R G S R A A
F Y R A N T A I E M U T A O L G N M
A N N O M N O R N T R L O O D O I O
I S M E I O O M O A O A G M O M A R
N M H A C M G M A M M O H M A A I O
A A E T A O A O A N M O E P R N T D
M T F N I N M N L A I E H A A I I E
O H I E I G I A N F E A N T N A Y A
T A N A D A N I N A O O N O Y W F N
I O E A I N A M O I N O A S C M A E
S A G D O Y T A I N A M O G A H P A
```

ABLUTOMANIA	HEDONOMANIA	NOSTOMANIA
CHREMATOMANIA	LOGOMANIA	OINOMANIA
DOROMANIA	MEGALOMANIA	ONIOMANIA
ELEUTHEROMANIA	MELOMANIA	PHAGOMANIA
ERGOMANIA	MONOMANIA	PHARMACOMANIA
GYNECOMANIA	MYTHOMANIA	SITOMANIA

I BEFORE E, EXCEPT...

3

```
N E B S P S O T H E V E I R T E R D
D E C E N W H H E T E N V T T F L I
F D B E L I E F E I O O E E O E P H
S D G A E S R C O H F W D R I S I C
C R S S R E N R E T I L B Y O E E E
O T R A L E E V E I H C A S A U D I
N O A I I O I A E C G R I E V E C L
T D E C R W E F P V E T E E F D O I
O F S U G G E A E E I S O H E N N
T T E D E R V V D T R I V T E C C G
T E T I A D I S V R D C L E Y E E P
H E S V C E E E D I L E E E E I I L
I R C H E F C C F H E B F I B O T N
E P I E I R N B E T I C C V V H W S
F E I E O H O S O I W P E A N E E E
F H R E E T C N T T V A N R E V I I
I C D E C E I T S K V E I R G C R Z
E Y I A E E D E N E A T S I N O D E
```

ACHIEVE	DECEIVE	RETRIEVE
BELIEF	FIERCE	SCIENCE
BELIEVE	GRIEF	SEIZE
CEILING	GRIEVE	SIEGE
CHIEF	PERCEIVE	THIEF
CONCEIT	PIECE	WEIRD
CONCEIVE	RECEIVE	WIELD
DECEIT	RELIEF	YIELD

OOH, NO!

```
G O O F U C A Y D S E N O O B T I N
C W O D T M W M V P U R R E O N A K
H N D E I G H O O D S O O T I A O T
T O O K I U O E S I R G T R N O R M
E T N E A A U O F E O M O L B N O N
S M S D R D N D D T N O R T H H O B
H N E O I X N L E T P L O O C G W O
W O F P M O O B E N I E C I N O S O
S L X O N R E E O D R A R O E O Y T
L O I K O O R O I W I I O E E E C C
T O I O O T K D C V L G O T K B O E
H W F A S H K O O H O C T O R I M H
N O S D D O J A A T O A O O A E P K
G R F I Y O L W K O N L R M U T O W
T D O O C P G O T D N O N P B O E I
I W G O O E L S O E O F L O C G O D
I S R E B D H O Y I A A E F O O L O
F C D F O O W U E M O O L S A M S T
```

BOOK	GOOD	NOOK
BOOM	GOOF	POOR
BOON	GOON	ROOF
BOOR	HOOD	ROOK
BOOT	HOOK	ROOT
COOK	HOOP	SOON
COOL	LOOK	SOOT
COOT	LOOM	TOOK
FOOD	LOON	WOOD
FOOL	MOON	WOOF
FOOT	MOOT	WOOL

SOME LOOKALIKES

```
I H C O A R S N E D O N C D R T E E
N E L I C I T C R S A C E A E I L R
A O I U X C A N O G R S A R N I I A
D C T A R A C A A U S U A P C O M T
T E E R C S I D A E E C O P I C N L
E R B T D I S C R E T E T C O T M A
B U A N A R H T L A I T E M E I O E
B E E A R A R E E C S N P B O R E L
R M B R R O T N E M I L P M O C E R
E I R R A B C X A I E L L R U O S O
A G E E N N C R L M T C E O K V R S
C R E E T A O L E N S F E A A A A N
H A C D P C I N E G G C R N U O O E
F N H I O C T S N D U A I G S B C C
I T T M I E S A F A T A U T R U N A
O A P T A A L T E R C R A S E M R E
L H I D E S E R T N A R G I M M I E
S T O L T H T N E C S A S I C U P I
```

ALTAR	BREECH	COARSE
ALTER	CANNON	COURSE
ARRANT	CANON	COMPLEMENT
ERRANT	CAPITAL	COMPLIMENT
ASCENT	CAPITOL	DESERT
ASSENT	CARAT	DESSERT
AUGER	CARET	DISCREET
AUGUR	KARAT	DISCRETE
BOAR	CENSOR	ELICIT
BOOR	CENSURE	ILLICIT
BORE	CITE	EMIGRANT
BREACH	SITE	IMMIGRANT

5

SHERLOCK HOLMES

6

```
R E L D A E N E R I N F A S H M D T
E L Y O D H L A U E O E S B N Y E N
E L E M E N T A R Y S E E A H S Y N
G I I I A I E H H R D M L S E T A I
A E R I R A E T E D U O L I Y E M S
D O L E S T R A D E H R I L R R U E
T E N D W A T S O N S I V R E Y Y D
T E E M E N S C R T R A R A O E I N
G E S R O T R W L H M R E T O C R I
D R N W S E E L O F E T K H I A E G
A E N I E T K C P B F Y S B I L N E
T R D P L E A R T O T I A O C A E L
O S E U I O B L R I N S B N S B A B
R R O B C I I C K N V C A E S A D R
C T O E N T Y V E E H E D L S S L U
I C A E H M I D P M R P L S S H E C
S P I D E R W O M A N U M E D I V E
H A R L I S A B N D E T E C T F H D
```

BAKER STREET	DETECTIVE	MRS HUDSON
BASIL RATHBONE	DOYLE	MYCROFT
BASKERVILLES	ELEMENTARY	MYSTERY
CALABASH	HIS LAST BOW	NIGEL BRUCE
CREEPER	IRENE ADLER	SPIDER WOMAN
DEDUCTION	LESTRADE	VIOLIN
DEERSTALKER	MORIARTY	WATSON
DENNIS HOEY		

MAGAZINES

7

```
F T E O T E S N U S E D M S A F E S
O E E D M E D T D Y R E M E R S L T
P U U S H N J O N E A O E L R L I A
R E V O C S I D U B T D B F E L F U
S R U O M A L G O O T U S R I A E D
L C F C C B S N R V S G S N S C I U
I O D O U R A T G I Y E O B A C N B
A C E L E P R U N E B O K U M M C O
T P L P P E I E P R R A B K R N O N
E A R E N D S M O Y P U O Y E M A W
D A T D E S A F F E N P L W A P E R
H I F A W V E O O B S O S L E L C T
T C S E O S R P E I O W B A A M P A
D N E G P T L S E V E N T E E N I N
E K U O U E E S S E R S I N N E T T
C E R N O E C A K R E D B O O K C T
A T E D L R O W C P H X O O B D E R
E L L E T I F R I A F Y T I N A V O
```

ALLURE	HARPERS	SELF
AUDUBON	INC	SEVENTEEN
BON APPETIT	JET	SIERRA
BUSINESS WEEK	LIFE	SPORT
DETAILS	MCCALLS	SUNSET
DISCOVER	MOTOR TREND	TENNIS
EBONY	NEWSWEEK	TIME
ELLE	OMNI	TV GUIDE
FORBES	PC WORLD	VANITY FAIR
FORTUNE	PEOPLE	VOGUE
GLAMOUR	PLAYBOY	WOMANS DAY
GOURMET	REDBOOK	

U.S. CITIES

8

```
O M N E I T S O H S L N O R K A E N
R U U M A M O C A T A A H I K R C E
A I B O A F G E P S A G T I E O Y P
S A R N T N G Y N N A M R D E Y K S
B U Y N A B L A S R B E A L G O R A
A K E P O T T A Y I M F A C B H A U
E P E W E O L O I N F I P N O E W U
W E L O T L E S L N E A M P E N E N
I D T U A E O R L E R D A M P W N A
H L T D E P U T I T D D T E F D A S
S E M I A M I C O E A O R L L E I S
E C A I T E W S N M U E E A I U A C
H H N S E T E E P S S E S N E D S
E I R L O C A S U W T D L T T R A I
A C A R D T A S U O I E C J E O Y A
E A S O T I A A L D N I N P D A T H
D G A M E B N E F U N Y I F N A O C
F O G O C A W E U O T S O N E R N O
```

AKRON	ENID	RENO
ALBANY	ERIE	SALEM
AMES	FLINT	TACOMA
ASPEN	GARY	TAMPA
AUSTIN	MACON	TOLEDO
CHICAGO	MIAMI	TOPEKA
DALLAS	NEWARK	TULSA
DAYTON	NOME	WACO

HERBS & SPICES

9

```
A N W I D H L E N N E F A N A E N E
E E E N Y O R M A C E S Y D K T S T
P T S J A R P E H E I H R C I G N N
L C H Z L A A I M V T A A E R E U U
N H T S R S V M R U T R C F P S T A
M R O S A E O E E S G N H O A I M L
A I L S S F H E U S C A E B P N E E
B E N E O C F M E E O A R A A A Z N
Y T D T C E Y R R C O R V R H S I D
H E G A S R G M O E N H I S A M R E
C R T O O I R R A N A O L V U T E T
R D R C N S I A U R L A G C A S R H
W N I G G A G Y T I J S S A V O R Y
E H E T N E G A C S T O L O R O I M
C R M D M R M E R M I O R L T R O E
S A E T A N Y T R L M E H A I H A P
B R L I S A B S U O L A D I M D V T
H I O S E V O L C N T G A R L I C G
```

ANISE	FENNEL	PAPRIKA
BASIL	GARLIC	PARSLEY
CHERVIL	GINGER	ROSEMARY
CHICORY	MACE	SAFFRON
CHIVES	MARJORAM	SAGE
CLOVES	MINT	SAVORY
CORIANDER	MUSTARD	TARRAGON
CUMIN	NUTMEG	THYME
DILL	OREGANO	

GOLFSPEAK

10

```
D C A N T F I I H E N L D H A E M H
U C H I P O E O E E D H D F E H R T
N M F R O S N I P E E A V U O T V C
K G C P H L E T D S O E F O H Y S M
D N S H Y B B I P U S A L O E I V H
A E O E T R S I S N B A F F Y E O E
Q I G O B A Y O A A S P O O K O R S
R O H O P S H K A E C E A O K E T C
B U E C B S E A S E T E F I C I D N
F E W E T I E K F B I T O F B A S J
D I P R I E D F E L B C O E Y S T K
B E A C H H E E N A B T I V E T N A
E N N B S L S A N A A A N S I L R N
E I E P G W G A O D R R T O S D T S
P S O A R H B U M E I D R I B A I H
P O E P E I B C H S E L G G A W R D
G E H E G F A S X F F U R C S E S B
N A E C Y F R H D D E O R T G U T H
```

ACE	CHOP	RABBIT
BAFFY	DIVOT	SCRUFF
BEACH	DUB	SNAKE
BIRDIE	DUNK	SNIPE
BOGEY	EAGLE	SPOON
BRASSIE	FADE	WAGGLE
BYE	HOOK	WHIFF
CAN	MASHIE	YIPS
CHIP		

WANNA DANCE?

11

```
S E N A L O B M A M E C A U N I M N
T T A F T L O S T V A K O O G N A T
A S O M A O I M H B R N H N H O C I
F L A M E N C O M U N O W U G A A A
N O H S P G D A Z L H R A I L A R F
A O H U D U S A R S A U L E W A E U
T A N P X B M A N S R M B I B T N D
O R A A H R O D L G E B B O M E A T
R T K I F E G L U S O A L A I B S B
T T L O T T A S I D A E T S D I B W
O H O S H T H E E N R D H F W A A E
R B P N T I S C F O D O K T N L E M
T A A A I J R T A F R Y A D T T X A
X S C A R I O C A A F T P Z S W I Z
O W I E T O C O N V C V E E N I X U
F O H D I C A R I O S N R I N S A R
M Y M M I H S L I M B O T U H D M K
L T T C O M I N U E T A H I S D H H
```

BOLERO	LIMBO	SALSA
CARIOCA	LINDY	SAMBA
CONGA	MACARENA	SHAG
FANDANGO	MAMBO	SHIMMY
FLAMENCO	MAXIXE	STOMP
FOXTROT	MAZURKA	TANGO
HORA	MINUET	TREPAK
HULA	POLKA	TWIST
JITTERBUG	RUMBA	WALTZ
LAMBADA		

BRIT LIT 101

12

```
O E E N E S W Y N O I F M T E I E D
T P D B T D D O T R E E N R E T S E
O O E A G R R T R H E T N O R B N S
I P E G A A O Y C D A M A E O O H T
L K H H D C Y S D L S C E I S A S F
E O C A S I A E W E S W K N K T D I
G N I N W O R B D I N L O E E F T N
F E T T C L E E N F K J S R R R T O
N M R F T H F A L R I P P E T A R S
E I O I E O Y N I O E E Q R A H Y Y
T L L W E N A C O A C H L P T A S N
S T L S U W H U R E T O T D R J L N
U O O B E A E E P O I A H G I O C E
A N P L R C H A U C E R L E T N B T
E A E D T E B H A I D O N N E S G E
T U S Y E N D I S I T H R M A N E T
M O M H S N E K C I D O E N O R Y B
N E E S R H S W I F Q S P E N S E R
```

AUSTEN	ELIOT	SCOTT
BRONTE	FIELDING	SHAKESPEARE
BROWNING	GAY	SIDNEY
BUNYAN	GRAY	SPENSER
BYRON	HARDY	STERNE
CHAUCER	JONSON	SWIFT
COLERIDGE	KEATS	TENNYSON
DEFOE	MILTON	THACKERAY
DICKENS	POPE	TROLLOPE
DONNE	RICHARDSON	WORDSWORTH
DRYDEN		

ROUNDABOUT

13

```
N O I T U C O L M U C R I C H E A J
O S D A M P H I B I O U S T E E S E
I E T Y R E H P I R E P N F B Y T U
E P N A R E T E M I R E P I N A S R
E S E H S U C R I C V E R R L I E N
L C U H C M E O E M E C C U O A O A
T I L P A I E O U P S I B C S N M I
C R F E E B R C U M R M I I D P F N
E C M R E O R C U C A E S T H U T I
P U U I C I R C U M N A V I G A T E
S M C S C S R M U M R N T C M I M P
M F R T R I F C S H S P P H C O O
U L I Y C E R O P E E T H A O E B C
C E C L R I S I M A A I A E D U I S
R X L E C O R S T T B N E N G N H I
I O N U R E E E D O O R H A C F P R
C C I E P E R R L R L D E A N E M E
E E O N Y S G Y V O B I H P M A A P
```

AMPHIBIOUS
AMPHIBOLY
AMPHITHEATER
CIRCUMAMBULATE
CIRCUMFERENCE
CIRCUMFLEX
CIRCUMFLUENT

CIRCUMLOCUTION
CIRCUMNAVIGATE
CIRCUMSCRIBE
CIRCUMSPECT
CIRCUMSTANCE
CIRCUMVENT

CIRCUS
PERIMETER
PERIPHERY
PERIPHRASIS
PERISCOPE
PERISTYLE

ANTI & ANTE

```
R O A C N F A A H C A N T E R O O M
E A O A E O N N I A A N E D X A E U
A D N H N T D T T L O A T A M T A L
W N T T I T P I A E N G M I T N N L
M N T D I E I N T T M I M C T E T E
A U O E S R T T E N L E N A E H E B
M T I I M A A P H C A E R N T A R E
E S T D R E E N I E T E A I Y N I T
A N I C N N R T T A S I T A D T O N
A N T N U E N I P A V I N N A I R A
A I T L O A P I D U R T M T N P E U
C M T H O G C E L I I S T E T A F M
O E O I E I A I T N A R I C H T R S
H H U O T L D T O N T N P E E H B O
E T D N Y E I M N L A H I D L E D L
H N A P T L Y K E A R E N E I T U N
E A A N T I T H E S I S S S N O I E A
R H A O N A N T E D A T E T N C A T
```

ANTAGONISM
ANTARCTIC
ANTARES
ANTE MERIDIEM
ANTEBELLUM
ANTECEDENT
ANTEDATE
ANTEDILUVIAN

ANTEMERIDIAN
ANTEPENDIUM
ANTEPENULT
ANTERIOR
ANTEROOM
ANTHELION
ANTHEM

ANTICIPATE
ANTICLIMAX
ANTIDOTE
ANTINOMY
ANTIPATHETIC
ANTISEPTIC
ANTITHESIS

BIG BANDS

15

```
O D R A B M O L Y U G L E N G R A Y
V E S T Y E S R O D Y M M I J H I S
N N A M E T I H W L U A P T I E E I
O O O A S T B E I S A B T N U O C H
R A T T N E B E N N Y G O O D M A N
H T R N G I E R N D O I A E E P R R
N W E W I N T Y O N V S A Y S M T E
S A O N T L I R A R I O O A I E I L
H R G O R O C L A K A E E E O K E L
E O L I D A M Y L M Y Y M A A L S I
P T L E R Y B M R E Y M N O H A H M
F S I R S E H E Y R E D M O T H A N
I A A Y U B B E I D A K D A B E W N
E P A E L N R Y R L O L U E S L N E
L Y E G R P A O N M R R E D R E E L
D N L E S B R O W N A A S H N F E G
S O Q M E K L A H R U N H E O A T A
S T A N K E N T O N B B N C Y D T O
```

GLENN MILLER	STAN KENTON	HAL KEMP
ARTIE SHAW	LES BROWN	TONY PASTOR
TOMMY DORSEY	GLEN GRAY	SHEP FIELDS
JIMMY DORSEY	PAUL WHITEMAN	LARRY CLINTON
DUKE ELLINGTON	BENNIE MOTEN	BUNNY BERIGAN
BENNY GOODMAN	GUY LOMBARDO	CHARLIE BARNET
COUNT BASIE	SAMMY KAYE	RAY NOBLE
WOODY HERMAN	FREDDY MARTIN	

2. Missing Vowels

You may have to search a little harder in these puzzles. To make it more fun, we left out all the vowels. But things could be worse—we were going to leave out the consonants, too.

Answers begin on page 295.

GET-TOGETHERS

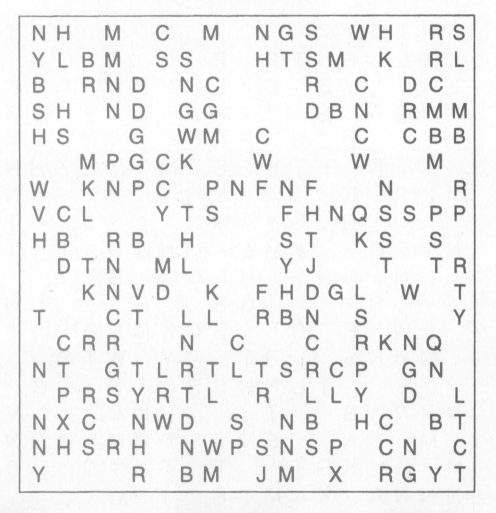

```
N H   M   C   M   N G S   W H   R S
Y L B M   S S   H T S M   K   R L
B   R N D   N C       R   C   D C
S H   N D   G G       D B N   R M M
H S   G   W M   C       C   C B B
    M P G C K     W     W     M
W   K N P C   P N F N F     N     R
V C L     Y T S     F H N Q S S P P
H B   R B   H       S T   K S   S
    D T N   M L       Y J     T   T R
    K N V D   K   F H D G L   W     T
T     C T   L L   R B N   S     Y
    C R R     N   C     C   R K N Q
N T   G T L R T L T S R C P   G N
    P R S Y R T L   R   L L Y   D   L
N X C   N W D   S   N B   H C   B T
N H S R H   N W P S N S P   C N   C
Y     R   B M   J M   X   R G Y T
```

ASSEMBLY	HAPPY HOUR	POTLUCK
ASSIGNATION	HOEDOWN	RALLY
BANQUET	HOMECOMING	RECEPTION
BARN DANCE	HOOTENANNY	REUNION
CLAMBAKE	JAMBOREE	SHINDIG
COFFEE KLATSCH	MASKED BALL	SHOWER
CONVENTION	MIXER	SLUMBER PARTY
COOKOUT	OPEN HOUSE	SMOKER
COUNTY FAIR	ORGY	TRACK MEET
FIELD TRIP	PICNIC	WINGDING

MUSICALS

```
R T J T Z     G F     L D           K T
K T L     R   T R   P     L     C S G N
L W   L Y G   C   R B Y N N     F   N
  N S S   S       T H P   C     F   C G
H Y     L   B   R N S T     N   N X
  T   N   F T H   S T M     T R Z H N
M L R   K   W   Y H       V         N
      R L S Y   M N         D       T
N T C G     Y M L   M N W D   T   T
  H N   B R     H L G       B R
T     N Y       G B       R     L N
  L W   B   C     B C K M S B
  M H K S     R T     Y   W T S
      S     T L N N S R     N T   G
N R R W B     T       H H C         V
  M   F N     S M   S D H M H G R N
M   G   K R T     T   T L T D     P
N N N R   K   M   R   J L W V
```

ASTAIRE   ETHEL MERMAN   JEROME KERN
BERNSTEIN   FANNY BRICE   JOLSON
BUSBY BERKELEY   GENE KELLY   MARY MARTIN
CAROUSEL   GERSHWIN   OKLAHOMA
COHAN   GIGI   SHOW BOAT
COLE PORTER   HAMMERSTEIN   SOUTH PACIFIC
EDDIE CANTOR   IRVING BERLIN   ZIEGFELD

TV WESTERNS

```
H   K C   R   V   M P   S L P L
C   N H S       X   N N C G G       Z T
W           N L Y N   N N       N R T G
    S S       T   L       N       F
S L   L B V V L V K H S R G R     N N
K S W D M       Y S       S     Z T
S   L S D D D K F T N R D W N N
    N Y T Y S S S G Y       G
W N D T D D       D   V N   N   T
  N   N T N F R R N B T R   S       R
  M     N   N Y Y P P   H F   B     Y
S R   G   R Y   R     N     D L   P
  L D   K   C S   C   H T   R H   X
F   L   N N       K L   Y D T D
M H G   N S M   K   W   L D B   L L
  N     S T H   R   F L   M   N L T
    T C W   L   G W Y   T T     R P
R   W G   N T R     N   H   S S
```

ANDY DEVINE
ANNIE OAKLEY
BONANZA
DALE EVANS
FESTUS
GENE AUTRY
GUNSMOKE

HOPPY
HOSS
LONE RANGER
MATT DILLON
MAVERICK
ROY ROGERS
SKY KING

THE CISCO KID
THE RIFLEMAN
TONTO
WAGON TRAIN
WILD BILL
WYATT EARP

HATS

```
L T   R   B D   B P H   F D N C S
  F H N K K N   D           D     P
V   D L     M T T T R L   L M J
B   M Z     L F   R   M X P B H   B
H R H   S     L R   S     R S   P T
  V B C N   R C Y L   C       P
H G N     T G S M B S R L X     J M
P   Y   L L     T Y       L   D   N
      V L R M C X R   C P L     B P N
R   G   H     C B L L B     T     D
K H R G L   D R R     K N X B G M B
P     H R       X       Y Q R
  P     F T C B F L   W F R T   B R
    B R F Y   K   B Y B R   D B
  N   N B     M   N T   R   M G T
S N G S T     G   B   S L     N T
      T M   T C H T   Q     H J
D B R B R   T   N   T C R   N N   P
```

BALMORAL
BEANIE
BERET
BIRETTA
BOATER
BRETON
BUSBY
CALASH
CALPAC
CAUL
CLOCHE
DEERSTALKER

DERBY
DINK
FEDORA
FEZ
GIBUS
HAVELOCK
HOMBURG
JIPIJAPA
KELLY
LEGHORN
MONTERO

MUTCH
PETASUS
PILLBOX
PINNER
PIXIE
PORKPIE
SOMBRERO
SUGARLOAF
TAM
TRILBY
TUQUE

JUST FOR FUN

5

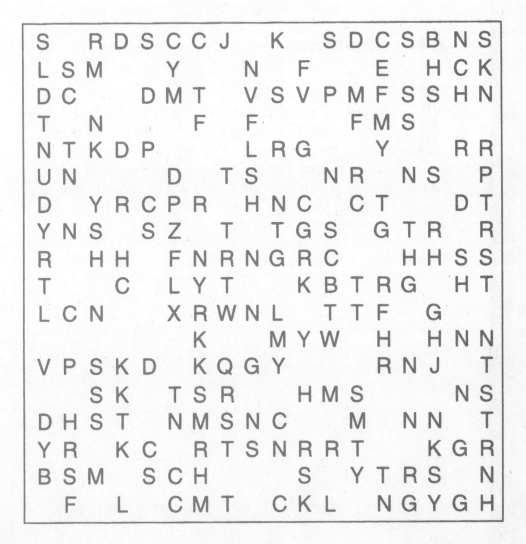

```
S   R D S C C J   K   S D C S B N S
L S M       Y       N   F       E   H C K
D C       D M T   V S V P M F S S H N
T   N       F       F           F M S
N T K D P           L R G           Y       R R
U N       D   T S       N R   N S       P
D   Y R C P R   H N C   C T       D T
Y N S   S Z   T   T G S   G T R       R
R   H H   F N R N G R C       H H S S
T     C   L Y T       K B T R G   H T
L C N     X R W N L   T T F   G
            K   M Y W   H   H N N
V P S K D   K Q G Y       R N J   T
    S K   T S R     H M S       N S
D H S T   N M S N C   M   N N   T
Y R   K C   R T S N R R T   K G R
B S M   S C H       S   Y T R S   N
    F   L   C M T   C K L   N G Y G H
```

ANTICS	JOKES	SHENANIGANS
BUFFOONERY	MISCHIEF	SKITS
CAPERS	MONKEYSHINES	SPOOFS
CHARADES	MUMMERY	STUNTS
DEVILTRY	NAUGHTINESS	TICKLING
ESCAPADES	PRANKS	TRICKERY
GAMES	RASCALITY	WAGGERY
HIGH JINKS	ROGUERY	

3. Missing Words

In the puzzles that follow, the idea is to think of the appropriate word or words for each blank(s) and then search for the words in the diagram. That's the easy way—unless, of course, you can't fill in all the blanks. If that's the case, try approaching the problem from a different direction: by searching for words in the grid that will fit the blanks. (They're all in there somewhere!)

Answers begin on page 296.

CLICHES 1

```
R E E R G A T N D L U O C T A W E
O H G H D E O N I A T R E C N U D P
U E E N R E M B C H N E E D L E S S
O C L R I S R O L Y I L O C E S F D
H S U D T Y N E T E B D I T E I F I
A F P N M T A I D A S R D O E G P I
P L A E R O C S E N C S R E N H D C
P T O A R A R E T U E U I O N O N E
A L R N P S S E M U N R I N U F R C
R T I A G E P S W N O T E N G R V O
E F C M R S T E I A A H C U C E N N
N O O O I A T N C U Y E T U I L E T
T I F R N T G O T T R S T I M I S R
C O D C E H E I R T I D I P W E A A
C U E I I B S D A Y V V M F O F R R
O S O A D G N I T A U N E T X E H Y
S N O I T O M E H T A S R E P S P E
I S U O I C I V Q A T R E C N U A T
```

Clues

1. TO COIN _____ (2 words)
2. TO MAKE _____ SHORT (3 words)
3. _____ TO SAY (1 word)
4. IT GOES _____ (2 words)
5. A _____ IN DISGUISE (1 word)
6. _____ TO POPULAR OPINION (1 word)
7. DUE TO _____ BEYOND OUR CONTROL (1 word)
8. A HOSTAGE _____ (1 word)
9. _____ CIRCUMSTANCES (1 word)
10. WE FACE AN _____ FUTURE (1 word)
11. IN THE _____ FUTURE (1 word)
12. FILLED _____ (2 words)
13. FOR A _____ TIME ONLY (1 word)
14. FOR NO _____ REASON (1 word)
15. HIT THE GROUND _____ (1 word)
16. JUST GOING THROUGH _____ (2 words)
17. HEAVE A BIG _____ (3 words)
18. TO PUT THINGS IN _____ (1 word)
19. TO HAVE A _____ AGENDA (1 word)
20. I _____ WITH YOU MORE (2 words)
21. FOR SERVICES _____ (1 word)
22. IN _____ THAN ONE (2 words)
23. A _____ CIRCLE (1 word)

HEADLINES

2

```
O S W A L D R M R B R E Z H N E I L
G O A D I D O E E H A B K H I T L S
L C H R E O T A H V I H Y T T W C C
L O S O N R R T R C R T B R A T O O
P N C F A H O O T U T R L R R O O H
A N U C A M O A S G E A R E L C L M
T O B L I S D H O Z D E H T R H I A
T R A H E A C R H S N R E T L U D N
O E S V S H B N N T C N Y A E R G T
N U E O E A E N D D E H N B H C E E
B L H V C V A E H X E A O E A H I I
T J T H B G G N E A C G R O T I M V
C C E T A A Y O S A W G A H L L F N
S V Y E U L H T M T U A E U A L D A
N W R L A A L A S K A E I O L R P P
A E L E C T N S R R P L A I R L T A
H P P A N A M L E O N D I H O G E J
D E H S P N C O T A G N F N A L E G
```

Clues

1. _____ TAKES OATH OF OFFICE (1.21.89)
2. _____ AND _____ SIGN MISSILE TREATY (12.9.87)
3. _____ ASSASSINATED AT ARMY PARADE (10.7.81)
4. REAGAN NOMINATES _____ TO SERVE ON SUPREME COURT (7.8.81)
5. _____ IS BRITAIN'S NEW PRIME MINISTER (5.4.79)
6. SENATE VOTES TO GIVE UP _____ _____ (4.19.78)
7. _____ DEFEATS _____ IN TIGHT RACE (11.3.76)
8. _____ PEACE PACTS SIGNED (1.28.73)
9. MEN WALK ON _____ (7.21.69)
10. _____ OUSTED; _____ GETS TOP PARTY POST (10.16.64)
11. _____ COMMISSION FINDS_____ ACTED ALONE (9.28.64)
12. U.S. BREAKS DIPLOMATIC TIES WITH _____ (1.4.61)
13. _____ TO JOIN UNION (3.13.59)

14. _____ VOTED INTO UNION (7.1.58)
15. _____ _____ NAMED PREMIER (6.2.58)
16. _____ QUITS AS PRIME MINISTER (4.6.55)
17. HIGH COURT BANS _____ SEGREGATION (5.18.54)
18. _____ DIES AFTER 29-YEAR RULE (3.6.53)
19. KING _____ VI DIES IN SLEEP (2.7.52)
20. IRISH PLAYWRIGHT _____ DIES (11.2.50)
21. _____ SURRENDERS (8.15.45)
22. _____ CROSSES RHINE (8.15.45)
23. PRESIDENT _____ IS DEAD (4.13.45)
24. VON HINDENBURG DIES; _____ TAKES PRESIDENCY (8.2.34)
25. _____ FLIES ATLANTIC (6.19.28)
26. _____ DOES NOT CHOOSE TO RUN (8.3.27)
27. _____ FLIES TO NORTH POLE AND BACK (5.10.26)

FILMS OF THE FIFTIES

W	E	S	T	H	O	P	S	E	T	S	U	N	S	E
E	S	A	U	C	K	I	P	R	H	U	N	E	P	N
S	U	B	R	I	D	G	E	R	I	N	O	N	O	N
T	R	A	N	S	P	I	E	H	E	S	T	I	E	T
B	A	G	Y	D	O	B	C	E	F	E	S	E	Q	E
S	T	O	H	T	A	T	H	I	U	A	U	Q	U	R
T	O	L	E	D	I	E	S	T	U	Q	Q	U	E	S
S	A	D	G	O	A	N	S	S	U	Q	U	E	E	M
E	V	E	R	S	P	U	R	E	R	U	N	V	E	R
W	I	N	E	S	N	E	O	E	O	E	E	C	A	F
H	A	L	D	S	P	U	B	A	T	N	T	E	R	D
T	H	E	E	S	C	R	E	A	N	E	R	S	E	L
R	A	T	N	O	R	F	R	E	T	A	W	H	I	R
O	U	T	U	N	E	C	T	U	A	L	E	C	E	O
N	I	N	E	C	A	U	S	E	L	E	C	D	O	W
S	T	H	I	E	R	A	S	U	B	L	R	I	G	H
Y	R	E	I	A	F	S	E	T	N	U	S	T	U	N
H	O	N	U	S	S	E	T	E	M	E	S	N	U	S

Clues

1. THE AFRICAN _____ (1951)
2. AROUND THE _____ IN 80 DAYS (1956)
3. THE _____ COUNTRY (1958)
4. THE _____ ON THE RIVER KWAI (1957)
5. _____ STOP (1956)
6. THE COUNTRY _____ (1954)
7. DIAL M FOR _____ (1955)
8. EAST OF _____ (1955)
9. FRIENDLY _____ (1956)
10. FUNNY _____ (1957)
11. INVASION OF THE _____ SNATCHERS (1956)
12. THE _____ AND I (1956)
13. THE LONG _____ SUMMER (1958)
14. THE MAGNIFICENT _____ (1954)
15. THE MAN WITH THE _____ ARM (1955)
16. MISTER _____ (1955)
17. NORTH BY _____ (1959)
18. ON THE _____ (1954)
19. RAINTREE _____ (1957)
20. _____ WINDOW (1954)
21. REBEL WITHOUT A _____ (1955)
22. THE RED _____ OF COURAGE (1951)
23. THE SEVEN YEAR _____ (1955)
24. _____ BOULEVARD (1950)
25. TO CATCH A _____ (1955)

CLICHES 2

4

```
E V I R T U E P L H N I H T O O T Y
F E H N H P D U G D E D E E A R U P
F T R W Y L L R S C R I F A B H A F
I C T P A H L P E T A P T S M I O R
R E U O P I Q O C T A A S E A R O A
S P W M M R W S G F H N S F T I R E
V S A B N S A E O T G S D H T F A E
H E V R I N L S T F A C E I I F S L
T R E P L D L C T G N C M R N Y S G
I E L C M H A N E E O O S V R G E N
A U E I L F Q A U U F T R A S N C I
F D N X E I I R R D E A S E U A E Y
F S G H P R G S E M A S E N T E N L
O U T A O R E H A E E E E L L U K F
U A H N B T E G T C C S C R W C R E
H K S O S D N S E A O T D S M E A N
S E N A W A S N S O T V R U P O N A
T A F I S O R E L E N T J O N F O A
```

Clues

1. TURN OVER _____ (3 words)
2. WITH ALL _____ (2 words)
3. MERE WORDS CAN'T _____ (1 word)
4. LIFE IN THE _____ LANE (1 word)
5. FIRST THINGS _____ (1 word)
6. WITH _____ COLORS (1 word)
7. PAR _____ (3 words)
8. A NEW _____ PLAN (1 word)
9. TOO MANY _____ IN THE FIRE (1 word)
10. SEE _____ THE END OF THE TUNNEL (2 words)
11. GO OUT ON A _____ (1 word)
12. A _____ CANNON (1 word)
13. SEND A _____ TO (1 word)
14. A _____ EVIL (1 word)
15. A LEAP _____ (2 words)
16. PAST THE POINT _____ (3 words)
17. FOR ALL INTENTS AND _____ (1 word)
18. A _____ OVATION (1 word)
19. IN VIEW OF (or DESPITE) (3 words)
20. DON'T SPREAD YOURSELF _____ (2 words)
21. MAKE A _____ OF NECESSITY (1 word)
22. OFF THE _____ (1 word)
23. ON A DIFFERENT (1 word)

CHAPTER 12

LOST AND FOUND

The missing letters in each grid have been found—but they haven't been put back where they belong. If you put them in the right places, you'll find that every word crosses another, horizontally or vertically, at least once. (Some letters will be used more than once.)

Answers begin on page 297.

1

Missing Letters

N	E	R	I
E	X	S	H
A	R	C	E
L	S	U	E

2

Missing Letters

L	D	L	S
E	E	M	E
O	L	Y	E
M	N	P	A

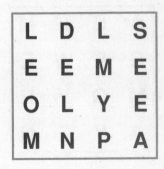

3

Missing Letters

H	E	I	C
M	M	A	E
X	J	I	H
A	L	T	Y

				C		S		
	O	U	E		O		E	O
I		D		C	H	A	R	
A			N			R	E	
S	I			A	R	M		T
		I	D	L				O
		A		K		W	A	
L		R				R		
	S		Z	Y	G	Y		C

4

Missing Letters

A	S	M	M
S	E	W	E
M	G	Y	R
A	Y	E	U

	P			J	U		B	O
P			T	A				
	N	C	O	M	I			
W	E	E				N	O	R
		N	A	T		D	O	
R		E			C		D	E
			O	U	R			A
L	I		O		B			S
	C	A	U				A	Y

5

Missing Letters

P	A	R	M
E	L	L	P
P	D	R	O
A	C	U	D

6

Missing Letters

Y	Y	Y	Y
Y	Y	Y	Y
Y	Y	Y	Y
Y	Y	Y	Y

7

Missing Letters

Q	Q	Q	Z
Z	Z	Z	X
X	X	X	X
U	U	U	Y

			E	U	E	S		A
		I			R	E	A	P
	I	N				O		
A	N	T				E	U	S
	C		T			S	A	P
		L	E				L	A
	N							D
E		I	T				H	E

8

Missing Letters

S	E	F	R
A	L	Q	U
S	T	R	E
Y	E	B	S

	O		S			U	M	S
A	B			R	U	S		
	T		A		M			
B		S	Y		M			
U	S				O		U	M
		C	O	N		A		
B				R			R	
	P	R	A					
E				Y			Y	

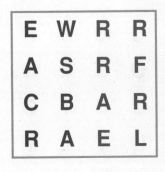

9

Missing Letters

E	W	R	R
A	S	R	F
C	B	A	R
R	A	E	L

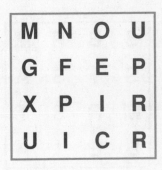

10

Missing Letters

M	N	O	U
G	F	E	P
X	P	I	R
U	I	C	R

11

Missing Letters

U	D	M	R
O	G	E	N
O	U	I	O
U	T	L	M

	I	O	N			B		
I	N				U			S
	G	L	E	E		A	P	E
F	E	E	D	S				
O	N			T		I	T	E
L		T			E			
D			R	E		O	T	E
		E			I			N
A	S	C	E	N	T			

12

Missing Letters

S	B	R	M
S	I	S	A
M	R	S	T
B	E	I	A

P		G			A		T
A	H	A		A	S	T	E
G	A		N	I		H	A
A		N		E		A	
N	A		V	E		A	C	E
		E	S	A		E	
	H				B		A
	E			B	I	B	
	H	E	R		E	T	

Puzzle 13

S	T	E	W		A	S	
	E		R	A	C	K	W
D	T	A			I	T	
I			T	E	T	S	
	I	N	K	N	D		
P				T	E	M	
	A	P	I			E	
	D	I	T		P		
S	N		E	R	A		

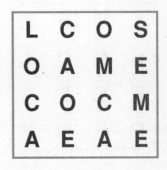

Missing Letters

L	C	O	S
O	A	M	E
C	O	C	M
A	E	A	E

Puzzle 14

	T	A		S	O		
	R	T	I	O	N		T
I	A			A	D		
	M		B	A		E	
N	A	P	R		W	E	
	N		B	A	D		R
	G			C	E		
B	E	A		H			
	Y		T	H	E	M	E

Missing Letters

G	O	A	T
P	P	O	E
A	R	E	T
O	L	A	R

15

Missing Letters

K	O	J	A
S	C	O	I
E	E	F	A
P	P	M	R

			A	B		U	R	E
L	I		P					
	M	O			V			E
O	P		O	S	I	T	E	
F		E	S		A		E	
	L		I		L	I	K	
O		A	T	E		A		X
		D	E		T		H	
T		D				V	E	T

16

Missing Letters

F	I	T	L
A	D	W	E
I	U	E	T
E	R	C	D

A		L	A	Y		O		D
T	O		U				I	
	A		G	U	R		S	O
	T		E		E		C	H
	H	O	R	D	S		O	
C		U		A		O	M	S
E	A	T		N				
			C	A	V			L
E	E						T	

17

Missing Letters

			W		A		S
		S		E	R	B	
E	X		O	L		R	R
S		R		A	O	M	A
S	C	A		T	G		I
	H	I		E	X	A	T
S		G			T		
	S	Y			E		O
H	E	T		R		D	

N	O	L	T
H	R	X	E
E	A	O	T
E	H	H	C

18

Missing Letters

		I	S		R	E	
			U			O	
S	T	E	R	I	S	K	S
	C			T			E
E	R		S	V	E	N	
	E	E	P		V		E
B	E		N			K	
		A	N		R		M
		E	A		T		

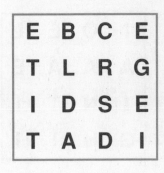

E	B	C	E
T	L	R	G
I	D	S	E
T	A	D	I

19

Missing Letters

I	T	Y	A
D	S	A	R
A	R	D	I
E	I	C	I

V	I	E	D			P		
	N	V	I			O	U	S
O	S		G	E		D		P
L	I	D		T		I	T	E
	D			R		U		R
S		D	E	A		M		
	O						A	
A	U		I	T		W	R	
					S	E	C	

20

Missing Letters

I	O	E	L
A	A	A	E
I	N	T	I
G	H	T	I

		S	L		I			
			L		N	E	A	R
		P		N	A	L	T	Y
	F	R		E		D		S
	L		G		E		A	
P		T	H				W	
	W	E	T			B		T
	E				L			
	D		Y		B	L		C

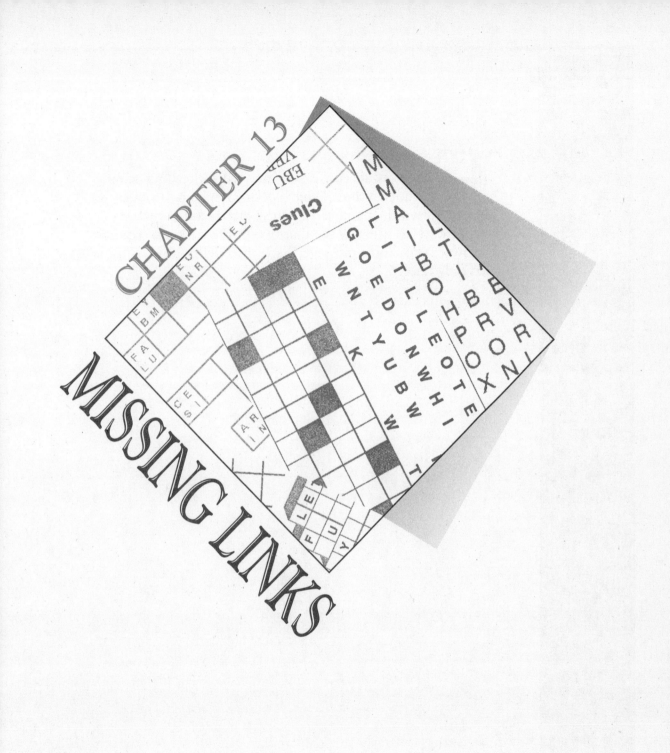

CHAPTER 13

MISSING LINKS

E ach puzzle consists of nine words, reading across, but two three-letter blocks are missing from each word. If you can find the pieces and put them where they belong you'll see that two of the columns (reading downward) contain a message. Each three-letter block is to be used only once.

Answers begin on page 301.

1

```
P H E
F U S
B R O
C U B
C O N
P R O
N O M
I M P
S C A
```

NDS	ELY	TOR	FOU
FUS	ING	BYH	INA
LAW	ADL	OOM	UGN
AGS	OLE	ILL	ROM
ONE	ADE		

2

```
U S C
L O G
A L A
C T I
N C H
R O X
A P A
O Q U
S C R
```

SUB	ATE	IPT	IES
DES	OBL	BAL	NEO
OBF	ESC	LIO	HYD
ISM	PUN	IKA	STA
ING	IDE		

3

```
W A R F
R T F
R I M
R E U
O R E
E P O
T H W
N T I
H B A
```

REF	LLS	THE	MOT
HEA	SCI	BUL	SOU
KED	LLA	NUT	EST
FIR	PON	ENT	WER
ELT	STS		

4

```
C A L
O N E
A T E
E S S
T E S
O S E
N I C
I N S
T T I
```

BEG	GHE	NCI	ENU
IDE	STO	SPA	JUX
NTI	ICA	WOE	UTN
ABD	MAN	TAP	PHO
NIK	SYM		

5

D	A	C				
T	H	E				
S	H	I				
W	A	T				
M	A	C				
U	N	C				
E	B	U				
V	I	N				
D	I	S				

LLI	PHY	HED	HLY
OSO	ENT	PMA	OUT
TES	ATE	HSH	HIN
DIC	UND	SUA	ERY
ERS	DES		

6

P	O	L				
M	E	L				
O	M	B				
L	I	B				
H	O	P				
U	N	P				
C	A	R				
A	F	T				
O	B	E				

AMA	RAR	MAN	UDS
EFU	ODR	NAT	OPU
NAL	LAR	LLY	NCE
ERN	YGO	ION	OON
IAN	ISA		

7

		P	E	G		
		R	A	T		
		C	O	N		
		R	O	W		
		M	A	T		
		L	W	E		
		I	O	N		
		I	G	I		
		T	H	W		

RAT	ALE	LIT	ABS
IVE	LUC	EDE	EAR
ORM	OAT	IAN	DAL
DED	SCA	ISS	EST
NAR	OUS		

8

		N	O	I		
		I	O	R		
		N	G	E		
		B	I	N		
		E	N	T		
		M	E	T		
		S	E	R		
		F	I	G		
		N	O	U		

HAR	NCY	DYS	ADE
DAL	HEI	GER	ATE
ISO	ERY	PRE	CAS
RIC	PLA	SLY	MEL
OLE	URE		

Puzzle 9

						P	H	S
						T	I	C
						A	G	M
						A	T	E
						I	U	M
						O	W	N
						T	R	Y
						T	T	E
						A	G	E

ALU	DEC	ISO	VIS
ATA	QUE	MOR	DIA
PHR	MAR	STA	NSD
TUE	OUP	MIN	SWA
CTU	FLU		

Puzzle 10

V	E	N						
P	A	R						
A	D	V						
S	I	N						
D	E	C						
C	O	L						
L	A	U						
D	R	A						
C	I	G						

DAT	ANT	ADE	TIL
GLE	TOR	ATE	CON
IAL	OCH	ORY	TON
AGE	TTE	IAN	ONN
ARE	ORA		

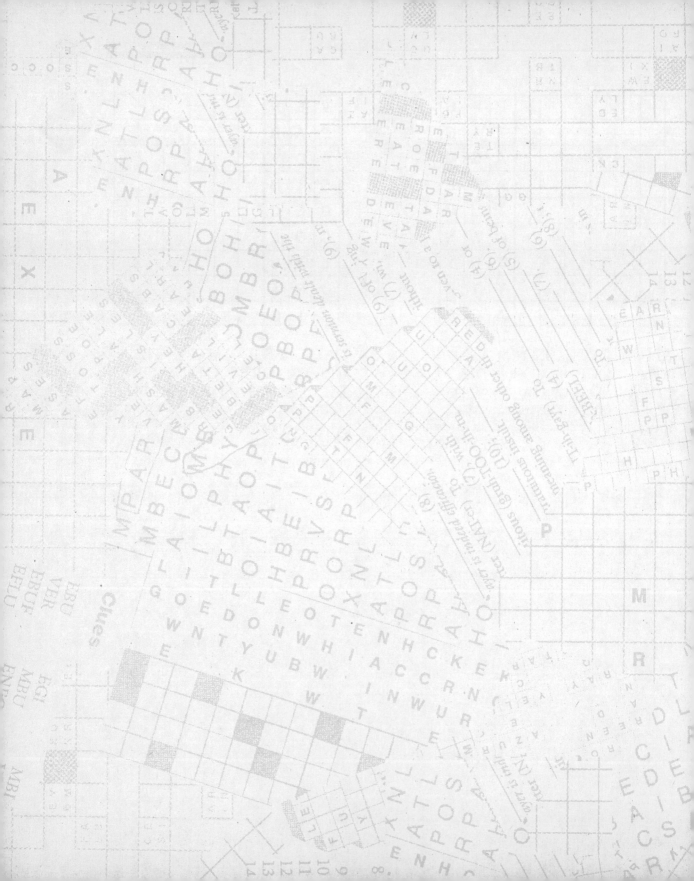

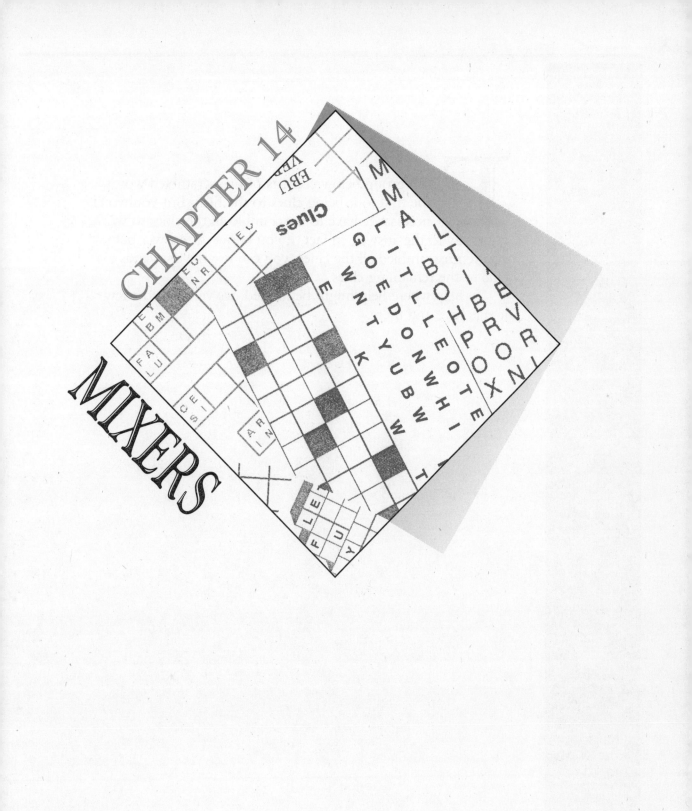

CHAPTER 14

MIXERS

E ach group below consists of five scrambled words, the first four being clues to the fifth. But you won't necessarily have to unscramble all the clues to work your way to the answer. In fact, if you know the answer before you've unscrambled all the clues, you can use the answer as a clue to the remaining clues.

To help where help might be needed, we've inserted a few letters here and there.

Answers begin on page 303.

Clues

LAPER
`_ _ A _ _`

CATTOUS
`_ _ _ _ _ _ T`

DYURATEL
`_ _ _ _ _ _ _ Y`

SMITERNI
`_ _ _ I _ _ _ _`

Answer (3 words)

TEACHTERTRELLEST
`T _ _   S _ _ _ _ _ _`
`L _ _ _ _ _`

Clues

MUPIOD
`_ _ D _ _ _`

GRSSINT
`_ _ _ _ _ G _`

RCOTCONUD
`_ _ _ _ _ _ _ O _`

SWOONDWID
`_ _ _ D _ _ _ _`

Answer (2 words)

SCRANYTHESOMORPHY
`_ Y _ _ _ _ _ _`
`_ _ C _ _ _ _ _ _`

Clues

SMAAB
`_ _ M _ _`

ABLADAM
`_ _ M _ _ _ _`

ACACIOR
`_ _ _ I _ _ _`

SNOOBAVAS (2 words)
`_ _ S _ _   _ O _ _`

Answer (2 words)

CRISABLANDAZINE
`_ _ _ Z _ _ _ _ _`
`_ _ _ _ _ _`

Clues

LITED
`_ _ L _ _`

VARGE
`_ _ A _ _`

CROMNA
`_ _ C _ _ _`

REXFUMCLIC
`_ _ _ C _ _ _ _ _ _`

Answer (2 words)

CLAMCRASITIKARID
`_ I _ _ _ _ _ _ _ _`
`_ _ _ K _`

Clues

5

IRROUCE
_ O _ _ _ _ _

LETINNES
_ _ _ _ _ _ E _

VERBRESO
_ _ _ _ _ _ E _

CROATPETS
_ _ _ C _ _ _ _ _

Answer (2 words)

SNEEMPAWSPANER
_ _ _ _ _ _ P _ _
_ _ M _ _

Clues

6

CEMI
_ _ C _

SPAGER
_ _ _ P _ _

TAILTROL
_ _ _ T _ _ _ _

DESSIPRONE
_ _ P _ _ _ _ _ _

Answer (2 words)

BENKISTHONJEC
_ O _ _   _ T _ _ _ _ _ _ _

Clues

7

INAR
_ _ I _

STHOGS
_ _ O _ _ _

FRENETERENIC
_ _ _ _ _ _ _ _ _ _ C _

GLOPINTRILUCER (2 words)
_ _ L _ _ _ _   _ _ C _ _ _ _

Answer (2 words)

MOOTENBEPILLSIVERS
_ E _ _ _ _ _ _ _ _
_ _ _ _ _ _ M _

Clues

8

ORLIE
_ _ L _ _

SHRUB
_ _ _ S _

CRAHOB
_ _ _ _ _ H

STREWZEE
_ _ _ _ Z _ _ _

Answer (2 words)

SMOOKSHATTLECRAW
_ _ _ _ H _ _ _ _ _ ' _
_ _ _ L _

Clues

9

PULIT

_ _ _ _ P

TUFLE

_ L _ _ _

POUCE

_ _ _ P _

CARUSE

_ _ _ C _ _

Answer (2 words)

MAGALSPEECHSNAGS

_ H _ _ _ _ _ _ _ _

_ L _ _ _ _ _

Clues

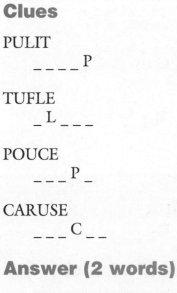

10

PLEAM

_ _ P _ _

TOCULS

_ _ _ _ S _

PROALP

_ _ P _ _ _

STUNETCH

_ _ _ _ _ _ U _

Answer (2 words)

CEROUSEDUSTIED

_ _ C _ _ _ _ _   _ _ E _ _

Clues

11

NETURE

_ _ _ _ E _

REGARCH

_ _ _ _ G _ _

POOMCET

_ _ _ _ _ T _

ENTRACED

_ _ _ _ _ T _ _

Answer (2 words)

VICONNESTRAINGERS

_ _ _ V _ _ _

_ _ N _ _ _ _ _ _ _

Clues

12

EPPI

_ _ P _

STOCKE

_ _ _ K _ _

KYMONE

_ _ N _ _ _

FROOTCOW

_ _ _ W _ _ _ _

Answer (3 words)

SCHORKSWINFEEND

_ _ _ D _   O _

_ R _ _ _ H _ _

Clues

13

SNIBARA
_ _ B _ _ _ _

FATFINYS
_ _ _ _ _ _ Y _

RADEACH
_ _ _ _ _ D _

DYRAMIAFLY (3 words)
_ _   _ _ I _   _ _ D _

Answer (2 words)

HAURBENPUERDY
_ _ _ R _ _   _ _ _ B _ _ _

Clues

15

SNOG
_ _ _ G

SPAWM
_ _ _ M _

VERPES
_ _ S _ _ _

CLONNIL
_ _ _ C _ _ _

Answer (3 words)

SPRONKWASFORIDS
_ _ N _ _   O _
_ P _ _ _ _ _ _

Clues

14

UNJO
_ _ N _

ADANI
_ _ A _ _

STAVE
_ _ _ T _

RAUFONT
_ _ _ _ _ N _

Answer (2 words)

SOOMDERSGASEND
_ _ M _ _   _ _ D _ _ _ _ _

Clues

16

SKATE
_ _ A _ _

ROBYN
_ _ _ O _

LESLEHY
_ _ _ _ _ E _

SONNENTY
_ _ _ _ Y _ _ _

Answer (2 words)

SHELOPENTIGS
_ _ G _ _ _ _   _ _ E _ _

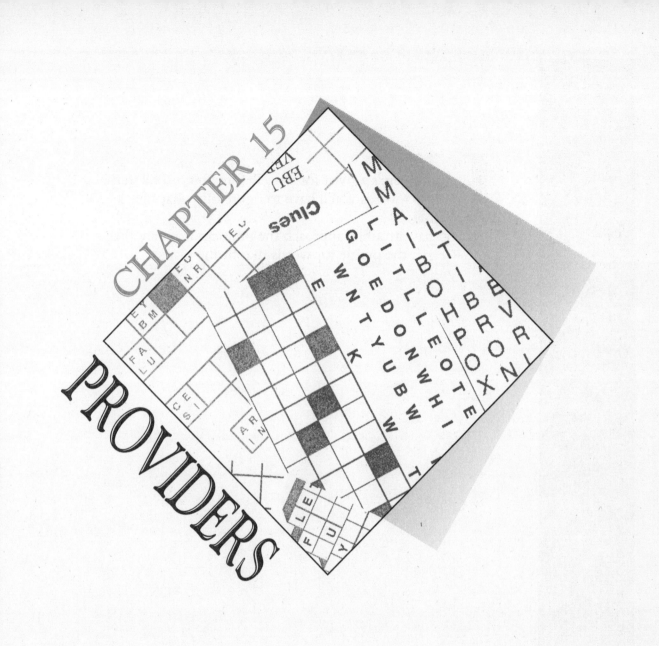

CHAPTER 15

PROVIDERS

H ere's a twist for you. Before you can fill in the words you'll have to figure out what they are.

If you have trouble, approach the problem from another angle—search the puzzle for words that fit the blanks.

Answers begin on page 304.

The grid begins with the letters **T A J**.

Clues
TAJ

3 Letters

aah
aha
air
ala
ale
ama
amp
ate
atm
bet
bra
can

cod
cpu
day
eat
eau
end
ere
icy
lib
qua
rec
set
sky
spy
tab
taj

tao
tet
the
tnt
use

4 Letters

aloe
arty
else
jade
oats
quay
race
rink

sand
stab
tact
taut
teed
than
tomb
yeas

5 Letters

adieu
arbor
coble
perse
roast

sores
suede
tacet
talcs
trade

6 Letters

adored
celery
echoed
edited
hearts
orator
teeter
terror

Clues

PEA

3 Letters

air
ave
can
cob
den
dew
doe
don
eke
elm
era
eve
ewe

fan
gam
gyp
hem
ire
lid
man
mid
mud
our
owe
pea
pep
pop
pro
red
run

sit
tad
tam
tan
toe
too
uke
yet

4 Letters

date
diet
hand
many
poor

putt
scam
tied

5 Letters

adorn
aloha
aroma
awoke
circa
enemy
felon
scrum
slash
token

6 Letters

abased
amazed
creamy
errata
orator
pestle
sanity
zipper

7 Letters

aerates
idiotic
painted
persona

3

R	A	G	S								

Clues
RAGS

3 Letters

aah
aft
ala
ale
arb
arm
ave
bat
bio
bra
crt
esp

eve
god
hey
hie
lad
map
mrs
ova
poe
rag
ran
raw
rbi
rec
ref
sly

til
ufo

4 Letters

abbe
afar
aloe
ante
arcs
atop
bare
bass
beta
brae
bulb

cabs
cell
cloy
dais
earl
evil
hall
imps
lamb
mash
opal
rags
rams
ryes
seer
sees

shay
soda
sole
toss
wade

5 Letters

abase
adage
brace
cases
isles
rebec
seems
syces

C	A	D									

Clues
CAD

3 Letters

abc
ala
ale
ama
apo
apr
art
bar
boa
cab
cad
cbs

coo
eau
end
ere
far
ham
ire
lit
oat
rbi
rid
rot
sac
tip
ufo
urn

use
vet

4 Letters

aloe
also
amen
atop
avis
bate
beau
bomb
cabs
cafe
card

crab
data
dear
dens
ebon
elan
lure
pace
rent
safe
scan
scot
sere
shed
sous
spec

stay
stet
tass
ware
yaps

5 Letters

asset
popes
secco
septa
serum
sibyl
swami
tabby

5

| A | B | M | | | | | | | | | |

Clues
ABM

3 Letters

aah
abm
acm
act
aha
air
ala
ale
and
ann
bat

bmw
boo
bra
cad
cia
con
coo
eke
end
ere
esp
fda
hem
hog
ira
mac
mci

men
oaf
ova
tab
tho
tow

4 Letters

abbe
abcs
aces
ages
alas
alma
area
brae

cams
coke
coma
ends
even
fact
late
lava
made
mesa
pace
rand
raps
safe
sash
semi
sloe

snap
soma
sore
talc
teed
toes
visa

5 Letters

moses
roses
seems
serra

6

| S | P | A | | | | | | | | | |

Clues

SPA

3 Letters

aah
abc
aha
aim
ala
ale
ama
amy
apo
arb
art
ash

ate
bar
bra
eat
end
eon
ere
fan
hmo
mot
ova
pre
pst
raw
rig
rpm
rum

sam
sba
spa
tea
tug

4 Letters

abet
ages
alas
alma
also
anew
anta
anti
ares

baas
brae
cafe
cats
ebon
eggs
elan
hang
late
lime
mesa
near
pool
rave
sacs
sand
seam

semi
sire
smog
then
user
uses

5 Letters

bases
gates
iliac
syces

The grid begins with: M A G

Clues
MAG

3 Letters

aha
ala
ale
ama
ana
bet
bra
cab
can
end
get
let

mac
mad
mag
mob
mtv
oct
our
pub
sam
tut

4 Letters

ache
ales
alma
anas
anew
ares
baas
babe
beta
cham
elan
emit
epic
gabs
halo
hems
item
kale
loss

mace
mags
mete
odes
pace
rite
road
sack
sand
sane
sari
seam
sere
shah
soda
star

subs
thee
tune
unit
vats

5 Letters

aorta
arose
asses
basso
esses
lasso
rapes
swear

8

O	F	F							

Clues
OFF

3 Letters

ale
and
ant
baa
bra
bus
dad
day
dim
eau
eec
eon

esp
faa
fee
fro
ion
mao
mod
odd
off
orb
pfc
pst
rod
sac
san
yea

4 Letters

abbe
aeon
alas
alma
amen
anas
anna
arcs
aunt
baas
base
bore
dabs
dead
dear

dram
ease
else
fete
gala
lass
mesa
pass
peso
pine
rage
rift
roam
sure
toed
tots
tsar

5 Letters

deeps
drama
sated
septa

6 Letters

diesel
erased
mantel
senior

9

| A | N | A | S | | | | | | | | |

Clues
ANAS

3 Letters

act
air
aka
ala
ale
ama
amp
and
ann
apo
ate
cad
cbs

cio
cob
col
die
don
eke
end
faa
fie
get
mci
med
men
non
nor
opt
rbi

rep
rot
sky
tab
tee
toe

4 Letters

able
anas
bomb
cope
crab
crag
dank
eddy

fiat
ices
stay
trod

5 Letters

arena
cafes
cairn
diana
modal
oared
opine
ramps
sofas
stead

tabby
taint

6 Letters

cooled
cosmos
iodide
sedate
states
stator

7 Letters

foreman
panacea

10

F	D	A									

Clues
FDA

3 Letters

ala
ale
all
ann
art
ave
aye
con
dad
dag
den
dey
dig

dna
eye
fda
gad
gem
hem
keg
meg
mom
ran
rbi
tho
use

4 Letters

able
aloe

anas
anna
anti
baas
bead
brad
brae
darn
data
draw
dual
edge
ever
ewes
frau
gees
isle
lays

lien
lily
pear
sack
semi
snag
tang
yams

5 Letters

cabal
media
sable
sages
tease
units

6 Letters

arrays
basses
recess
sables
satire
sorely

7 Letters

deposed
gardens

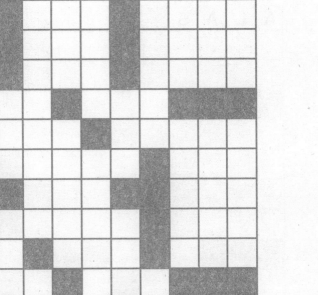

Clues
THOU

3 Letters

aha
ale
ama
amp
arc
ate
ave
baa
ban
bar
bin
cad
cob

din
eec
ell
end
ere
fur
hag
has
ira
lee
ohm
oil
ova
pta
rue
sag
sam
set

sou
tab
tat
tho
try
tug
ufo
use

4 Letters

abbe
alma
arab
baas
beta
bibb
cain

each
hair
hand
nary
ogle
putt
seam
thou
urea

5 Letters

asses
bases
chats
eagle
eerie
otter

sahib
scent
seeds
stale
tabby
teeth
upset

8 Letters

cataract
ideology

12

	A	L	A	S							

Clues
ALAS

3 Letters

aah
abc
air
ale
ate
aye
bib
bra
cab
cad
car
cbs
cia

crt
eat
eel
end
esp
fbi
fda
fro
hmo
its
key
law
let
mrs
nor
nyc
orb

set
spa

4 Letters

alas
aman
ames
arty
cobs
dale
earn
ease
edit
egos
ewer
eyes

gabs
halo
ices
mesa
pale
rapt
rely
rows
sack
safe
shad
shod
stay
talc
than
wire

5 Letters

arbor
awash
carob
cider
cosec
esses
ethic
meaty
scrim
swami

13

U	R	G	E							

Clues
URGE

3 Letters

aha
air
ala
all
ama
bet
bra
dey
ere
eye
han
imp
lot

met
mpg
mrs
nor
rye
sba
spa
tan
tat
try
ufo
ugh

4 Letters

ably
alma

chug
copy
ebon
elms
eras
gala
goal
hock
holm
kale
knee
lent
nope
oboe
pipe
root
safe

shoe
tail
taps
tsar
urge

5 Letters

ashen
atlas
beret
discs
eager
massy
meaty
melee
sense

state
takes
taste
terse

6 Letters

rebate
sitter

7 Letters

emerald
grandee

14

| A | J | A | R | | | | | | | | | | | |

Clues
AJAR

3 Letters

act
aft
ama
apo
arb
ave
bbc
boa
eat
elf
ely
ere
fda

few
han
ill
joe
kob
mad
med
mid
mil
not
oar
oft
old
ova
rag
ray
rec
rob

roe
rot
rue
rye
tin
try
use
woo

4 Letters

abbe
ajar
chow
chub
coma
dewy
dole

epic
ever
fete
halo
mama
race
taft
team
undo

5 Letters

arose
dante
eerie
enact
erode
ethos

hotly
ivies
motet
motto
troll

6 Letters

orated
ramrod

7 Letters

backlog
referee

15

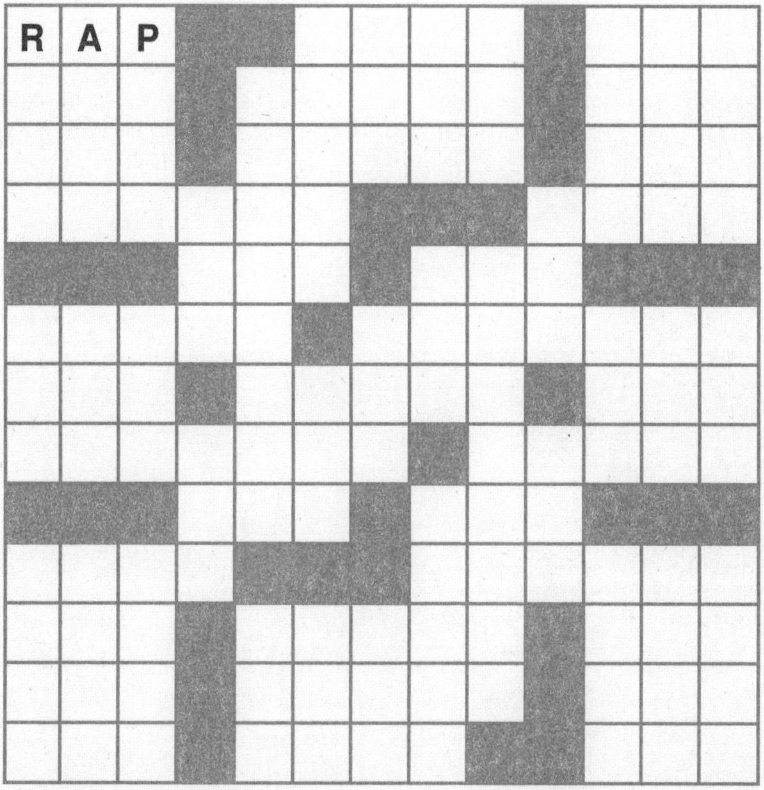

R A P

Clues
RAP

3 Letters

ala
ale
ama
amy
arb
arm
ate
ave
boa
ell
err
fda
goa

han
imp
ivy
lys
map
mci
mon
nag
nne
old
ova
rag
rap
rep
rib
rid
rom
tan

tee
ten
tet
tot
ufo
wad

4 Letters

abet
aloe
cole
crab
half
imps
kale
mama
nabs

pays
peat
raft
rags
thou
thug
undo

5 Letters

elves
manna
midas
outdo
pleat
raise
ruler
ruses

trite

6 Letters

settee
unpack

7 Letters

negroid
renewal

8 Letters

anemones
operator

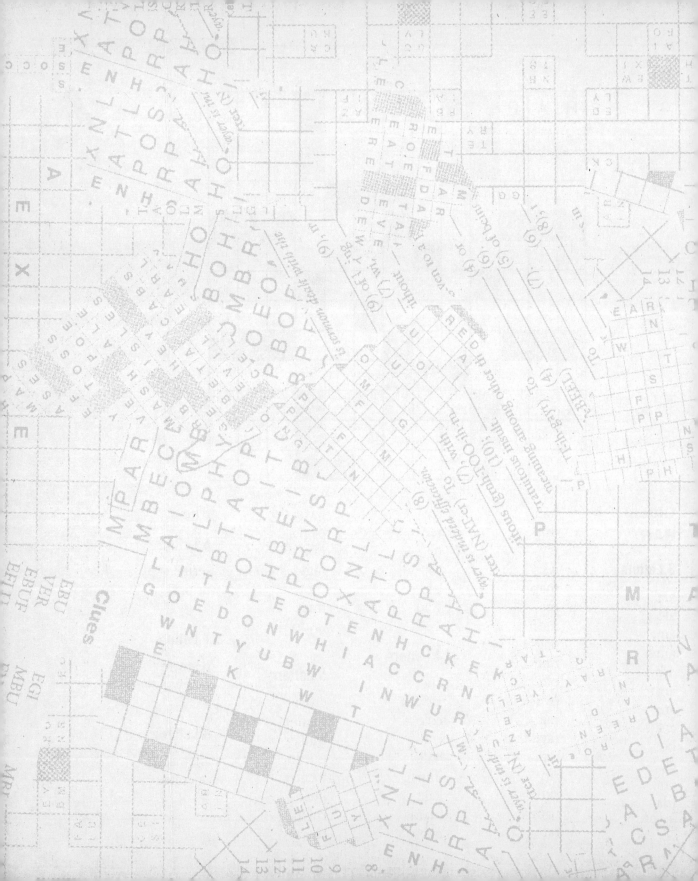

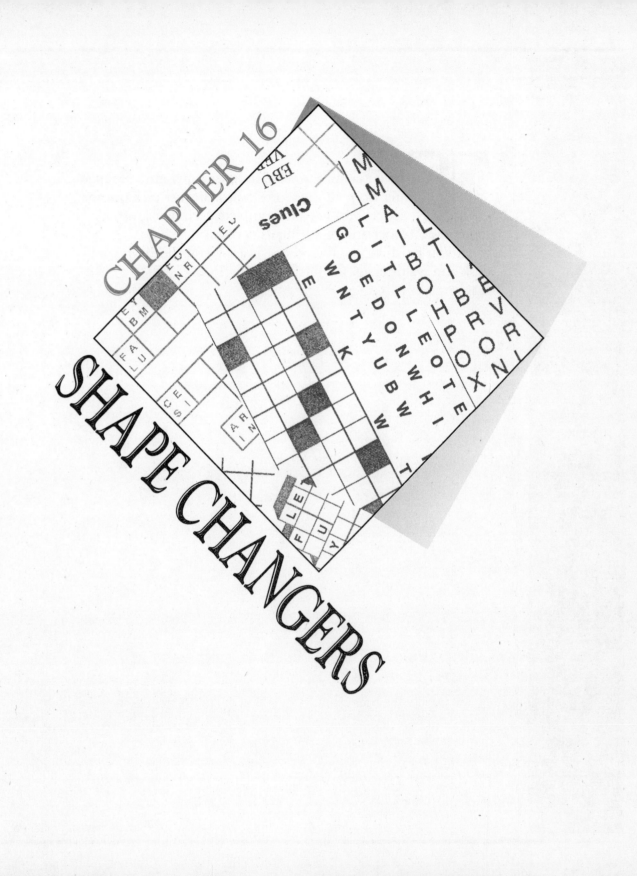

CHAPTER 16

SHAPE CHANGERS

he letters in the word atop each pyramid are missing from all the words below it. Just pick out the letters you need to complete each word, using them in any order and repeating as necessary.

If you finish before the others, just lay your head on your desk and wait quietly for further instructions.

Answers begin on page 308.

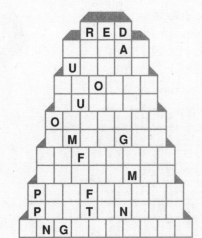

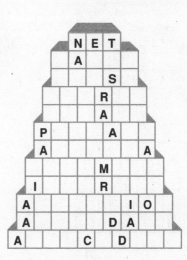

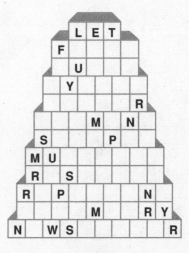

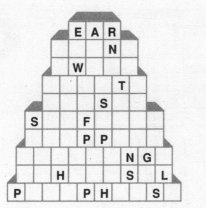

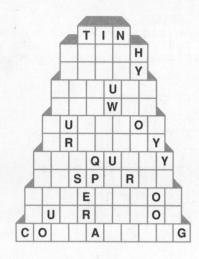

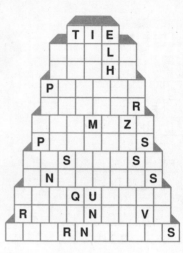

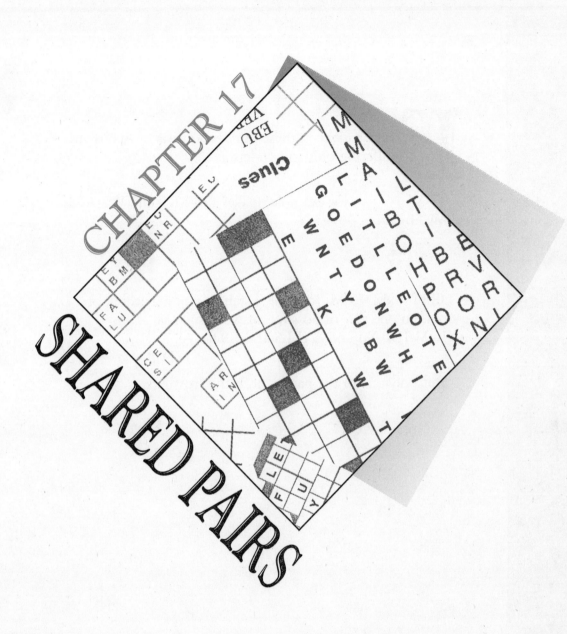

CHAPTER 17

SHARED PAIRS

Every answer in these puzzles consists of two words differing only in two letters.

$\frac{\text{D W}}{\text{W H}}$ _ _ _, for example, makes DWARF and WHARF.

_ _ $\frac{\text{B T}}{\text{EM}}$

is DEBT and DEEM. In some instances you may think of more than one pair of possible answers, such as AXIOM/IDIOM and AXLES/IDLES for $\underline{\text{A X}}$ _ _ _ .
$\phantom{\text{AXIOM/IDIOM and AXLES/IDLES for A X}}\text{I D}$

But only one of the pairs will fit the crossings.

Answers begin on page 310.

1

6

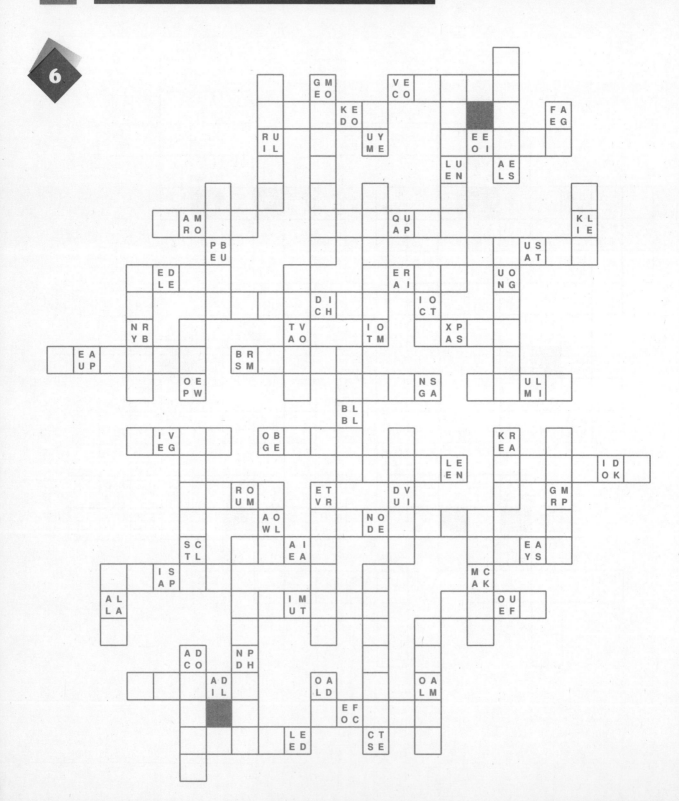

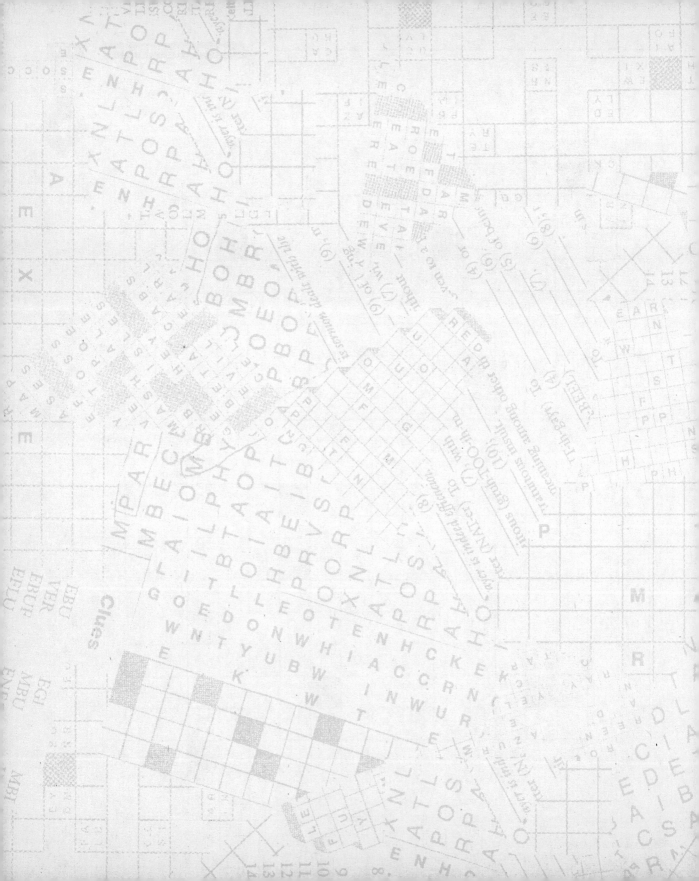

CHAPTER 18

WORDS WITHIN WORDS

This is the perfect game for people who like to take things apart and put them together again—and don't mind having some parts left over.

The goal is to reorganize on a separate piece of paper the letters in the "mother" word to make as many shorter words as you can.

Here are some rules to limit your creativity:

(1) No proper nouns (i.e., capitalized words such as *Tracy*, *Yukon*, *Serb*).
(2) No words of fewer than four letters.
(3) No plurals of two- or three-letter words to form four-letter words (e.g., *goes*, *gets*, *eggs*, etc.).
(4) Only one form of each word. For example, *farm*, but not *farms* or *farmed* (which differ only in number and tense). But *farmer*, which has a different meaning, would be OK.

Answers begin on page 317.

ABROGATE
(AB-ruh-gayt)
Repeal; annul; abolish.

Best score so far: 50

ACRIMONY
(AK-rih-moh-nee)
Bitterness; sharpness.

Best score so far: 57

ADUMBRATE
(uh-DUM-brayt)
Cast a shadow; emerge faintly.

Best score so far: 91

ALLEVIATE
(uh-LEE-vee-ayt)
To lessen or relieve.

Best score so far: 36

ALLOGRAPH
(AL-uh-graf)
A signature made for another person.

Best score so far: 24

AMBIGUOUS
(am-BIG-yoo-us)
Having more than one possible interpretation.

Best score so far: 17

ANTIPATHY
(an-TIP-uh-thee)
Strong aversion; repugnance.

Best score so far: 28

APOCRYPHAL
(uh-POK-rih-ful)
Of doubtful authenticity.

Best score so far: 64

ARROGATE

(AIR-uh-gayt)

To claim without right.

Best score so far: 33

AUSPICIOUS

(aws-PISH-us)

Favorable; auguring success.

Best score so far: 16

CHRONOLOGY

(kruh-NOL-uh-jee)

An arrangement based on
sequence of occurrence.

Best score so far: 32

CIRCUITOUS

(ser-KYOO-ih-tus)

Roundabout.

Best score so far: 40

COMPUNCTION

(k'm-PUNK-sh'n)

Remorse; contrition.

Best score so far: 54

CONDUCIVE

(kun-DOO-siv)

Favorable; helpful.

Best score so far: 40

CONGRESS

(KON-gress)

Formal meeting or conference;
nation's legislature.

Best score so far: 26

CONSPICUOUS

(kun-SPIK-yoo-us)

Easily seen.

Best score so far: 38

DIONYSIAN
(dy-uh-NIH-zhee-un)
Sensual; unrestrained; passionate.

Best score so far: 16

EFFICACIOUS
(ef-ih-KAY-shus)
Producing the desired result.

Best score so far: 22

EGREGIOUS
(eh-GREE-jus)
Very bad; flagrant.

Best score so far: 35

EPHEMERAL
(uh-FEM-er-'l)
Existing only a short time.

Best score so far: 58

EQUIVOCATE
(eh-KWIV-uh-kayt)
To be ambiguous; mislead.

Best score so far: 36

EXACERBATE
(eg-ZASS-er-bayt)
To make worse; aggravate.

Best score so far: 48

FACTIOUS
(FAK-shus)
Marked by faction and dissent.

Best score so far: 31

FEASIBLE
(FEEZ-ih-b'l)
Capable of being done; advis-
able.

Best score so far: 36

25 HOMOLOGOUS
(hoh-MOL-uh-gus)
Similar in structure, position,
etc., to something else.

Best score so far: 23

29 OPPROBRIUM
(uh-PROH-bree-um)
Infamy resulting from disgraceful
conduct.

Best score so far: 27

26 IGNOMINIOUS
(ig-noh-MIN-ee-us)
Shameful; deserving of contempt.

Best score so far: 34

30 PEREMPTORY
(per-EMP-tor-ee)
Dictatorial; imperious.

Best score so far: 75

27 LOGOGRIPH
(LOH-goh-grif)
A word puzzle.

Best score so far: 18

31 SOPHOMORIC
(sof-uh-MOR-ik)
Immaturely pretentious.

Best score so far: 44

28 LOQUACIOUS
(loh-KWAY-shus)
Talkative.

Best score so far: 21

32 TEMPORIZE
(TEM-per-yze)
To put off making a decision or
commitment to gain time.

Best score so far: 75

CHAPTER 19

CROSSWORDS

H ere is the main course—classic crosswords, and they're edited by one of the best in the business, Herb Ettenson of *The Chicago Tribune*.

Ettenson sold his first crossword to the *New York Herald Tribune* when he was only 16. Besides editing crossword puzzles and crossword puzzle magazines, he has worked as a lexicographer and written vocabulary books.

Answers begin on page 323.

ACROSS

1 Biblical spy
6 Garlands
10 Reverberate
14 Where the action is
15 Badly
16 Guinness
17 Noble fish?
19 Carry on
20 Have a meal
21 Kingston, perhaps
22 Join
24 Edible root
25 Plumed bird
26 Poet Teasdale
29 More gaudy
33 Cafe —
34 Type of optimist?
38 Biblical preposition
39 Nevada lake
41 Ono
42 Tall, skinny person
44 Cal. abbr.
45 Became too large for, as clothes
48 Gaelic
49 Up high
52 "A Doll's House" mistress
54 Suspicions
56 Pound the poet
57 Priest's robe
60 Troubadour's instrument
61 Noble dessert?
64 Poetic land
65 Ant of rock
66 Chutzpah
67 Great Barrier, for one
68 Wild animals
69 Gravely sober

DOWN

1 Dessert item
2 — da capo
3 Furnished
4 Sch. subj.
5 Sew lightly
6 Adam's first wife, in folklore
7 Sailor's patron saint
8 Workmen's gp.
9 Thesaurus items: abbr.
10 Noble beverage?
11 Filmmaker René
12 Therefore
13 Musical group
18 God of war
23 Furtive glance
24 Noble meat?
26 Insult
27 First-class
28 Moreno or Hayworth
30 Earthy color
31 Court
32 Freebie at motels
35 Hold — horses!
36 Scrapes by
37 Amount of medicine
39 Small drink
40 Math subj.
43 Greens stroke
46 Pepsin or rennin
47 Michael Dorn on "Star Trek: the Next Generation"
49 Polly or Alfred
50 Donald Duck's nephew
51 Bizarre
53 Showers
55 Smelting residue
56 Mild cheese
57 City on the Jumna
58 Anthropologist — -Strauss
59 Reared
62 Computer language
63 Fishing aid

© 1996 Tribune Media Services, Inc.
All rights reserved.

2

ACROSS

1 Conflict
6 Mantle
11 Swift canine
13 Comforts
15 Bullies
16 Pro bono —
17 December 24, e.g.
18 Walks unsteadily
20 Train term.
21 Peel
23 Dazes
24 Beehive
25 Red dye
27 Norm: abbr.
28 Rich Little's forte
29 Cylindrical and tapering
31 Induce to commit perjury
33 Novelist Umberto
34 Male heir
35 Croquet arch
38 Forces out of bed
41 Vaccinations
42 Otto's emp.
44 Concave, like some arches
46 Cans
47 Mustang, for short
49 NV city
50 Helm dir.
51 Blunders
53 Corp.'s superior
54 Greek letter
56 Referee's signaling device
58 Discourse
59 Border city
60 " Days of wine and — "
61 Destroy documents

DOWN

1 Breed of sheep
2 Imprimatur
3 Appropriate
4 Dalmatian's name
5 Toast starter
6 Certain cocktails
7 Fireplace ledges
8 Ocean: abbr.
9 Narrow margin
10 Podium
11 " — are the snows of yesteryear?"
12 Nagana carrier
13 Shells out
14 Lathery
19 Tongue-clicking sound
22 Superintends
24 Angel
26 Violin parts
28 Circa
30 "Eye of newt, and — of frog"
32 GI hangout
35 Murmur
36 Playwright Eugene
37 Cathedra
38 Distinction
39 Framework
40 Made a one-base hit
41 Harden
43 Take as booty
45 Sheepfolds
47 Roughnecks
48 Some salmon
51 Despondent
52 Deep breath
55 " — about time! "
57 Patriotic org.

3

ACROSS

1 Son of Noah
5 Legislate
10 Party nosh
14 Party giver
15 "Robinson Crusoe" author
16 On — with (equal to)
17 Astronaut/cosmonaut turf
19 Tattered
20 Strong effort
21 Impart fragrance to
23 Iron will?
25 Turner and Louise
26 Unrefined
28 Bridge position
31 Explosive letters
32 Show excessive love
33 Infinite
36 Novel by 13D
41 Certain bird
42 Little — (Dickens heroine)
43 Newhart
46 Karate prize
47 Equally
49 Tropical palm
51 Fairy tale monster
53 See 13D
56 Observed
59 Stravinsky ballet
60 That can be told
62 Sound of distress
63 Copywriter
64 Silent one
65 Magnani or Moffo
66 Inventor Nikola
67 Wriggly

DOWN

1 Like tame horses
2 Time period
3 Approximate calculation
4 Earth's highest peak
5 Copy chiefs: abbr.
6 Katmandu's land
7 Novel by 13D
8 Tropical tree
9 Swarm
10 Page of song
11 Stretch — (make an exception)
12 Jungle hero
13 US novelist (with 53A)
18 Soaks
22 Perfume
24 — -weenie
26 Chicago summer time: abbr.
27 Partner of aah
29 Gaelic
30 Sound sleeper
34 Extravagant
35 Typewriter feature
37 Of the city
38 Rational
39 Building wing
40 Cagey
43 — Islands
44 Salem's state
45 Lament
48 Waistcoat
50 Character in "Julius Caesar"
52 Circular
54 Pesky insect
55 Move diligently forward
57 Israeli airline
58 Paper size
61 Collection of anecdotes

4

ACROSS

1 Director who won three Oscars
6 Being: Lat.
10 H.H. Munro
14 At right angles to the keel
15 Burmese tribesman
16 Burden
17 1995 Stanley Cup winners
20 Part of the UN
21 Org.
22 Greek letter
23 Chocolate dessert
27 "— Town"
28 Cover girl Carol
29 Mink or ermine
30 Final Four org.
32 Killer whales
35 Tolled
38 Ferocious marsupials
42 17A, e.g.
43 Defendant's statement
44 Selves
45 "— Woman" (Reddy hit)
47 100 square meters
49 Ram's mate
50 Typesetters' assistants
56 Poetic contraction
57 Draft status
58 Allen of "Home Improvement"
59 Argumentative types
65 Eager
66 Hun leader
67 Certain suit in bridge
68 Horne or Olin
69 Places
70 Cardinal number

DOWN

1 Container
2 Actor Vigoda
3 Church seat
4 Gandhi assassinated in 1991
5 Aviatrix Earhart
6 Curve
7 Bundle
8 Dictum
9 "From the — the earth!" (Kipling)
10 Part of USSR: abbr.
11 Singer Baker
12 Former Russian farmer
13 Offspring
18 Deodorant type
19 Last
23 Old coin
24 Make a change
25 Gaza —
26 Desire
27 Can. prov.
31 Forcefully
33 Baseball's Ripken
34 Three-time PGA winner
36 Late actor Bruce
37 Shines
39 Powerful explosive
40 "Do I — eat a peach?" (Eliot)
41 Comp. pt.
46 Used at the table
48 Throws out
50 Bike part
51 He played Superman
52 Hall of Famer, Monte
53 Lariat
54 Unfortunately
55 Japanese porcelain
60 Muckraker Tarbell
61 Nobleman: abbr.
62 Formal suit, briefly
63 Ambulance attendant: abbr.
64 Mole

5

ACROSS

1 Kind of bandage
6 Food
10 Son of Noah
14 Old Greek city
15 Swiss river
16 In —
(completely)
17 Appears
magnified
18 Exclude
20 Valued
22 Rumor
23 Levin and
Gershwin
24 Bullets
26 Lean-to
29 Mop
30 Greek letter
33 Orient
34 Lambchop's
Lewis
35 Max — Sydow
36 Tiny part
40 Hawaiian guitar,
briefly
41 Cancel
42 Poker money
43 Paronomasia
44 Rank
45 Fireplace facing
47 Strays
48 Knave
49 Italian commune
52 Incensed
56 Type of flat
59 — Gay
60 Marsh plant
61 Rainbow
62 Fishing line
63 Box
64 Masculine
65 Demi- —

DOWN

1 Bargain event
2 Players for pay
3 "— Rhythm"
4 Acquire
5 Say strongly
6 Bistros
7 Stubborn
8 Mineral earth
9 Tiny
10 Office employee
11 Gangster
12 Small case
13 US feminist,
Lucretia
19 Mixed drink
21 Springtime
24 Expect
25 Chagall
26 Frame
27 Japanese
verse
28 Poplar
29 Author Hite
30 Happening
31 Rich cake
32 Heavenly one
34 Attempts
37 Litter of pigs
38 Ski lift
39 Colored
handkerchief
45 Rug
46 Nab
47 Church official
48 Jinx
49 Biblical book
50 Dinner course
51 Earthenware
crock
52 — -de-boeuf
(oval window)
53 Departs
54 Annexes
55 Valley
57 Goal
58 — la la

© 1996 Tribune Media Services, Inc.
All rights reserved.

6

ACROSS
1 Lake in Italy
5 Communications word
9 River in Germany
12 Lulu
13 Insulting putdowns
14 Gam or Tushingham
16 Canopy for a boat
17 1996 Oscar for original music
19 Clothe
20 Tall and thin
21 Lurches
22 Impart zest to
24 — hound
25 Poison
26 — and switch
28 Indian group
30 Calendar word
35 Scads
36 Intolerant one
37 Hard to handle
38 Was useful
40 Count in music
41 Drive the getaway car, e.g.
42 Seasoning
43 Islands around lagoons
47 Roof style
50 Washes
51 Trademark
53 British miler, Sebastian
54 1996 Oscar for best picture
56 Particle
57 Fill up
58 Puzo subject
59 Middling
60 Poker call
61 Preminger
62 Part of B.A.

DOWN
1 Terra —
2 Pungent bulb
3 1996 Oscar for best director
4 Table scrap
5 Solo
6 Las Vegas need
7 Tatter
8 Residue
9 Piscivorous flyers
10 Very small contributions
11 Far from fresh
13 Outburst
15 Aide: abbr.
18 Declaim
20 Bowling alley
23 Flat finish
24 Nautical post
26 Sire
27 Like peas in —
28 Tractor part
29 Pub drink
30 Location
31 Repasts
32 Nicolas Cage in 1996
33 Wallach or Whitney
34 Whiskey
36 Apron parts
39 Test answer
40 Rock group
42 Barbara or Clara
43 Mass robes
44 "— Bulba" (Gogol)
45 Egg-shaped
46 Embankment
47 Former governor, Cuomo
48 Perch
49 Some auto sales
51 Thrash
52 George of Hollywood
55 Med. provider
56 Sharp — tack

7

ACROSS

1 Annie Oakley
5 Biblical name of Syria
9 Taxis
13 Self-evident truth
15 Be defeated
16 Site of Taj Mahal
17 Fitzgerald's wife
18 Dutch colonist
19 Brad
20 Book by Tolstoy
23 — carte
26 Theater award
27 Literary device
28 Fine
30 Tribe
31 Silky fabric
32 Lads
33 Lady of Spain: abbr.
36 Dill, old style
37 College professor
38 And others: abbr.
39 Dictionary: abbr.
40 River in Hades
42 Moon goddess
44 Additional
45 More grouchy
46 Greek philosopher
48 Baseball stadium
49 After deductions
50 Book by Pearl Buck
53 Horse
54 Couple
55 Spooky
59 Last of the Stuarts
60 Sea eagle
61 Oxeye
62 Annoying person
63 Oboe
64 Cupola

DOWN

1 La —, Bolivia
2 Hatchet
3 Part of RSVP
4 Carbonated water
5 City on the Hudson
6 Abounding in certain birds
7 Confused
8 Lightheartedly
9 Howitzer
10 Encore!
11 Salty
12 Room in a casa
14 Cloak
21 Memo
22 Time periods
23 Shock: var.
24 Sierra —
25 Ell
29 Envoy: abbr.
30 Swindle
32 Fight in the ring
33 Mug
34 Wife of a rajah
35 Wide awake
37 Stain
38 Moose
40 Explorer De —
41 Policeman
42 Court litigant
43 Jubilant
44 Lodestone
45 Divided
46 Call
47 Has a tendency
48 Large fishing net
50 Two-wheeled carriage
51 Confront boldly
52 Uppermost part
56 — de Janeiro
57 Doctrine
58 Needle opening

8

ACROSS

1 S.A. rodent
5 Relief carving
10 Military bugle call
14 Image
15 Transmit from sea
16 Evening wear
17 Bowler's milieu
18 Ruhr Valley city
19 Japanese native
20 Hill dweller
21 Actor Vigoda
22 Ire
24 Rod Stewart 1989 hit
28 Ms. Gardner
29 King of Israel
30 Greek letter
33 — out (settle, in a way)
36 "Faerie Queene" maiden
37 Asian sea
38 Estefan '90s remake
41 Accustomed
42 Utmost degree
43 Declined in price
44 Vane letters
45 U.S. author
46 Agreeing with
47 1988 Bangles tune
52 Small sword
55 Feel sorrow
56 English dress style
57 During
58 Sustain
61 Lyon friend
62 Celebration
63 Noted weeper
64 Shoulder
65 Emperor
66 English composer
67 Rug type

DOWN

1 Rice dish
2 Bell town
3 Oppose
4 Strong brew
5 Loon relative
6 Surgical tool, of a kind
7 Length measures: abbr.
8 Comedic prop
9 Tegucigalpa people
10 Bowstring sound
11 Jejune
12 Glass panel
13 Incite
21 Advantage
23 Black cuckoo
25 Turn outward
26 Renew
27 Sports arena
30 Code writer
31 Except
32 "— Three Lives"
33 Cut down
34 English county
35 Reddish-orange
37 Variable star
39 Game or joke finish
40 Faux pas
45 Took lunch
47 Down source
48 Resort island
49 Siren
50 Wavy fabric
51 Bodily swelling
52 Great number
53 IA city
54 Flat bread
59 Zilch
60 Gear tooth
61 Legal assn.

9

ACROSS

1 Yemen's capital
5 Oaths of old
10 Promote successfully
14 Goddess of discord
15 Cordage fiber
16 Kind of bargain
17 Parade confetti, at times
19 Disembark
20 Volcanic fallout
21 Trials
22 Exquisitely fragile
24 Wobbles
26 Move rapidly and nimbly
27 1040 supplier
28 More insubstantial
32 Confidence games
35 Fiber source
36 Icelandic literary work
37 Soliloquy start
38 Biblical weapon
39 Fountain throwaway
40 Tangy fish sauce
41 Steal a look
42 Dispensed as charity
43 Take the lead
45 Weekday abbr.
46 Versifier
47 Debarkation
51 Pursued
54 No great shakes
55 Overly
56 Lima land
57 Guard's post
60 Spoken
61 Wide-eyed
62 Glade
63 "Kemo —" (Tonto)
64 Affirmatives
65 Part of P.T.A.: abbr.

DOWN

1 — ease (make comfortable)
2 Greet the day
3 Cubbyhole
4 Request
5 Oversights
6 Revolutionary general
7 Amo, —, amat
8 Party nosh
9 Young plant
10 Instant
11 Spirit
12 40-day period
13 Baronet's spouse
18 Pitchers
23 Ready follower
25 Cornerstone content
26 Steak cut
28 Like onion rings
29 Adored one
30 Adams or McClurg
31 Author Ayn
32 Men-only affair
33 Singer Natalie
34 Sanction misdeeds
35 Sheepish comment
38 Indianapolis, e.g.
42 — pass go
44 Weed remover
45 Converts into pulp
47 Actress Sondra —
48 "— just one of those things"
49 Coward and Harrison
50 Late bridge maven
51 Naval noncoms: abbr.
52 Wife of Zeus
53 Hebron native
54 R.R. terminals
58 Fill with wonder
59 Harem room

10

ACROSS
1 Some alley cats
5 Attempt to avoid the inevitable
10 "Thin Man" canine
14 Needle case
15 Ancient Greek region
16 Highway warning
17 Like — of bricks
18 Suppress
19 Curtail
20 A Sound place?
22 Wife of Geraint
23 Ballads
24 Transmit
26 Paris' victim
29 Sentry's command
31 Wane
34 Woe is me!
35 Type of card
37 Peggy of TV
38 Sloe —
39 The Sunshine State
40 Former secret org.
41 Supplement
42 Represent with a symbol
43 Fat
44 Kinsman: abbr.
45 A terrible leader?
46 Jai alai basket
47 Nursery rhyme opener
49 Taj Mahal site
51 Shillelagh
53 Sea fearer?
59 Diving birds
60 A place to remember
61 Roof overhang
62 Waste allowance
63 Ninth day before the ides
64 Ashtabula's waterfront
65 Small amounts
66 School bigwigs
67 Order to a broker

DOWN
1 Freshwater duck
2 Holy Roman emperor
3 Elementary particle
4 Diamond hits
5 Spacek of films
6 Works the land
7 Rectangular pilaster
8 Celebrity
9 Overwhelming victory
10 CO city
11 Defamatory
12 Convex moldings
13 Inspired with reverence
21 Author Fleming
25 Cartoon's Kett
26 Ishmael's mother
27 Slur over
28 Like some countries
29 Long-necked wader
30 Mine exit
32 Harass
33 Trump, in card games
35 American League team
36 A Barrett
39 Bank agcy.
43 Naval builders
46 French vineyard
48 Aeries
49 Madison street minions
50 Sheen
51 O.T. book: abbr.
52 Gloriole
54 — vera
55 Wendy's dog
56 Expose to the public
57 Satanic
58 Lively dance

11

ACROSS

1 Lady of rank
5 Dervish
10 Garden item
14 Give approval
15 Cream of the crop
16 Reps.
17 Holland sight
18 Pulls out the stops
20 "— for the money..."
21 Paddy plant
22 Queen of mystery
23 Show appreciation
25 Auctioneer's aim
26 Sedan shelter
28 Move with urgency
32 Fill with awe
33 Fischer's game
34 Bygone Mideast coalition
35 "I Love —" (old TV show)
36 Call up
37 Snare, for one
38 "— and ye shall receive"
39 Prattle
40 — hand (help)
41 Convention meetings
43 Particular styles
44 Latvia native
45 Certain African
46 Grief relief
49 Pond plant
50 Kind of Jazz
53 Gets a move on
55 Up to the task
56 Tide's partner
57 Court event
58 Professional charges
59 Sorrowful sounds
60 Contest prize
61 Horse gait

DOWN

1 Stupid fellow
2 Related
3 Hotfoot it
4 Storm center
5 Puma or civet
6 Smart — (wise guy)
7 High flier
8 "— a Wonderful Life"
9 Practice a role
10 Globetrotters' home
11 Fairy tale beast
12 To-do
13 Catch site of
19 Raines and Fitzgerald
21 Current fashion
24 Indistinct
25 Public tiff
26 Elegant events
27 Entertain
28 Gunfire
29 Roar off
30 Magna cum —
31 Bombeck et al.
33 Intone
36 Objects
37 Bumper boo-boo
39 Recital number
40 Musical Horne
42 Quenches
43 Geese group
45 "— House" (Dickens)
46 Atl. fliers
47 Indiana neighbor
48 Barnyard baby
49 Inter —
51 Bread spread
52 Annoying person
54 Museum display
55 Toward the stern

12

ACROSS
1 Hot tubs
5 Las Vegas main street
10 Hourglass filling
14 Word on a door
15 Instant
16 "Now — me down to sleep..."
17 Song from Placido
18 Leader
19 Alaskan city
20 Maris to Mantle
22 In a chair
24 Trail
25 Dad's sister
26 Asian temples
29 Indian fabric
32 Dairy case choice
33 Vacation home
35 Reason for overtime
36 — glass
39 "— Maria"
40 Meetings
42 Forehead
43 Necessary
44 Lifetime pursuits
47 Refuse
48 Spoken
49 Fleet of warships
52 Like an amoeba?
56 Castle defense
57 Reputation
59 Heavenly hat?
60 Axlike tool
61 Fernando or Lorenzo
62 Ellipse
63 Obey
64 Perfume
65 Cucumber, e.g.

DOWN
1 Tiff
2 Immaculate
3 Europe's neighbor
4 Beauty parlor item
5 Layers
6 "We hold these —..."
7 Annoy
8 Rink surface
9 Talk into
10 Ol' Blue Eyes
11 Thanks —!
12 Point out
13 Colored
21 Furious
23 Concluded
25 Despot Idi —
26 Kitchen items
27 Sigourney Weaver movie
28 Barnyard honkers
30 Cognizant
31 Taste
33 That guy's
34 Evergreen shrubs
36 Took up one's cause
37 Pedicure targets
38 Opie's dad
41 Calmed, in a way
42 Hotel lobby figure
44 "—'s Bluff" (film)
45 Collar
46 Battering —
49 Oriental nanny
50 Traveled
51 Labyrinth
52 Notoriety
53 Roof overhang
54 Sharp blow
55 Fly alone
58 Unknown guy

© 1996 Tribune Media Services, Inc.
All rights reserved.

ACROSS

1 Grocers' competition
6 Math course
10 Fed. mail handler
13 Spartan square
14 Jam makers?
16 Gun engines
17 Fun task
19 Mesozoic, e.g.
20 Stretch
21 Involve
23 Dame Myra —
24 Feature
25 Altered organism
28 Argues against
31 "Frankly, my dear, — give..."
32 Creek craft
33 Tall tale
34 Domestic
35 Candle
36 "— Time, Next Year"
37 Indisposed
38 Was wrong
39 Approve of
40 Take to the — (impoverish)
42 Coe and Bannister
43 Rip and red
44 Author Morrison
45 Large rodent
47 New York lakes
51 Egg: pref.
52 Melanie Griffith film
54 Compete
55 Neighbor of Andorra
56 "Vive —!"
57 McMahon and Ames
58 Conveyed
59 Construct

DOWN

1 Valley
2 Equal, in Quebec
3 Gray wolf
4 Strict control
5 Artist John
6 First family in 1910
7 Call the tune
8 Legal Lance
9 Speed regulator
10 — Lake, Canada
11 Scope or meter beginning
12 White House office
15 Upper house
18 Malt kiln
22 Deadlock
24 — down (softened)
25 Parrot
26 Former US Secretary of the Interior
27 Grooming aids
28 Cod and Horn
29 Indonesian island
30 Visionaries
32 Darleen and Vikki
35 Perches for peregrines
36 Pierre or J.D.
38 Furnishes funds
39 Trick
41 Zero in
42 Forenoon
44 Sully
45 Arouse emotions
46 Enthusiastic
47 — and bones
48 After million or billion
49 Large reptile, briefly
50 Trench type
53 "Norma —"

© 1996 Tribune Media Services, Inc. All rights reserved.

14

ACROSS
1 Benedictine title
4 Ulan —
9 Trial car
13 Family member
14 Abscond
15 Dry
16 Stupid persons
17 Played a flute
18 Trick
19 If perhaps
22 Morse dash
23 Before
24 Vane dir.
25 Parisiennes' magazine
27 Switch positions
32 Basics
34 Trampled
35 To and —
36 Vendetta
37 "...— in the fountain"
38 Distant
39 Ump's kin
40 Amerind
41 Tuxedo accouterment
42 Intermittently
45 Cut
47 Molokai garland
48 Branch
49 Hellenic letter
52 Avant-garde theater
57 Always
58 Like classical architecture
59 Breathing sound
60 — noire
61 Obliterate
62 Troubles
63 Reared
64 Schussboomer
65 Use diligently

DOWN
1 Princess of Wales
2 Extemporaneous
3 Engage
4 Ere
5 "Get —!"
6 London dandy
7 Oil cartel
8 Skelton and Buttons
9 Became morning
10 Norwegian navigator
11 Highway measure
12 Shelley piece
13 Driver
20 Conger
21 Sothern or Jillian
26 Hallucinogen
27 Heavenly hunter
28 Not any
29 Outlandish
30 13A, in Bonn
31 Cross
32 Continental prefix
33 Gripe
34 Dorothy's pooch
37 Classifies
38 Burro
43 — the Great
44 Classical beginning
45 Food merchant
46 Drs.' gp.
48 Leave the arms of Morpheus
50 Score
51 Votes for
52 Done
53 Holiday
54 Tined implement
55 — B'rith
56 Plumbing problem
57 Flag

ACROSS

1 Move about
5 "Dear —" (advice column)
9 Long-legged bird
14 Phoenician city
15 Mrs. Copperfield
16 Lofty nest
17 Saga
18 In a lively fashion
20 Ancient Persian
21 Defamatory charges
22 Makes over
23 Sows
25 Waldorf or Caesar
27 — trap for
29 Toss
30 Electrical units
34 List extender
36 Animated
38 — barrel (at a disadvantage)
39 Joan Crawford-Franchot Tone film
42 Prongs
43 Legal claims
44 Cereal grain
45 Before: pref.
46 Dolores — Rio
47 Loyalist
49 Peons
51 Staircase support
54 Suppose
58 Mimic
60 — monster
61 City
63 First garden
64 Go-between
65 Fruit decay
66 Not a soul
67 Palomino
68 Capri, e.g.
69 "— the night before..."

DOWN

1 Stalks
2 Melville opus
3 Lustrous
4 Ebb
5 "— Bede"
6 Premium
7 Yosemite cascade
8 Sweet potato
9 Surfeited
10 — off (irate)
11 Church calender
12 Irritate
13 FL feature
19 Certain Asian
24 Has the lead
26 Lerner's partner
28 — Baba
30 "— Maria"
31 Franz Lehar operetta (with "The")
32 Quarry
33 Marquis de —
34 Ms. Kett
35 Slender
37 Lazy person
38 Actor Welles
40 Busy insect
41 Can. prov.
46 Profound
48 Ruler
49 Chastised, old style
50 Sales pitch
52 Ms. Verdugo of TV
53 Country paths
54 Eastern nurse
55 Kind of lily
56 Ham or lob end
57 Footed vases
59 Titled Italian family
62 Oriental sash

15

16

ACROSS
1 The area between
6 Significant period
9 Willowy
13 Church instrument
14 Stubborn critter
16 Decorate again
17 Certain tournament
19 Golf club
20 Sheepfold occupant
21 On the — (no longer friendly)
22 Fit for cultivation
24 Tiny
25 So be it
26 Decorative hangings
30 Took care of nestlings
33 Type of seal
34 Influence
35 Atop
37 Of the same length
38 Equine ladies
39 Bowling alley feature
40 Encounter
41 Soon
42 Certain horse
43 Malicious report
45 Diverged
46 Lethal items
47 Tennis term
48 Item for TV control
51 Tempo
52 That girl
55 Bridge feature
56 Serious eating
59 Fluid carrier, anatomically
60 Certain heavenly bodies
61 Wanders
62 Rind
63 Devoured
64 Scandinavian people

DOWN
1 Suffering pain
2 Ship's front
3 Chills and fever
4 Is capable
5 Bestowed naturally
6 Ham it up
7 Applies with friction
8 — Baba
9 Three-sided
10 Ginseng, e.g.
11 Object of worship
12 Not any part
15 Glossy paints
18 Regrets
23 Blushing
25 Ethan of the Green Mountain Boys
26 Consider
27 Certain critiques
28 Swaying dizzily
29 Five-sided
30 Extreme rage
31 Heavenly time period
32 Gift receiver
34 Window areas
36 Social misfit
38 Loss of sanity
42 Model for imitation
44 Pecan
45 Fruit
47 Landlord's concern
48 Certain reply letters
49 Dueler's weapon
50 Leonine feature
51 Batter's ploy
52 Cause to wither
53 Smokehouse items
54 Other
57 Sine — non
58 Pasture sound

17

ACROSS

1 Summoned
6 Sharp bark
10 Intention
14 Rope plant
15 Butterine
16 — Royale
17 Angler's basket
18 Ancient Greek coin
19 Pleased
20 Patti Page hit
23 Also
24 — de mer
25 NASA theme song?
33 Brings up
34 — avis
35 — in the bud
37 Oohs and —
38 Boosts one's product
40 Head: Fr.
41 GI's hangout
42 Jog
43 Subway
44 Astronaut's question?
48 Towel word
49 Actor Linden
50 Jimmy Johnson's favorite song?
57 Formal dance
58 Agatha Christie's "Death on the —"
59 Trunk item
61 Seed covering
62 Fitzgerald of note
63 Type of battery
64 Contradict
65 Oliver or Rex
66 Freud follower

DOWN

1 Moccasin
2 City on the Jumna
3 Celt
4 Daredevil Knievel
5 Takes out
6 Hello, there!
7 Czech river
8 Uris
9 Chemical compounds
10 "American —" (Gere movie)
11 Capital of Norway
12 Ladd
13 Conducted
21 "I — Rhythm"
22 "I Remember —"
25 Teutonic title
26 Tether
27 "Gulliver's Travels" creature
28 25D in the USA
29 Verity
30 Crone
31 — a customer
32 Yegg's explosive
36 Lowly laborer
38 James Brown's "— of Love"
39 Ship's record
40 Pro —
42 Slender
43 Musical Manchester
45 Altogether
46 Hang by a —
47 Pork product
50 Old, grey beast?
51 Actor Ken, of "thirtysomething"
52 Base
53 Fashion magazine
54 Like peas in —
55 Stores galore
56 Dies —
57 Rotten
60 Goof

© 1996 Tribune Media Services, Inc.
All rights reserved.

18

ACROSS
1 Stringed instrument
5 Swiss city
10 North European
14 Russian city
15 Negatively charged particle
16 Not at home
17 1955 Disney classic
20 Self-esteem
21 Wild ox
22 Concur
23 Concoct
24 Vocations
26 More indelicate
29 Lifts to judge the weight of
30 Image
31 Stiller and — of comedy
32 Copy
35 Flynn and Gardner film of '57
39 Letter from England
40 Strained food
41 Shipshape
42 English forest
43 Property
45 Maxims
48 Christiania
49 Loos or Bryant
50 Self: pref.
51 Craze
54 One of the "Star Wars" trilogy
58 Mideast nation
59 Without — in the world
60 Greek liqueur
61 Thrall of yore
62 Wearing less
63 River in Germany

DOWN
1 Cavity
2 "To — and a bone" (Kipling)
3 Make over
4 Layer
5 Pennant
6 Supply
7 Actress Moreno
8 Japanese drama
9 Comp. pt.
10 Scows
11 Cognizant
12 Debussy opus
13 Categories
18 Swiss river
19 Violent one
23 Containers
24 Terminate
25 Hair style
26 Elegant display
27 Yearn
28 Campus belle
29 — of Troy
31 Equines
32 Puzzled
33 Irish fuel
34 Punta del —
36 Rumpus
37 Artist's model
38 Division word
42 Adjust
43 Williams or Rolle
44 — gin
45 A Curie
46 Dillies
47 Giant
48 Bizarre
50 At a distance
51 Vendetta
52 Tool with a curved blade
53 Name in fashion
55 Arrest
56 Edible tuber
57 — Blow (average citizen)

19

ACROSS

1 Rhine feeder
5 Male party
9 Short haircut
12 Willow
14 Ponder (over)
15 Source of the Blue Nile
16 Fish
17 Raises
19 Cabinet wood
21 Certain racers
22 Skin protuberances
23 Bog
24 Fall
26 Guiding principle
30 Climbing plant
31 Crowns
33 "A — 'clock scholar"
34 Cupolas
36 Receive
37 Viral disease
38 — out (made do)
39 Lightweight paper
41 Superlative suffix
42 Lawmakers
44 Drudges
46 Mr. Sagan
47 Spyri work
48 Store, as fodder
51 Stupors
54 Auto adjunct
56 Like an old woman
57 Call it —
58 Honolulu is here
59 Daughter of Tantalus
60 Lease
61 Writer's enc.
62 Easy job

DOWN

1 Wander
2 Annapolis letters
3 Certain robbers
4 Put in more bullets
5 Rotates
6 Theater award
7 Jeanne d' —
8 Cousins of the mouse
9 Headquarters
10 Doozy
11 Opera voice
13 Rues
15 Is attracted by
18 Ireland
20 Italian commune
23 Castle adjuncts
24 Secretes
25 Call to mind
26 Fourth estate
27 Medium
28 Ouzo flavoring
29 Haley work
32 "It's —!"
35 Voraciousness
37 Web-footed bird
39 Bullfighters
40 Addict
43 "A — of Two Cities"
45 Handsome youth
47 Netherlands city (with "The")
48 Israeli airline
49 Brood of pheasants
50 RBI, e.g.
51 Slangy negatives
52 Exile island
53 Ooze
55 Comment from the lea

© 1996 Tribune Media Services, Inc.
All rights reserved.

20

ACROSS
1 Counterpart
6 Town near Des Moines
10 Open a bit
14 Hilo howdy
15 Bygone
16 Moderate
17 Author of "Ulysses"
19 Look over
20 Commercial pact: abbr.
21 — Rafael, CA
22 Enameled metalware
23 Mexican border town
27 Fit to imbibe
29 Bedouin
30 Gaelic
32 Alphabet run
33 Thrashes
34 601
35 Threaten
38 Verse or lateral starter
39 First U.S. chief justice
41 Tub
42 Slip-up
44 U.S. troops
45 Entree, e.g.
46 Run for the health of it
47 Fine fellow
48 "Leave — Beaver"
49 Underwriter
52 Unbeatable foes
54 Stanley and America's
55 "Maude" portrayer
57 Angling need
58 — Stanley Gardner
59 Colleague of Ricki Lake
64 Fritz's refusal
65 Outward: pref.
66 Olympic great, Jesse
67 Bivouac shelter
68 Midterm
69 Scoff

DOWN
1 Army off.
2 Chicken —king
3 Cruise
4 Angels
5 "— la vista!"
6 Address for 44A
7 Giant Hall-of-Famer
8 Bust out
9 Courtroom asst.
10 Practice self-denial
11 Four-term N.Y. senator
12 In any way
13 Actress Taylor
18 Anonymous female, legally
23 Actress O'Neal
24 Tabriz resident
25 "Cry Baby" singer
26 Foot feature
28 "— Call the Wind Maria"
31 Char
35 Adeptness
36 Hindu social class
37 Body of beliefs
39 Amphorae
40 Lamp spirits
43 Permission
45 Abate
47 Country on the Aegean
49 Whiff
50 Thick soup
51 — d'art (museum piece)
53 Voodoo amulets
56 Tiny toilers
60 Negative
61 Society column word
62 Comp. pt.
63 Latvia, formerly: abbr.

© 1996 Tribune Media Services, Inc.
All rights reserved.

ACROSS

1 Financial nabob
6 Made a high grade
10 Ski lift
14 Texas shrine
15 Money on hand
16 Trick
17 Baseball teams
18 Salad fish
19 Clumsy vessels
20 Elvis hit
23 French department
24 Simian
25 Softens the noise
27 6-pointers
29 Before Castro
31 Headache remedy letters
34 Boot-shaped country
37 Ken or Lena
38 Brimless hat
40 Period
41 Make into law
42 — go bragh
43 Reside
45 Calendar sections: abbr.
46 Indian drums
49 Russian river
51 Towel cloth
52 Legendary bird
54 Small glass container
58 Johnson/Miles film
61 Fellow
63 Cover with concrete
64 Body cavities
65 In —
66 Bakery worker
67 Entices
68 "— a man with..."
69 Irish forefather
70 Fermenting agent

DOWN

1 Uke's kin
2 "... — or a madman" (Rousseau)
3 Took into custody
4 Egg dish
5 Snack between meals
6 Misbehave
7 Make happen
8 Slave of old
9 Buddhist teachings
10 Tire friction
11 Gene Barry TV show
12 Inquire
13 — judicata
21 Kiln
22 Away
26 Adhere
28 Telegraph code item
29 Computer unit
30 Formicary occupants
31 Assist, in felony
32 1992 election figure
33 Hayden/Nelson film
35 Makes a summation
36 Underhanded
39 Warehouse
41 Antlered animal
44 Centers of activity
47 Globe
48 Nearsighted
50 Boulevard
52 Make merry
53 Apparent
55 Within: pref.
56 Large quantities
57 Smallest amount
59 Grimace
60 Tyne of TV
61 106
62 That guy

21

22

ACROSS
1 Agent 007
5 — Bill,
   legendary
   cowboy
10 Beehive State
14 Region
15 Glorify
16 Egyptian river
17 Word difficult to
   pronounce
19 Fido's bane
20 Capp and
   Capone
21 Formerly
22 Lucky piece
24 Seashore
26 Asterisk
27 Burn with a hot
   liquid
29 Of the highest
   quality
33 Desert havens
34 Hoodlums
35 Born
36 Doing
37 Glossy
38 "Terrible" ruler
39 Witness
40 To pieces
41 Longest river of
   France
42 Supercilious
44 Feeling of
   dread
45 Violin part
46 Authority
48 Withdraw
51 Comic Kaplan
52 Unpleasantly
   chilly
55 Declare
56 Nonsense
59 Isinglass
60 "Let's Make —"
61 Singer James
62 Frolic
63 Frenchman's
   income
64 Not diluted

DOWN
1 — California
2 Spoken
3 Dan Rather, e.g.
4 Touch lightly
5 Hammer parts
6 Precise
7 Birthday dessert
8 Spanish cheer
9 Game plan
10 Spread open
11 Cash box
12 Not aweather
13 Preliminary
   contest
18 Streets
23 A planet
25 Margarine
26 Daring feat
27 "March King"
28 Prank
29 Article of
   apparel
30 Pep up
31 Approaches
32 Mammal with a
   ringed tail
34 Be grateful
37 Typewriter part
38 Charged
   particles
40 Old
41 Hen
43 Road sign
46 Former Egyptian
   leader
47 White poplar
   tree
48 Freeway exit
49 Sinful
50 Comic Imogene
51 Singer Campbell
53 Nora Charles'
   dog
54 Reporter's
   question
57 Summer drink
58 Study room

23

ACROSS
1 Ecstatic
5 Greatest amount
9 Egged
14 Wide-mouthed jar
15 Sheltered
16 Singer Judd
17 Astringent
18 Window part
19 Defeat decisively
20 Clerical item
23 "My Gal —"
24 Hi-fi
25 Climb
27 List ender
30 Kitchen gadget
33 Indistinct
37 Burn the surface of
39 TV part
40 Large landmass
41 Type of letter or saw
42 School letters
43 Rendezvous
44 Throng
45 Inquired
46 Convince
48 —-do-well
50 "Le Nozze di Figaro"
52 Radiation devices
57 Summer need
59 Necktie feature, sometimes
62 Mountain crest
64 Singing pair
65 Lazily
66 Tolerated
67 Fleuret
68 Soothe
69 Pavilions
70 Transmit
71 — majesty

DOWN
1 Laughs heartily
2 Parcel out
3 Feather
4 Daughter of David
5 Team charm?
6 Hodgepodge
7 Vend
8 Relates
9 Open a gift
10 College cheer
11 Part of a certain lamp
12 Lazarus or Bovary
13 Government representative: abbr.
21 Lack
22 Baby oak
26 "— have peace" (Ulysses S. Grant)
28 Tennis great
29 Find out
31 Fashion magazine
32 Enjoy a novel
33 "I Remember —"
34 Applies
35 Gets soused
36 Consume
38 General's gofer
41 Darling: Fr.
45 Sandarac tree
47 Marries again
49 Overacted
51 Mountain range of South America
53 Know-how
54 Clothe
55 Croissants
56 Class
57 Eat nothing
58 Comedian Johnson
60 Easily deceived one
61 Noticed
63 Youngster

© 1996 Tribune Media Services, Inc.
All rights reserved.

24

ACROSS
1 Grouch
6 Floats
11 Apportioned
12 Printing mistakes
14 Pedicure item
15 — tear
17 Historic time
18 Totally conspicuous
20 Vive le —!
21 Legal reps.
23 Quick drink
24 School jacket
25 Hunts
27 Deity
28 VCR button
29 Arcaro and Cantor
31 One who speaks a certain way
32 Mormon initials
33 Quantity: abbr.
34 Pill
37 Cosset
41 Actress Stella
42 Hood's gun
45 Rush forth
46 Clod
47 Is sympathetic
49 Require
50 Globe
51 Tremulous light
53 St.
54 Interstellar dust masses
56 Laundry worker
58 Reply sharply
59 Kind of fungus
60 Thin in tone
61 Stage direction

DOWN
1 Broke rules
2 Managed
3 Spirited horse
4 Simon and Diamond
5 Canadian songstress
6 Bonus kin
7 "— we all?"
8 College club
9 Paving stuff
10 Pick a fight

11 Categorized
13 "Marriage is —" (Don Quixote)
14 Rib
16 Eatery
19 In addition
22 Spider
24 Photography VIP
26 Passover meal
28 Certain cottons
30 Rapid transport
31 Once around the track
34 Bird's weapon
35 Worshiper
36 Fat
38 Gratifying one
39 Pigskin number
40 Cup, in golf
42 Glee
43 Branch

44 Place of worship
47 Leaf vegetable
48 Finch
51 — gin fizz

52 Geometric figure: abbr.
55 Indian
57 Haggard title

ACROSS
1 Earth
5 Zoo denizens
9 Drink of booze
13 Employer
14 Citified
15 Shredded
16 Essays of —
17 Mother-of-pearl
18 Summit
19 Good-bye parties
21 Take into custody
23 Give off
24 Stage show part
25 Run
28 Game piece
32 Tehran native
33 At what place
34 "— if by..."
35 Tattered duds
36 Embers
37 Ice cream holder
38 Summer: Fr.
39 Holiday song
40 Sensational
41 Falls
43 Athletic shirt
44 Insects
45 Layer
46 Show of respect
49 Cry heard at sea
53 Like a bump on —
54 John of song
56 Charged particles
57 Hankering
58 Approaches
59 City in Alaska
60 Spoils
61 Flavoring plant
62 Young or old ending

DOWN
1 Club charge
2 Ait
3 Check
4 Certain commercial transactions
5 Kind of union
6 Rudiments
7 Sailor
8 Gym shoes
9 Begins
10 Kind of chest
11 Minerals
12 Printed matter
14 Not suitable
20 Sports arena
22 Small hill
24 Hard outer covering
25 Fathered
26 Talk long and idly
27 Storms
28 Disorder
29 Anchors
30 "— Get Your Gun"
31 Poor
33 Sentence elements
36 Flasks for water
37 The end
39 Penny
40 Spring
42 Captured
43 Puts together
45 Job
46 Go by boat
47 Singing voice
48 Crazy
49 For men only
50 Owl sound
51 "Don't Tread —"
52 River in Belgium
55 Pasture

2

ACROSS

1 Sound of disapproval
5 Waited
10 Cudgels
14 Stake
15 Animated
16 Butterine
17 Roman: abbr.
18 Fundamental
19 Mountain lake
20 Haughty
22 Things worn
24 Feed for horses
26 Female hare
27 Dormitory occupant
31 Goofs
35 Loan charge: abbr.
36 Smudges
38 Estrada or Satie
39 Rests
41 Grows together
43 Letterman, familiarly
44 Was aware of
45 Tutor
47 Playing marble
48 Unruffled
51 Fruit-filled pastries
53 Corn spike
54 Relaxation
55 Living things
60 Stages
64 ——de-camp
65 Inexpensive
67 Period of calm
68 Venerated women: abbr.
69 Taut
70 — Stanley Gardner
71 Try out
72 Cloyed
73 Peruse

DOWN

1 Greet
2 Division word
3 Leading actor
4 Not very often
5 "Mama," "Dada," etc.
6 Stevedores' org.
7 Kind of jockey
8 Maleficent
9 Solve a cipher
10 Troubled
11 Jai —
12 Gull-like bird
13 Ballad
21 Farm animal
23 Rocky hill
25 Daring feat
27 Hazards
28 Cat- —-tails
29 Fish-eating mammal
30 American Indians
32 Speak eloquently
33 Competitor
34 Distorts
37 Condition
40 Most sugary
42 Discarded
46 Quiet!
49 — King Cole
50 Puts up
52 Seller
55 Actors and actresses
56 Ceremony
57 — of March
58 Flightless bird
59 Caused to go
61 Positive
62 Singer Fitzgerald
63 Toboggan
66 Ibsen character

© 1996 Tribune Media Services, Inc.
All rights reserved.

3

ACROSS

1 Wood strip
5 Theme
10 Orem's state
14 Arch with a point
15 "— Paris in..."
16 Isben character
17 Great anger
18 Finch
19 Certain flowers, briefly
20 Proffer
22 Delicious drinks
24 Border on
26 College VIP
27 Dark color
31 Radar's cousin
34 Yield from a mine
35 Transmits
37 Passover feast
39 Dagger
41 Psychological self
42 — out (distribute)
43 Roof part
45 Jewish teacher
48 Clear
49 Percolates
51 Interpretations
53 Brad the actor
55 Feels remorse
56 Kind of plaster
59 Aromatic substance
63 Teasdale
64 Danger
66 — mater
67 Big piece
68 Part of AWOL
69 Refusals
70 If not
71 Rims
72 Office furniture

DOWN

1 Attic's cousin
2 Fever
3 Coastal bird
4 Time of glory
5 Disorder
6 Cry heard at bullfights
7 Ripped
8 Like college walls
9 Barriers
10 Like some NASA flights
11 — de force
12 Weapons
13 Possesses
21 Becomes less
23 City in New Mexico
25 Radio receiver
27 Stem joint
28 Operatic songs
29 Liveliness
30 — Rice Burroughs
32 Decorate
33 Faith: abbr.
36 Not at all tipsy
38 Ohio team
40 Memento
44 Rod for roasting
46 Trinkets
47 Notion
50 Paper clip relative
52 Ait
54 Brought to bay
56 Handle roughly
57 Samovars
58 Kind of race
60 Blackthorn
61 Singer Ed
62 False face
63 That girl
65 Common contraction

4

ACROSS
1 Farm building
5 — Park, CO
10 Lump of clay
14 Border lake
15 Feel malicious pleasure
16 Theater box
17 So long
18 Spiny European shrub
19 Swiss river
20 Siskel's partner
22 Describing most wallpaper
24 Stooge name
26 German region
27 Most vigorous
31 Lists of names
35 Some sheep
36 Yellowish pigment
38 Murray or West
39 Riata
41 Cartographer's abbr.
42 Pine for
44 Adherent: suff.
45 Handles the helm
48 Variegated
49 Slave
51 Figures of speech
53 Employer
55 Small dog
56 Readied for the play
60 Reverie
64 First grandfather
65 "Lou Grant"
67 Cosmetic ingredient
68 Weed
69 Wash
70 — colada
71 Electric units
72 Gazers
73 Pay attention

DOWN
1 — noire
2 Semite
3 Ceremony
4 Close shave
5 Hen's output
6 Unappetizing food
7 Religious scroll
8 Certain U.S. natives
9 Hat
10 Red wine
11 Kind of shark
12 Fairy tail demon
13 Title instrument
21 Digit
23 School paper
25 Curve
27 Object of veneration
28 Overflowing
29 Jai alai item
30 Indefatigably
32 Communication of a kind
33 Street show
34 Dispatches
37 Summer: Fr.
40 Site of ancient port of Rome
43 Building inscription
46 Patio
47 Taste
50 Motifs
52 Mire
54 Adoree or Taylor
56 Pro —
57 Cheese type
58 Stringed instrument
59 Letter opener
61 Writer Wiesel
62 First-rate
63 Honey beverage
66 TLC providers

5

ACROSS

1 Weaving material
5 Larceny
10 Plummet
14 As strong as —
15 Nest on a height
16 Relaxation
17 Kind of fountain
18 Fuse
19 Poker stake
20 Settle comfortably
22 Loquacious one
24 Gallery in London
25 Additional
26 Negligent
29 Say again and again
33 Flower cluster
34 Polynesian dances
36 Extinct bird
37 Monarch
38 Inn
39 Piece
40 Antiquity, old style
41 Rabbits
42 Illegal act
43 Solar and Dewey decimal
45 Black eye
46 Mature
47 Goatee location
48 Harsh
51 Work at
55 Portent
56 Harder to find
58 Unyielding
59 Discover
60 Run off to marry
61 Fragrant ointment
62 Dilettantish
63 Change purse items
64 Letters

DOWN

1 Instance
2 Before long
3 Shows approval
4 Requiring precision
5 Jeers at
6 Therefore
7 Great Lake
8 In good shape
9 Practicing abstinence from alcohol
10 Seller
11 Give a rating to
12 Bone: pref.
13 Equal
21 Oven
23 Greek war god
25 Distance measures
26 Libertines
27 Post or Dickinson
28 Knits
30 With full force
31 Mel the singer
32 Hungry one
34 Draft animal
35 Western Indian
38 Impeded
39 Kind of press
41 — apparent
42 Stylish
44 Up-to-date
45 Uses with others
47 Thin pancake
48 Davenport
49 Arab VIP
50 Express
51 School dance
52 Dies —
53 Apple remnant
54 Ceases
57 Fourth caliph

6

ACROSS

1 Glided
5 Stores
10 Underground growth
14 Dove's home
15 Greek marketplace
16 Rim
17 Assist in wrongdoing
18 Soccer and tennis, e.g.
19 Burrowing animal
20 Stay behind
22 Teased
24 People looked up to
26 Corn unit
27 Stringed instrument
30 Sides
34 Nancy's husband
35 Located
37 Search in secret
38 Hairless
40 Leading
42 Mislead
43 Aware of danger
45 Have a spat
47 Recent
48 Inborn
50 Large land holdings
52 Clatter
53 Cease by legal means
54 Having a slanted direction
58 Foray
62 Goad
63 Entertain
65 Musical instrument
66 Forest animal
67 Ore veins
68 Columbus' ship
69 Whirlpool
70 Trapshooting
71 Young or old end

DOWN

1 Injury memento
2 Ear section
3 Thing
4 Individual part
5 Blooming tree
6 Muslim prince
7 Plays merrily
8 Corner
9 Talks back impudently
10 Clerical title
11 Scent
12 Stare at
13 — off (irate)
21 15th of March
23 Spigots
25 Deadly
27 Located in a city
28 Australian animal
29 Not leased
30 Old sayings
31 Nobleman
32 Jungle hat
33 Emits
36 Always, poetically
39 Tiresome labor
41 Most powdery
44 Small group
46 Short jacket
49 Records
51 Protective garments
53 Avoid capture
54 City man
55 Angry
56 Ancient
57 Out of control
59 Death notice
60 Top-notch
61 Cherished
64 Witness

ACROSS

1 Military meal
5 Dance from Brazil
10 Chickpea
14 "L. —" (TV show)
15 So long, amigo
16 Rounded part
17 Evans or Robertson of films
18 Veins of metal
19 Fateful date
20 A Roosevelt
22 — Paix
24 Weighty book
25 Reverence
26 Give one's consent
29 Patrons of OTBs
34 Coastline
35 Bus riders
36 Dyer's equipment
37 — Brinker
38 Hamlet and his family
39 Singer Horne
40 Remnant
41 Playthings
42 Gaffe
43 Certain passenger
45 Part of one's specs
46 — Arbor
47 Venture
48 Draw
52 Not in the house
56 Metal money
57 Lend — (help)
59 Russian city
60 Sea eagle
61 Bombay attire
62 Chicken feed
63 Farmer's need
64 Pooped
65 Poet Millay

DOWN

1 Constructed
2 Flyer to Tel Aviv
3 Transaction
4 Knitwear
5 Biblical dancer
6 Love greatly
7 Central
8 Certain South African
9 Pacifies
10 Hang —
11 Traveled
12 Cain's victim
13 Tableland
21 Protuberance
23 Some sheep
26 Fire residue
27 Intone
28 Certain dwelling, for short
29 In a sickly way
30 God of war
31 Straightens
32 Rajah's queen
33 Luminaries
35 White House dog, once
38 Dejected
39 Dejected
41 "Two Years Before the Mast" writer
42 Ernie's pal
44 Alerted
45 Praised
47 Recipient
48 Experts
49 Raced
50 Prong
51 Certain Asian
53 Miffed
54 College official
55 Scat lady
58 Timetable abbr.

7

8

ACROSS

1 Sword handle
5 Cozy places
10 Shoe bottom
14 Aroma
15 Consumed
16 Braid
17 Fountain drink
18 Wading bird
19 Harness strap
20 Raise
22 Pudding
  ingredient
24 Mild oath
25 Relatives
26 Fisherman
29 Refining ore
34 Worries
35 Frighten
36 Fish eggs
37 Layer
38 Walks
  laboriously
39 Symbol of peace
40 Adam's mate
41 Skirt style
42 Evergreens
43 Set off a bomb
45 Struggle
46 Army bed
47 Safe haven
48 Keepsake
52 Easy to get
  along with
56 Spoken
57 Act the ham
59 Holiday word
60 Farm
  storehouse
61 Passenger
62 Felines
63 Fit of temper
64 British guns
65 Gaelic

DOWN

1 Stockings
2 False god
3 Vein of ore
4 Tourist
5 Flower essence
6 Having hearing
  organs
7 Depot: abbr.
8 Camp home
9 Rubber-soled
  shoes
10 Run
11 Bread spread
12 Secular
13 Volcanic peak
21 Ripens
23 Heap
26 Performed
27 Unsophisticated
28 Say "hello" to
29 Tea biscuit
30 Manufactured
31 Presses
32 New
33 Honking birds
35 Small cut
38 Serving dishes
39 Mileage
41 Soon
42 —mutuel
44 Nocturnal
  wildcat
45 Baseball swats
47 Communion
  plate
48 Forest growth
49 Ireland
50 African country
51 Leave out
53 Wild pig
54 Permits
55 Otherwise
58 Poem

9

ACROSS

1 Sailors
5 Scorches
10 Fellow
14 Toward shelter
15 — of Troy
16 Country road
17 German city
18 Came up
19 Johnson of "Laugh-In"
20 Tranquilized state
22 Spring holiday
24 "— the season..."
25 Bacteria
27 Worship
30 Leaves in the lurch
34 Flavoring plant
35 Maturing agent
37 Oxford, e.g.
38 — in the bag!
39 Protection
42 Tina's ex
43 — precedent
45 Lawyers: abbr.
46 Faded
48 Deletion
50 Somewhat tart
51 Agassi of tennis
53 Historic time
54 One who worships
57 Bedroom furniture
62 Lima's country
63 Below
65 Quarrel
66 Israeli airline
67 Bangor's state
68 Ireland
69 Irritate
70 Celerity
71 Swindle

DOWN

1 Labels
2 Tropical plant
3 Split apart
4 Law-making bodies
5 — lounge
6 Idol
7 Forward
8 Legal thing
9 Those who scoff
10 Genera
11 Deer
12 Pay up
13 Equal
21 Weary
23 Morning hrs.
26 Idyllic places
27 Lift
28 Come in
29 View
31 Horned animal, familiarly
32 Symbol
33 Threadbare
35 Following
36 Obtain
40 Tympanic membranes
41 Jugs
44 Usually
47 Piles up
49 One: Fr.
50 Ogled
52 Cantor or Murphy
54 Mime
55 Cold cuts store
56 Verbal
58 Artist Magritte
59 Saga
60 — avis
61 Flower part
64 Snooze

10

ACROSS

1 Exchange
5 Outbuildings
10 Beach cover
14 Dalai ——
15 West Point student
16 Singing group
17 Malevolent
18 Linda Lavin role on TV
19 Heap
20 Singer Arnaz
21 Procession of vehicles
23 Atlas entries
25 "—— Grant"
26 Puzzle direction
29 Divulged
33 Satellites
34 Position
35 Prune
37 Strategy
38 Existing
39 Cosmetic ingredient
40 Rds.
41 British titles
42 Go-between
43 Aspiring actress
45 Sparkles
46 Flange
47 Chesterfield
48 Taping device of a kind
52 Braid
56 Bull: Sp.
57 English novelist, Charles
58 Heckled
59 Gen. Bradley
60 Poker stakes
61 Baking place
62 Squirming
63 Minimal amount
64 Remain unresolved

DOWN

1 Arctic transport
2 Whitecap
3 Parisian pals
4 Support payment of a kind
5 Scalawags
6 Circles of light
7 Check copy
8 Art ——
9 Kind of silver
10 MN city
11 Saharan
12 Egyptian river
13 Bambi's mother
22 Unresponsive
24 Simpleton
26 Guitar enhancers, for short
27 Young horses
28 Rule the ——
29 Wading bird
30 Criticizes
31 Actress Burstyn
32 Lorna ——
34 Dry
36 Favorites
38 Brimless Scottish cap
39 Kind of doctrinaire information
41 —— the Red
42 Exclamation of surprise
44 Arsenal
45 Most angry
47 Surrenders possession of
48 Arrive
49 Russian sea
50 Fr. philosopher, Descartes
51 Info
53 Nothing, in tennis
54 Capital of South Yemen
55 Cultivate
56 Digit

ACROSS

1 Rings sonorously
6 Empty shell
9 Rigg or Ross
14 Pointer
15 Island instrument
16 Wrath
17 Shoshone transport
18 Curved wheel
19 European ermine
20 Type of craftsman
23 Fairy tale villain
24 Head: Fr.
25 Possess
27 Confronted
30 Coated with crumbs
34 Percussion cap
37 Musical composition
38 Came down to earth
39 Enticed
41 "Picnic" playwright
42 Simpletons
44 Some singers
46 French chemist Lavoisier
48 Weathercocks
49 Comp. pt.
50 Gore
52 Singer Ed
55 Self-governing
61 Dogma
63 Reel's partner
64 Incite
65 Willow used in basketry
66 Spanish lady: abbr.
67 Come in
68 Type of wagon
69 One of the Irvings
70 Demi—

DOWN

1 Moccasins
2 Part of QED
3 Florence's river
4 Diving bird
5 Add sugar to
6 Gold coin of the past
7 Tsar's edict
8 Floor model
9 "— Kapital"
10 Act of chanting
11 Eager
12 Approach
13 Comedian Johnson
21 Award of a kind
22 Conjunctive
26 Diminutive
27 Criminal
28 Like Pisa's tower
29 Oil source
30 — Rabbit
31 Irene of old movies
32 Rims
33 Sandra and Ruby
34 Art movement
35 Inner —
36 "...a man — mouse?"
40 Couch
43 Transgression
45 Low stool
47 Educators' org.
50 Tempest
51 The present
52 Above
53 Tableland
54 Author Bagnold
56 Minor or Major
57 — Lisa
58 On the — (unfriendly)
59 Expends
60 Withered
62 Bring before the court

12

ACROSS

1 Twirl
5 Sings a certain way
9 Incline
13 Source of starch
14 M. Zola
16 Ron Howard role
17 Arkin or Thicke
18 Antic
19 Plateau
20 Bible book
22 Goes
24 "— in the bag!"
25 Container
26 Make a speech
29 Kitchen utensils
31 Health farm
34 Garlic unit
35 Janitor
37 Bee's place
38 Made do
39 Grade
40 Catches up with
42 Lugs
43 Each
44 Dilly
45 Hermit
46 Finish
47 Coolidge, to friends
48 With courage
52 Controlling agents
57 Citrus fruit
58 Cafe patron
60 Length times width
61 Ajar
62 Blackboard
63 Phone
64 Left
65 Biblical home
66 Farm measure

DOWN

1 Kind of party
2 Too white
3 Mid-East nation
4 Nary a soul
5 Relate in detail
6 Pile up
7 Seed of a fruit
8 Winter vehicle
9 Italian citizen
10 Mime
11 Spray
12 Pod denizens
15 Built
21 Building location
23 Ago
26 — Oyl
27 Gadabout
28 State strongly
29 Official statement
30 Native metals
31 Glide on ice
32 Jennings or Falk
33 War god
34 Mince
35 Fuel
36 Elvis — Presley
38 Tapers
41 Musical sound
42 Revealed
45 Ms. Bacall
46 Happening
47 Mediterranean island
48 Huff
49 Ready for eating
50 Prayer word
51 New Haven campus
53 Artistic movement
54 Former skating champ, Heiden
55 Bring up
56 Vendition
59 Wee bit

13

ACROSS

1 Pedestal part
5 Young cow
9 Jabber
14 Algerian port
15 "—'s Irish Rose"
16 Like a tablet
17 Brutish one
18 Apple, for one
19 Rang down the curtain
20 Deceptive action
22 Hardhearted
23 Sonnet part
24 Explorer Hernando de —
26 Social dud
29 List
33 Toward the left side, nautically
37 Work for
39 Part of a roofline
40 What's for lunch
41 Gay —
42 — go bragh!
43 Persian Gulf land
44 Yemeni port
45 Designer Simpson
46 Meal
48 Love to excess
50 Orient
52 Semitic language
57 Scratch, at Canaveral
60 Magna Carta site
63 A code
64 Tournament type
65 Seed appendage
66 Acquire, as expenses
67 Siouan
68 Opening for coins
69 Cookies
70 Duck's milieu
71 Matched collections

DOWN

1 Means of access
2 Dispute
3 Repairs socks
4 — a time (singly)
5 "In Cold Blood" author
6 "— Ben Adhem"
7 Describe
8 Nourishes
9 Magician's word
10 Deteriorate
11 Actor Ray
12 Adolescent
13 Swirl
21 Landlord's income
25 Writer Sarah — Jewett
27 Pursue
28 Challenged
30 Weed
31 Sermon topic
32 Descartes
33 Surrounded by
34 Persian fairy
35 — even keel
36 Some competitors
38 NV city
41 Golf scores
45 Ethereal
47 Trenchermen
49 Thrashed
51 Group of soldiers
53 Hoard
54 Comic Milton
55 Fool
56 Gaels
57 Friends: Fr.
58 German capital
59 Killer whale
61 — - date (modern)
62 Store front sign

14

ACROSS

1 Labor Day mo.
5 Palm fruit
10 Stomach of an animal
14 Jai —
15 Parisian learning center
16 Mechanic's job, briefly
17 Shelve
19 Sleeping
20 Poker call
21 Try to lose weight
22 Distrusts
24 Hive dwellers
25 Forest open space
26 Sires
29 Can
32 Bitter drug
33 Banquet
34 Author John — Passos
35 Celebrity
36 Paton and Milne
37 Fit
38 Angeles or Alamos
39 Separated
40 Statue base
41 Hats
43 Quivers
44 Shake down
45 Cherished
46 Obliquely
48 Persian Gulf country
49 Cleo's undoing
52 Dregs
53 Top-flight barrister
56 Convert into pulp
57 Call up
58 Chair
59 Gray
60 Glutted
61 Gels

DOWN

1 Fools
2 Nobelist Wiesel
3 Leaf
4 Link
5 Gainsays
6 Hurts
7 Honk
8 House addition
9 Like some grapes
10 Actor Rains
11 Bubble bath companion?
12 Aid a felon
13 Marries
18 "Waiting for Lefty" author
23 Tobacco kiln
24 Auxiliary verb
25 Confer
26 Four is a walk
27 Part of TSE
28 Fright film sensation?
29 Fruit
30 Curtain material
31 — Park, CO
33 Side
36 Missionaries
37 Fly high
39 A — able
40 Ladd classic
42 Inferior
43 Closed tightly
45 English explorer, Francis
46 — mater
47 Seven —
48 "— plenty o'..."
49 "African Queen" script writer
50 Blind part
51 Cats and dogs
54 A Gabor
55 Burro

15

ACROSS

1 Juan's room
5 Robert or Alan
9 Frosted
13 On one's —
(alert)
14 Silk fabric
16 — contendere
17 Obsessively in
mind
19 Roughly
20 Legume
21 Pub potions
22 Oil transport
24 Hot spot
25 Comedian
Johnson
26 Copies
29 African plant
32 Superman, e.g.
33 Ballet movement
34 Hat feature
36 "— for All
Seasons"
37 Hints
38 Zhivago's love
39 Lug
40 Attila's people
41 Dilly
42 Savings
44 Shuns
46 Fair grades
47 Mr. Flintstone
48 Minnesota
native
51 Ravelings
52 Singer Davis
55 Eye
suggestively
56 Annoying
59 Mine finds
60 Fertile desert
spots
61 Staff officer
62 Great
achievement
63 — Trueheart
64 Cabbage salad

DOWN

1 Traffic sign
2 The best
3 "— smile be
your..."
4 Shade of blonde
5 Moseys
6 Actress Sophia
7 Portuguese
discoverer
8 Mr. Onassis
9 Natural
10 Bottle stopper
11 In addition
12 Revolving or
barn end
15 Main courses
18 Roof edge
23 Swallowed up
24 Troubling
25 Zodiac sign
26 Chew the fat
27 Sour fruit
28 Make a speech
29 Threw
30 Middle Eastern
native
31 Broadcast
33 Stoppers
35 Defaces
37 Good-bye
43 Golf item
44 "Gunsmoke" star
45 Old soldiers
47 Some penalties

48 Foul up
49 Fairy tale
monster
50 Entreaty
51 Misplace

52 Air or chain end
53 Verdi opera
54 Ship's gang
57 — King Cole
58 Possesses

16

ACROSS

1 Neck napkins
5 Unhappy
8 "— old cowhand..."
12 Suit to —
13 Fruit drinks
15 Egypt's river
16 Rent again
18 Mona —
19 Move smoothly
20 Errs
23 Motored
24 — Diego
25 Bog
29 Giggly sounds
33 Came up
34 On the briny
35 Statute
36 Disencumbers
37 Less in numbers
39 Excavation
40 Foot appendage
41 Burrowing mammal
42 Davis or Midler
43 Noisy sleepers
45 Most recent
46 Exist
47 Above
49 Succeeds
55 Caron film
56 Comparison word
57 Make very happy
59 — even keel
60 Kind
61 Man on a pedestal
62 Trill
63 Legal matter
64 Armored vehicle

DOWN

1 Legally stop
2 Small piece of news
3 Lugosi of films
4 Search
5 Side dish
6 — a dozen
7 Arnaz of television
8 Babe
9 Cow's product
10 Medicinal plant
11 Fresh
14 More impudent
17 Effectively concise
21 Distress signal at sea
22 British farewell
25 Trading centers
26 Sky hunter
27 Western show
28 Fool
29 Mao —tung
30 Upper crust
31 Carries on
32 Sugary
34 Wonder
37 Wooded areas
38 City railways
39 Encountered
41 Only
42 Wilkes—, PA
44 Gardener's chore
45 Part of a journey
47 Chicago's airport
48 Airs
49 Kind of skirt
50 Ladd or Alda
51 Thunder god
52 Landed
53 Artistic movement
54 British school
55 — Angeles, CA
58 Antlered animal

© 1996 Tribune Media Services, Inc.
All rights reserved.

ACROSS

1 Hookah
5 Not quite dry
9 Fast
14 Stratford-upon-
 —
15 Lamb, alternatively
16 Best part
17 Chimed
18 Price
19 Bird's claw
20 Fortitude
22 Common contraction
23 "Clair de —"
24 Slender
26 Hit repeatedly
29 Remove from office
33 Redding or Skinner
34 Speediness
37 Impair
38 A bone
39 Place of safety
41 Mine's output
42 Sherbet
43 New York's — Island
44 Colonnade
45 Bernhardt and Jewett
47 Kind of leather
49 Foot digits
51 Bill of fare
52 Poetic Muse
55 IOU holders
60 Part of the eye
61 — avis
62 Genuine
63 River in France
64 Indigo dye
65 Revise a text
66 Yielded by treaty
67 Fruit stones
68 Hollywood's Howard et al.

DOWN

1 Reduce
2 Pavlov or Lendl
3 Body of water
4 Overwhelms
5 Pour, as wine
6 Unaccompanied
7 Hodgepodge: abbr.
8 Spreads for crackers
9 Lawyer's fee
10 Frightens
11 Heap
12 "Go Tell — the Mountain"
13 Fender spoiler
21 Regret
25 Old instrument
26 "— Godunov"
27 City in New York
28 Roughage
30 Overact
31 Baseball great, Hank —
32 Special pleasure
34 Farm bird
35 Beery beverage
36 Piggery
39 Taught
40 Flexible tube
44 Speech disorder
46 What's worn
47 Bicycle parts
48 Cuckoo
50 Discarded piece
51 Be worthy of
52 Long poem
53 Trick
54 Mimicked
56 Indian queen
57 Church calender
58 Wreck
59 Hardens

© 1996 Tribune Media Services, Inc.
All rights reserved.

18

ACROSS
1 Underground growth
5 Leading
10 Prizefight
14 Poker stake
15 Blend together
16 Too
17 "I — man with..."
18 Window sections
19 Lively dance
20 Grow
22 Bring back
24 Section
25 Regret
26 Fight against
29 Able to read and write
34 State of turmoil
35 Gave up, as territory
36 Auction action
37 Ripped
38 Talked wildly
39 Sharp pain
40 Printing measures
41 Walking sticks
42 Stitch loosely
43 Go without booze
45 Great strain
46 Torrid
47 Canvas shelter
48 Large ape
52 Greek letter
56 Allege
57 Wed secretly
59 Grotto
60 Kitchen vessels
61 Mature
62 Reclines
63 Coin opening
64 Fast horse
65 Makes a mistake

DOWN
1 Inclined surface
2 Outstanding thing
3 — Preminger
4 Recipe amount
5 Electrical measure
6 Valentine symbol
7 Sea bird
8 Ripening agent
9 Left high and dry
10 Swap
11 Bread spread
12 Consumer
13 Painting on metal
21 Waive
23 Took court action
26 Group of eight
27 Call
28 Analyze grammatically
29 Even
30 15th of March
31 Lower in rank
32 Adds color
33 Rims
35 First miracle site
38 Poisonous snakes
39 Tiny speck
41 Chilly
42 Breakfast items
44 Desire for drink
45 Rely (upon)
47 Brave's home
48 Open spaces
49 Ellipse
50 Gambling mecca
51 Landed
53 Den
54 Finished
55 Loch — monster
58 Unclose, to poets

ACROSS

1 Practiced, as one's trade
6 Large food fish
12 Kissing sound
17 Quickly
18 Exact satisfaction for
19 Giants
21 Melodramatic espionage
23 Axilla
24 In a snit
25 Singer Billy and his family
26 Make diverse
28 Topsy's friend
29 Rainbow
30 Corporate outfits
31 Enjoyed happy hour
33 Gets a serve past
34 Chum
35 Bridges
36 Showy flower
37 Cymbals sound
38 Catching some Z's
40 Brag
41 Movie sleuth, Charlie —
42 Certain necklines
43 Like rotten food
44 Hymn
47 VCR function
50 — leaguer
51 Peevish
52 Man: Lat.
53 Glorify
54 Damage
55 Breathe
57 Alter —
58 Housing units: abbr.
59 Early A-bomb test site
61 Thin nail
62 Dessert choice
63 Hereditary
64 "— in the bag!"
65 Rickety car
66 Make a mistake
67 Diner sign
68 Yields
70 Howled
71 Strikers' requests
73 River to the Rio Grande
74 Encircle with a band
75 On the — (not on good terms)
76 Las —
77 News release
81 Treaties
83 Accumulated charges
84 Haughtiness
85 Comp. pt.
86 St. Louis tourist sight
87 Bugs —
88 Magna cum —
89 Mrs. Roy Rogers
90 Mexican Mrs.
91 Indian tribe
92 Prom
93 — 'Azur
94 Paper hanky
96 Movie house offerings
100 Fly
101 Cup holder
102 The family at Tara
103 Concluded
104 Merchant ship fleet
105 Wanderer

DOWN

1 Biographical essay
2 Goofs off
3 Black
4 Schedule letters
5 Lovers
6 West Pointers
7 Ellipses
8 Implores
9 Participial ending
10 Mature
11 Domestic
12 Extreme
13 Smeared with mud
14 Bank convenience: abbr.
15 NASA blast-off site
16 Cook's equipment
17 More than one
20 Hidden supplies
21 Salsa scoopers
22 Accomplishing
27 Indefinite amount
30 Worked for the CIA
31 — Scrolls
32 Optimistic
33 Winglike
35 Exhausted
36 Cold climate feature
37 Errand
39 Wicked acts
40 Spar
41 Oaf
43 Deserve
44 Spirals
45 Tie, in a way
46 Wore away
47 Harvested
48 Breathe out
49 Poisonous snake
50 Accepts
51 Sees
54 After-dinner candies
56 Pigpens
59 Wampum
60 One that finishes last, a la Durocher?
61 Altar figure
63 Chaps
65 Pianist Frankie
69 John — Passos
70 Dorian Gray's creator
72 Writer: abbr.
73 Actor Sean
74 Specially trained canine
76 Ms. Redgrave
77 Mr. Willis
78 Item at an afternoon function
79 Coves
80 Prerequisites
81 Linguini, for example
82 Achieve success
83 Actress McClanahan
84 Larder
87 Animal variety
88 Sneaker ties
89 Means of access
91 Precious
92 Art —
93 Chafe
95 Down in the dumps
97 Pitcher part
98 Tire screw
99 Like a shrinking violet

ACROSS

1 Lanky
5 Rip-off
9 Reception
12 Evergreen with large pods
17 Scope
18 Used a crowbar
20 Cubicle
21 The end
22 Nonsense
26 Bon — (high society)
27 The Wash feeder
28 Moat
29 Rich cakes
30 Mr. Perot
31 — Carlo
32 Johnnycake
33 Summary
36 Gay —
37 Is under the weather
38 Funny DeLuise
41 Nonsense
44 Gray wolf
45 Gave out
46 Genetic letters
47 Coterie
48 Sky flier
49 Jewish month
50 Nonsense
55 No longer working: abbr.
56 Takes unlawfully
57 On the — of (close)
58 Contracts
59 English river
60 Thicket
61 Stillness
62 Spheres of action
65 Pro football Hall-of-Famer
66 Face
67 Lard
70 Nonsense
73 — mater
74 War of the —
75 Wrath
76 Writer Fleming
77 Sweeper
78 The — of March
79 Nonsense
84 — Aviv
85 — Rabbit
86 Standing up
87 Wore away gradually
88 Skidded
89 Singer Brooks
90 Put away
91 Buddhist shrines
94 — far (exceed the limits)
95 Writer Uris
96 — Vegas
99 Nonsense
103 Slugger Banks
104 Make secure, nautically
105 — Gillis of TV
106 Curtail
107 Withdraws, as from a dependency
108 Youngster
109 Pod occupants
110 Once more

DOWN

1 Big name in Ohio
2 Singer Guthrie
3 Tilt
4 Circuit
5 Mates
6 Grouchy
7 Helper
8 Tillis or Torme
9 Uptight
10 Actress Sommer
11 Priestly vestment
12 Punctuation marks
13 "That's —" (Martin hit)
14 Flat rate
15 Curved molding
16 Howls
19 Actor Don
20 Little Bighorn victim
23 Lost
24 Studied hard
25 Coral island
30 Sovereign
31 Parrot
32 Religious painting
33 Detector
34 Lyric poem
35 Smacking noise
36 Sleighs
37 States firmly
38 Major- —
39 Much too heavy
40 Feathery insects
42 Sun-dried brick
43 Fiber plant
44 Water vessel used in India
48 Board game
50 Kind of opera
51 Take — of (grip)
52 Calyx leaf
53 Region of Germany
54 Partly melted snow
56 Money of Iran
59 S.A. mountain range
60 Military school student
61 — He (Chinese river)
62 Evil spirit, in mythology
63 — Janeiro
64 A Ford
65 City in Ethiopia
66 Wimple kin
67 Biblical event
68 Soap plant
69 Gentle
71 Entered
72 Deciduous tree
73 Pointer
77 Nobleman's domain
79 Zippy
80 Become intense
81 Late actor, Flynn
82 Narrated again
83 Doric frieze features
85 Loud sounds
88 Santander's land
89 Noble Peace Prize winner
90 Cuttlefish ink
91 Pintail duck
92 Weedy plant
93 Arm bone
94 Sandwich type
95 Ear part
96 Banking term
97 Farm measure
98 Twist
100 Immature newt
101 Soda —
102 Auditor, at times

© 1996 Tribune Media Services, Inc.
All rights reserved.

ACROSS

1 Franklin follower
7 Comice underside
13 Stigmas
18 Mammal coverings
19 Place for floats
20 Prince of the jungle?
21 Marx film
23 Cantankerous
24 Tabby
25 Author Fleming
26 Envelope gum, for example
28 State: abbr.
29 Play division
30 Behindhand
32 Argot
33 Glut
34 Nets
37 Small duck
39 Jeanne D'Arc: abbr.
40 Voice votes
41 — Flow (British naval base)
42 Typo kin
45 Buddhist king in India
47 Asta's mistress
49 503
50 Poseidon's son
53 Gaiters
56 Playhouse
59 Harem room
60 "Where the Boys —"
61 Sit
62 Zestful
63 Statutory
65 Marble
66 Steiger and Serling
67 Edible seaweed
68 Pepys work
69 Very small contribution
70 WWII's General Eaker
71 City on the Songka
72 Logic
73 IA city
74 Waterloo marshal
75 CBS logo
76 Decorative flaps
78 Peak
79 Exchanged
81 Spanish river
82 Common NV machine
84 "Kol —" (Yom Kippur prayer)
86 Earthquakes
89 Pseudonym
92 Norms: abbr.
94 Guido's note
96 Relating to the earth
97 Suede maker
99 Penny
100 Choir singers
103 Kind of fund
105 Literary collection
106 "Exodus" hero
107 Not as big
109 Zodiac sign
110 Like — of bricks
111 Entertain
113 Routine
117 Building stone
118 Silly smile
119 Conditional releases
120 Crazy
121 Bedeviled
122 Syrup spouts

DOWN

1 Infers
2 Garter material
3 Ballads
4 Turkish title
5 After expenses
6 Ancient port of Rome
7 Wastrel
8 Shell propeller
9 Brothers
10 Countenances
11 Exemplary
12 Units of magnetic induction
13 Crater on the face of the moon
14 Chaney of films
15 Sitcom with Bonnie Franklin
16 Smooth and cylindrical
17 Modes
18 Hollywood's Irene
20 "The —" (WWII film)
22 American author
27 Pilaster
30 Despot
31 What fullbacks gain
33 H.H. Munro
35 Port on the Loire
36 Epic poetry
38 Non-clerical folks
43 Four-in-hand
44 El Al, for one
46 Nuncupative
48 Bring into accord
51 Takes to the stump
52 Most modern
53 Dash
54 "For richer, for —"
55 As different —
57 Nimbus
58 Stores fodder
59 Monster of myth
64 "— of Eden"
67 Castle-builder
68 Removes from office
69 Mary, of "South Pacific"
71 Pay attention to
72 Small shoot
77 Lincoln
78 Soft drink
80 Kind of attorney: abbr.
83 Slat
85 Ms. Fitzgerald
87 Wild duck
88 Veered
90 France
91 Granada gentlemen
92 Sacred beetle
93 Mother —, Nobelist
95 Finally
98 Seeds
101 Stan's pal
102 Nobelist Lagerlof
104 TV features
107 Do in
108 Torn and Taylor
110 Mil. transgression
112 Hgt.
114 Formerly called
115 Bark sharply
116 — Lanka

4

ACROSS

1 Modify
6 Military hat
11 Instance
15 So-so golf scores
19 Relinquish
20 Recurrent artistic element
21 Mont Blanc's range
22 Zone
23 — Park, CO
24 Ready to work
27 Dearth
29 Litigate
30 Enumerates
31 Group of atoms: abbr.
32 Wrenches
35 Fastidiousness
36 Work
41 Walks to and fro
43 Rise on the hind legs
44 Grammarian's word group
45 Provide food service for
46 Immature newt
49 Estuary
51 Keystone's structure
52 Form concentric rings
53 Lamb
54 Stooge name
55 Put together
57 Work
60 Hag
61 Hodgepodge
62 Calms
63 Tilts
65 Renaissance
68 Carving wood
69 More mild and pleasant
71 Spanish province
72 Holmes' "— Venner"
74 Work
76 Dress carefully
77 Rocky crag
80 Flowery neckwear
81 Chignon's place
82 Hindu hero
83 Clearing
85 Put two and two together
86 Scoundrel
88 Light pastry
90 Computer picture, of a kind
91 Dump
92 Work
94 Take for granted
97 Sitka site
99 Rathskeller specialty
100 Black eyes
102 Mo.
103 Gave a stamp of approval
108 Start to work
112 French religious leader
113 Border
114 Achy
115 Fewest
116 Musical piece
117 Clairvoyant
118 Water jug
119 Easy gaits
120 Painter of ballet dancers

DOWN

1 Inspires with reverence
2 Secure with a rope
3 Josip Broz
4 Always
5 — one's laurels
6 Polluted air
7 Aspiration
8 Chowed
9 Relatives
10 Ahead of the ball
11 Proofreader's symbol
12 Linen robe
13 Incite
14 Crucial element
15 Freaks out
16 Mountain ridge
17 Change a timepiece
18 Pert
25 River to the Wash
26 Frostier
28 Baldwin
32 Suspension of hostilities
33 Bathe
34 Prado's locale
36 Proper
37 Woven fabric
38 Ivy League school
39 Overwhelmed with laughter
40 More pungent
42 Cartographer's work
45 French landscape painter
46 Upper crust
47 More delicate
48 Labels
50 Mustard family plant
52 Memorial mound
53 Give the slip
56 — Parker (busybody)
57 Prufrock poet
58 Charter
59 Lazing
60 "The Fall" author
61 Corpulent
63 Tightened shoes
64 — Campeador
66 Bolt together?
67 Troglodyte
69 Weighted rope
70 Extent
73 Restraint
75 Singer Abdul
76 Bearlike mammal
77 Tampico lunch
78 Reputation
79 Lacoste
82 Status
84 Educated
86 Tybalt's nemesis
87 Wear out
88 Purify
89 Designer Edith
91 Craving
92 Jet speed word
93 Retarded
94 Ruins
95 Sun screen
96 Burn
98 Unsuccessful one
101 Store for future use
103 Other
104 Court dividers
105 Garden pest
106 Icelandic literary work
107 Accomplishes
109 Exist
110 Recent: pref.
111 Mountain pass

ACROSS

1 Queried
6 Emergency procedure letters
9 Improvise
14 TX city
18 Evans or Blair
19 North or South
20 Kid
21 Lendl of tennis
22 Dandridge/Belafonte film
24 Class reunion passageway?
26 Bristle
27 Prepares the violin bow
29 Breathed heavily
30 NY school letters
32 Sometimes it's wild
34 Hangman's noose
38 Young men's org.
41 Burrows and Vigoda
44 Net
46 King of Tyre
47 Avian hooter
48 Change
49 Ukraine, once: abbr.
50 — Vegas
53 Bother
54 Part of "Chaplin" cast
57 State of wealth
60 Looked upon unfavorably
61 Mayday letters
62 Govt. org.
63 "Exodus" hero
64 Mild oath
65 Camera part
66 Pleads
68 Fabler of note
72 School for priests
74 Truancy letters
75 Island in the Lesser Antilles
78 Harder to find
79 Bill of fare
81 Tightly stretched
82 Enameled metalware
83 Inc.'s French cousin
85 Enrolled: abbr.
86 Type of tide
87 Fate
88 Locale of luxury
92 Beatles album
94 Reduce
95 Sailor
96 Hospital procedures, briefly
98 St. —'s fire
99 Beehive State Indian
100 Garbo of films
102 Dating from birth
104 Thing owed
105 D.C. VIP
106 Attack
108 Pancake topping
110 Legendary bird
112 Counterparts
115 Cheerless
118 On the summit of
122 Douglas/Sheen film
126 Barney Leason novel
128 Ashtabula waterfront
129 Calloused
130 Terminates
131 Send in money
132 Pub offering
133 Liquor rounds
134 Bad: pref.
135 Bjorn Borg, e.g.

DOWN

1 Priest's vestments
2 Respectful term of address
3 Join together closely
4 — Rice Burroughs
5 Morse code word
6 — Bay, OR
7 Kilt pattern
8 Primary color quality
9 Money outlet: abbr.
10 More profound
11 Tibetan priest
12 "When the Frost — the Punkin"
13 Sleeping place
14 Deer, in season, e.g.
15 Actress Gardner
16 Fire
17 Wallet item
19 Paid athlete
23 Clannish
25 Slangy affirmative
28 Swanson/Holden film
31 Surfaced a road
33 Small sailing ship
35 Loyal
36 Bridge hand
37 Leasing ad abbr.
38 Masses
39 Pleasure seeker
40 Montgomery's state
42 Pencil attachment
43 Thesaurus item
45 Tarzan portrayer
51 — the rule (normally)
52 Constricted
55 Lowest point
56 Curve
58 Droop
59 Nothing: Fr.
65 Cowboy's rope
67 Knifed
69 Lutelike instrument
70 Smelly
71 Web-footed
73 Bottle part
74 Yearly payment
76 Debris
77 Dull
80 Night, poetically
81 Pekoe, e.g.
84 Peron
87 Japanese city
88 Golf course standards
89 God of war
90 Merchant
91 Coastal flyer
93 Rudimentary stage
94 Golfers' org.
97 Passed over quickly and carelessly
101 Goals
103 Agreement
107 Narrow strips of wood
109 Showy flower
111 A baseball MVP
113 "Rhoda" cast regular
114 Architect Saarinen
116 Extends
117 — judicata
119 Clock
120 Roman poet
121 Rose or Fountain
122 Network
123 119.6 square yards
124 Prevaricate
125 Hardin and Cobb
127 AMA members

6

© 1996 Tribune Media Services, Inc.
All rights reserved.

ACROSS

1 Spanish painter
5 Bosc or Bartlett
9 Garment
14 Foray
18 Ardor
19 Ms. Turner of Hollywood
20 Eagle's nest
21 Lily plant
22 Travel for singer Don?
25 Gem for Sharon?
27 In a strict manner
28 Dresses carefully
30 Perfume ingredient
31 "Norma —"
32 Union general
33 Pie — mode
34 Pirate flags for Kenny?

39 Summer cooler for Jack?
45 Wild ox
46 Summarize, briefly
47 Midday
48 Barbara — Geddes
49 Singer Vikki
50 Surveillance system
51 Croc
53 Grasped
54 Humane
55 Horne of song
56 Tra —
57 Strainer
58 Vend used merchandise
60 Caravansary
61 Family member
62 Pampering Ms. Pitcher?

66 Part of a sonnet
70 United
71 Shoe with thongs
75 Attempts
76 Nota —
77 Spy Mata —
79 Organism modified by environment
81 Swiss river
82 Coastline
84 Panama or Suez
85 Son of Jacob
86 Alphabet run
87 Peevish
88 Comedienne Fields
89 Author Ambler
90 Bridal box for Ms. Lange?

93 School contest for Tori?
96 Thai language
97 Iowa county
99 Goddess: Lat.
100 "Exit, pursued by —" (Shakespeare)
103 Charm
105 Pygmalion's statue
109 Melee for singer Osmond?
111 Flowers for Rather?
114 Desertlike
115 French river
116 Tresses
117 "Peter Pan" dog
118 Beatty film
119 Actress Sharon
120 — and crafts
121 Small insect

DOWN

1 Morning moisture
2 Pub drinks
3 Endure
4 Diversifies, as a speech
5 Power machine
6 Title of nobility
7 Actor Griffith
8 School cheer
9 Challenged
10 Mend shoes, in a way
11 Moran or Gray
12 Vices
13 Observe
14 Wickerwork material
15 Thanks —!
16 Island off Scotland
17 Bambi
23 Fay of "King Kong"

24 "Carmen" and "Aida"
26 Drawing room
29 Grate
32 Center of interest
33 Cupid
34 Car trunk item
35 Walking — (elated)
36 Greene of "Bonanza"
37 Author of "Animal Farm"
38 Sweet cherry
40 Involve
41 Pasture sound
42 Red as —
43 Dig
44 Senior
50 Parcel out
51 En — (fencing term)

52 "When I was —, I served..."
53 Towel insignia
56 Sierra —
57 Poster
59 Linguistic units: suff.
60 Oatmeal cake
61 Slowpoke
63 Toils
64 Belgian river
65 Jordan's neighbor
66 Stow
67 Muse of poetry
68 Pancake topping
69 Golf gadget
72 Authorizing
73 Bitter
74 C'est —
77 One who detests
78 Blue dye
80 Gambling cubes
82 London district

83 Color
84 Duplicated
87 Frightening
88 Despot
91 African antelopes
92 Eagle's weapons
94 Loungers
95 Actress Patricia
98 "The — of Hazzard"
100 Jewish month
101 Tiresome one
102 Author Bagnold
103 Seed coat
104 Forfeit
105 Growl
106 Mine entrance
107 Of the dawn
108 "— Karenina"
110 Capture
112 Exclamation of triumph
113 Occupied a chair

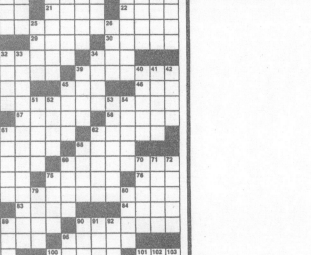

7

ACROSS

1 Fernando or Lorenzo
6 Hedonist
11 Look for
15 FDR's dog
19 Egg-shaped
20 Coeur d'—
21 Raison d'—
22 Smooth
23 1930s event
27 Previous to
28 Computer device
29 River to the Severn
30 Narrow street
31 "Mash" character
32 Associates socially
34 Before: pref.

35 Deli offering
38 Baseball teams
39 Drunken sprees
43 Again
44 Sedimentary material
45 Period of time
46 New Guinea port
47 1930s event
55 "Kookie" Byrnes
56 Lover boy
57 Barter
58 Methods
59 Reduced
61 Some lights
62 Extravagant speech
63 R — Roger
64 Pub game

65 — and Clark of TV
66 River deposit
68 Wharton's Ethan
69 O'Hara and Stapleton
73 Peasants' co-op in the USSR
74 City on Biscayne Bay
75 Fishing net
76 — of luxury
77 1930s event
81 Hostel
82 Have existence
83 Ballet by Stravinsky
84 Capital of Southern Yemen
85 Plunder
88 — with (tolerate)

90 Conduit
93 Pointed instrument
94 Gay —
95 Slender boat
96 Dwelling
99 Intellect
100 Roger of baseball
101 Short flight
104 1930s event
109 Nobleman
110 In — of
111 Yankee great
112 "Sesame Street" character
113 — majesty
114 Gossip
115 Footrest
116 Unfortunately

DOWN

1 Theater box
2 State strongly
3 Horse
4 Bank machine letters
5 Tar
6 Worker's delight
7 Horatio —
8 Microbe
9 Collection of anecdotes
10 Bird beak
11 Caters to
12 Character of a culture
13 The old sod
14 Range of vision
15 Satiated
16 Russian inland sea
17 Solitary
18 Warhol
24 Swelling
25 A marshal of France

26 Make, as money
31 English poet laureate, Nicholas
32 Ho Chi —
33 Lacking clarity
34 Remain undecided
35 Roll
36 Battery part
37 Provides a helping hand
38 Alliance acronym
39 Foretell
40 Get around
41 Badgerlike carnivore
42 Meeting: abbr.
44 Molt
45 Conclusions
48 Struggle
49 Ancient region of Asia Minor
50 Feds
51 Penned

52 Fleming and Hunter
53 Aggregates of nations
54 Idaho city
60 Markdowns
61 Mother-in-law of Ruth
62 In good health
64 Mild oath
65 Remained
66 Sluggard
67 Collars
68 Do clerical work
69 Small-minded
70 Skip over
71 Consumerist Ralph
72 Exhausted
73 Lacking moisture
74 Blackbird
75 Unappetizing food
78 Colorado ski area
79 Chills and fever

80 Bathe
86 Canoe need
87 Had debts
88 Be successful
89 Indic language
90 Earthly
91 Complete entity
92 Setbacks
94 Stingy one
95 City on the Nile
96 Seth's brother
97 Scottish hillside
98 Regatta items
99 1102
100 Member of a Malay tribe
101 Crew member
102 Trompe l'— (painting style)
103 Quarry
105 Aged
106 Cable network letters
107 Cosset
108 Bikini part

ACROSS

1 King of the kitchen
5 Ballet's Michael
0 Bear or cap
5 "Animal —
   (Orwell)
9 Steak order
20 Establish as
   correct
21 Personification of
   peace
22 — fixe
23 Eager
24 Type of seal
25 Adversary
26 Front
27 Expatriates'
   needs?
30 Pompous gait
31 Trapper's device
32 Sign maker's aid
33 Parthenon's place
34 St. Francis' place

37 Writer Rand
38 A Seton
39 Nav. off.
42 Turner or Danson
43 Tap gently
45 Utilize the crowbar
46 Low-down
50 Upper surface
52 Narrate once
   more
54 Table scrap
55 — Haute
56 Indian garment
57 Swiss river
58 Stowe's Simon
60 Relative
61 Show
64 Office cutback,
   tersely
65 Owing
66 Take to court
67 Wheel part

68 Kimono tie
69 Bus. org.
70 Diminishes
73 Uno, due, —
74 ESP
79 Grain for grinding
80 Thickets
82 Pitcher's stat
83 Cranny's partner
84 Harasses in a way
85 — longa, vita
   brevis
86 Agrees to
88 Type of metalware
89 Culture spot?
90 MDs
91 Dutch commune
92 List extender:
   abbr.
94 Cain's destination
95 Lake Michigan
   port

97 Joey was one
99 Howard of sports
102 Scary
105 Lei person?
107 Main artery
111 Moroccan
    capital
112 Time
115 — age
116 Climbing plant
117 Fix the hem
118 Trilled
119 Penny
120 Certain group
121 Waste away in a
    way
122 List extender:
    abbr.
123 Entry agents
124 Demi- —
125 Feudal serfs
126 Vendition

DOWN

1 Insensitive
2 Place of refuge
3 Author Jong
4 Felt hat
5 Went lickety-split
6 Verbal
7 Bog
8 Dusk
9 Type of grass
10 High seas crime
11 Genesis
12 Tear down
13 Literary
   collections
14 Kinsman: abbr.
15 Excuse for
   silence?
16 Worship
17 Summer TV fare
18 Has a session
28 Cozy corner
29 Powerless

30 Pig pen
33 Whatever it may
   be
35 Shawls
36 Model for
   achievement
38 Comedian
   Johnson
39 Formerly, once
40 Ark captain
41 Fern features
44 Asserts as true
45 Arranges in
   advance
47 Perry's creator
48 Semite
49 Salamander
51 Some career
   soldiers
53 Farm
   implements
54 African antelope

55 Louise and
   Yothers
59 — out
   (disgusted)
62 Some songs
63 Marine follower
65 Precipitately
70 Taj Mahal site
71 Naval prison
72 Verdi opera
75 Kilmer poem
76 "High —"
77 Aria
78 Supplemented
   (with "out")
80 Grant
81 Cringle relative
87 Alabama and
   Mississippi, once
90 Uninteresting
93 Tribal division
96 Inclined

97 Takes care of
   trees
98 Add the bubbles
   to
100 Prayer
101 Part of a bad
    streak
102 Neck discomfort
103 Street show
104 Hardwood
105 Joke objects
106 A crowd,
    sometimes
108 Lariat
109 Relating to sounds
110 Viewpoint
112 Paycheck reducer:
    abbr.
113 Ancient Persian
114 They had little
    lambs
116 Fate

9

ACROSS

1 Moderator
5 Ritzy
9 Batting great, Rod
14 Clearheaded
19 Judicial proceedings
20 Mafia boss
21 Flooded
22 Cache of riches
23 Paper measure
24 Shipping route since 1959
27 Modify
29 Environs
30 Coral isle
31 Trifling amount
32 Texas oil town
35 Eye doctor's field
39 '80s TV series
42 Take care of
43 Coloration
44 German number
45 Belief
47 Racing boat
49 Giant
52 Cinnamon or nutmeg, e.g.
55 Name in Cuba
56 Renowned Parisian designer
60 Lamb
62 Folk tales
63 Inflatable boats
64 Peril
66 Sch. subj.
69 Hesitant sounds
70 Consumed
71 Seasonal goddesses
72 "— Bravo"
73 Deli bread
74 Religious commune
76 Buenos —
77 Quay
78 Foe of Laver and Connors
79 1980 cataclysm site
82 Circumvent
85 "Jungle Fever" actor Davis
86 Concert waltz
87 Winery barrels
88 Make amends
91 Ajar
93 Verse or form starter
94 — incognita
96 Martyr with a February feast day
103 Lays waste to
105 Take offense
106 Boston's Red —
107 Water wheel
108 Daredevil act
110 Kiln
112 London landmark
118 Bio of remembrance
119 Ayatollah's subject
120 One-celled plants
121 Freedom from worry
122 War club
123 Musical ensembles
124 Far out!
125 Joie de vivre
126 — Rabbit

DOWN

1 Pester
2 Wild cat
3 The "Venus de Milo," e.g.
4 Tractable
5 CD-ROM users
6 Bit of granola
7 Toss water on
8 Gravelly voiced
9 "Fame" singer, Irene
10 Overwhelms
11 Sought office
12 Fugitive
13 Stimulated, as interest
14 Movie about college grads
15 Papal vestment
16 Archer's need
17 Zsa Zsa's sister
18 King, in Spain
25 Erosion
26 Flue buildup
28 Sticky compounds
33 Relaxation room
34 Lamb's mom
35 Sugar suffix
36 Sound of impact
37 Bylaw
38 Cry out
40 Rental agreement
41 — homo!
46 Tear asunder
48 Operative's org.
49 Tenth US president
50 Tusk material
51 Laconic
52 More secure
53 American Revolutionary general
54 1040A org.
57 Refuse
58 Woodworking machine
59 Part of French Polynesia
60 Plumed flier
61 Pet restraint
65 Like the Vikings
66 "The Tempest" sprite
67 Legal rights
68 Spiny shrub
70 City opposite the Gateway Arch
75 Cause of tides
76 Ques. response
77 Factory
78 Floating menagerie
80 Exploits
81 Social calendar list
82 Wind-driven clouds
83 "Citizen —"
84 Egyptian deity
88 Craftsperson
89 Sweet stuff
90 Western Hemisphere gp.
91 — Miss
92 Animal enclosure
95 Jazzman Hines
97 Factual
98 Buyer of goods
99 Star-related
100 Weather map line
101 Beginner
102 English cathedral city
104 — off (intermittently)
108 Bit of data
109 Lieutenant Kojak
111 Mausoleum
112 Relative
113 Singing syllable
114 Mythical piper
115 Muslim chief
116 Cute — button
117 Author Deighton

10

ACROSS

1 Italy's marble center
6 Fairy queen
9 300
12 Calyx parts
18 Maneuver
19 Algonquian
21 Climax
22 Accompany
23 Terry Bradshaw, once
24 Billiards shots
25 — lively!
26 Red Buttons in 1957
29 Horse's gait
30 Minus
31 — de la Plata
32 Stevedores' gp.
33 Reasonable
34 Upbeat, in music
36 "The Red Pony" author
42 Poet Egdar
43 Tree exudation
45 Alcazar site
46 Chum
47 '64 Hitchcock film
50 Clerical vest
51 Inappropriate
54 Eye part
55 Expert
58 Landscape painter
61 Average
63 Coin of Iran
64 Drama awards
65 Genuflected
66 An uncle for Pedro
67 Reading matter, briefly
68 Reed or Harrison
69 Fruit drink
70 Laine of song
71 Indian
72 Baldwin and Guinness
75 Early pope
77 Stone's "— for Life"
78 Tear apart
80 Twice a Pulitzer poet
81 Quay
82 Entr' —
83 — and all (nevertheless)
85 Site of Pago Pago
87 Lay in wait
89 Go all out
90 Makes for a particular purpose
92 Diva Sumac
93 Brooded
96 Redbirds
98 Make red-faced
102 Roman road
103 Party hack, for short
104 Actress Hagen
106 — Khan
107 Playwright Anita
108 Red Cloud
114 Vex
115 Australian parrots
117 — National Park
118 Harmonious
120 George and Thomas
121 The Barretts' street
122 Reds fan, for one
123 Rap session?
124 Perceive
125 Code alert
126 Dallas suburb

DOWN

1 Overcome
2 Entree
3 Red lights
4 — Michael Redgrave
5 Red Skelton, for one
6 Good luck charms
7 Greek city
8 Max or Buddy of boxing
9 Colombian city
10 Joan of "Twin Peaks"
11 Molding
12 Pelvic parts
13 Govt. org.
14 Red Sea stop
15 Public squares
16 Duds
17 Sonnet conclusion
18 Inventor Nikola
20 Church bench
27 Family member, briefly
28 Lodge member
35 — generis
37 Uncanny
38 "The Great" and "The Terrible"
39 Beak
40 Stendhal's "The Red and the —"
41 Rocker John
42 Rev
44 Red-letter
46 Red admiral
47 Whispered complaint
48 Travels on a plane
49 Certain chemical substance
52 Informal dining
53 Adriatic port
56 White poplar
57 Quarrelsome woman
59 Lariat
60 More aged
62 Brought up as a subject for debate
70 American Red Cross founder
73 Composer Franck
74 Decorous
75 Faint
76 Redhead Maureen
79 Red herring
84 Cover
86 1051
88 Actress Thurman
90 Fatty substances
91 Artificial channels
93 Thousands
94 Lord Jim portrayer
95 Bradley U. site
96 Tooth
97 Sault — Marie
99 Burrowing rodent
100 Excels
101 Prague coin
103 Horse thief pursuer
105 Red-hot
109 "I cannot tell —"
110 — Regis, England
111 Elec. unit
112 USN NCOs
113 Big Island city
116 And so on: abbr.
119 Negative prefix

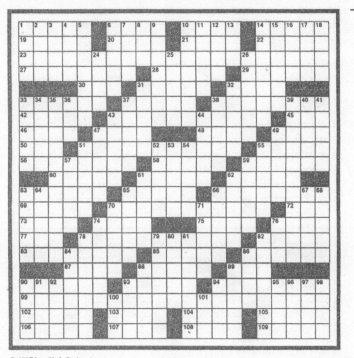

ACROSS

1 Certain computer instruction
6 Leave port
10 Prison
14 Decoys
19 Pale
20 School letters
21 Gofer
22 Light on one's feet
23 Old TV show
27 Discard
28 Rocket used as a probe
29 Rewards for workers
30 "— Haw"
31 Woodwind
32 Social gathering of a kind
33 Brief parts in pictures
37 Ninny
38 Ecclesiastical session
42 To pieces
43 Overwhelmed
45 Crude
46 Purchases
47 False god
48 Some votes
49 Off-Broadway award
50 Little planet
51 Bird
55 Lionhearted
56 Reeled
58 Shun
59 — owl
60 Machine part
61 Big party
62 Poisonous
63 Type of shepherd?
65 Show to be false
66 Acquits oneself
69 Martha and kin
70 Backroads
72 Armed conflict
73 Goes astray
74 Weary by being dull
75 Quarry
76 Advice columnist
77 Pixie
78 Backwoods
82 Boat peg
83 Hunting hounds
85 African antelope
86 Grace
87 Ages and ages
88 Set of steps over a fence
89 A feast — famine
90 Fortified building
93 Bargain
94 Raymond Burr TV role
99 Feuding families
102 Great reviews
103 Seed coat
104 It's clear to me
105 Dined
106 Pillar of stone
107 Retreats
108 — -do-well
109 Gaze fixedly

DOWN

1 Small rugs
2 Tennis great
3 Guitarist Atkins
4 Singer McEntire
5 Single appearance
6 Kid leather
7 "God's Little —"
8 Suffering
9 Slays
10 Idolized
11 Diacritical mark
12 Unemployed
13 Johnny —
14 NBA member
15 More hideous
16 U.S. social reformer
17 Gen. Robert —
18 Meeting: abbr.
24 Contends
25 Dwelling
26 Muslim decrees
31 — gold (pyrites)
32 Wet with moisture
33 Henry — Lodge
34 Orinoco feeder
35 Ken Berry sitcom
36 Sounds of hesitation
37 Thyroid, e.g.
38 Hair band
39 Travolta film
40 Innocent
41 Suiting
43 Kitchen gadget
44 Yet to be ignited
47 Man of great wealth
49 Fragrant rootstock
51 Greek letters
52 Half a WA city?
53 Profit
54 Runner-up
55 Crates
57 Large volumes
59 Comfortably inviting
61 Tam
62 Carried
63 Actress Garson
64 Football's — (Greasy) Neale
65 George or Robert
66 Healed
67 Aesopian tale
68 Young chicken
70 Libertines
71 Think
74 Farmerette's hat
76 So, that's it
78 — cucumber
79 Narrates again
80 Greek epic poem
81 Harmonizes (with)
82 Stupors
84 Sanctuary
86 School dance
88 Beer mug
89 Law and —
90 Hubs: abbr.
91 At the drop of —
92 Golfer Ballesteros
93 Father
94 Arrow poison
95 Begone!
96 Mite
97 Fabric worker
98 Slave of yore
100 Craze
101 Enzyme suffix

12

© 1996 Tribune Media Services, Inc.
All rights reserved.

ACROSS

1 Bilko or York: abbr.
4 Basset features
9 "You can — horse to..."
14 Makes high grades
18 Zodiac cat
19 Organic compounds
21 Stage figure
22 A U.S. president
23 Lennon's love
24 At that moment
26 Farm measure
27 Couch cushions
29 Giant hunter of myth
30 List of names
32 Aim high
33 "— the night before..."

34 Afternoon occasion
35 Lode largess
36 Heebie-jeebies
38 Leveret
39 Eating places
41 Gives it a go
42 Forays
44 Marble
47 Kitty's due
48 Eccentric
49 Pantywaist
50 Nordic tale
51 Humbug leader
52 Preserved meat
53 Cottage for Yeltsin
54 Room at the top
55 Foster or Crane
57 — and a promise
59 — soon (just in time)
61 Kind of fund

62 TNT word
63 Shepherded
64 Greek city
66 Librarian's gadget
67 Cross-current chop
70 Alas and —
71 Input item
73 Tittering laugh
75 Part of the psyche
76 Faction
77 Castor and Pollux
78 Islam units of weight
79 Ruckuses
80 Certain hold
81 Root or Yale
82 Marvelous!
83 Trunk inclusion
84 Lifeless and dull
85 Swellings

87 Adam's son
88 Bin's use
91 Formerly, formerly
92 Greens dishes
94 Fireplace feature
95 Peter or Jane
97 One of the fleet?
99 Libertine
100 Wriggle
103 Miss modifier
104 Takes advantage of
105 Ms. Lenya
106 Sweetheart
107 Renting abbr.
108 Tendency
109 Gave affirmative replies: var.
110 Computer units
111 — King Cole

DOWN

1 Slovenly one
2 Columbus' birthplace
3 Professional equipment
4 Landing wharves
5 Not us
6 Site query
7 Viewer's aid
8 Lady of Spain: abbr.
9 Not exactly prompt
10 Mythical nymph
11 "— o'clock scholar"
12 "Le Coq —"
13 "We always —" (David Garrick)
14 "— of Honey"
15 Desert plants

16 Violinist Zimbalist
17 Metric measure
20 Better for skiers
25 Lags behind
28 Drinking bout
31 Regatta implements
33 Well tested
34 Miscellany
36 Sometimes for all?
37 October demand
39 Trailer fronts
40 Med. sch. subj.
41 Change fortunes
43 Bat wood
44 Ragged
45 Exchange premium
46 Texas town
48 Knight's mission
49 — bleu!

50 Martin or Allen
52 Noteworthy quantity
53 Jaunty tune
54 Battery terminal
56 TV's "The — Is Right"
58 Tale-tellers
60 Bay window
64 Angler's maneuver
65 Medley
68 Mr. Stravinsky
69 Stance
72 Slangy negative
74 Greek letters
77 Just a bit
78 "— the Man" (Shaw)
79 Relating to bees

81 QED word
82 Frey's wife
83 Salt solutions
84 Haul to the hoosegow
86 Damaged, in a way
87 Famous Nation
88 Bonsai material
89 Plump a hairdo
90 Made of certain wood
92 Small gush
93 Alabama city
95 By — and starts
96 Bone: pref.
97 Corset feature
98 Musical pause
101 Distress cry
102 Society girl, briefly

13

ACROSS

1 Ingots
5 Indicate
10 Cassini
14 Troubadour's love song
18 Concerning
19 Sinbad, for one
20 "— Few Dollars More" (film)
21 Pretense
22 Gershwin tune
24 Gershwin tune
26 Tropical tree
27 Raced
29 Actress Greer
30 Police lab evidence
32 One who appraises
34 "— as a compass needle" (Lowell)
35 Do a cobbler's thing
36 Sheer fabric
37 Localities
38 Musical groups
39 Gershwin song from 61D
41 Sty denizens
45 — -bitty
46 Discharge
47 Part of ACLU: abbr.
48 Supporter
49 Payment for the needy: abbr.
50 Gershwin tune
54 Fr. city
55 Foot part
57 Carries on
58 Prairie animal
60 Soccer VIPs
62 Walks back and forth
63 Prominent
64 Largesse for teachers?
65 Jai alai basket
66 Endeavor
67 Micronesia offerings
68 Gershwin tune
70 Suppositions
73 Aesthetic pursuit
74 Half a dietary ailment
75 — Harbor, Guam
76 Academic exam letters
77 "To — thing in one sentence..." (William James)
79 Gershwin tune
83 Piece of cake
84 Coup —
86 Legionnaires' refuges
87 Scottish lords
88 Gym wear
90 Places for murals
91 Humans
92 Charlotte — (Virgin Islands capital)
93 Dray
94 Herb
95 Gershwin musical
97 "— You" (Gershwin song from 95A)
103 Can. prov.
104 Author Milne
105 Piccalilli
106 Pelvic bones
107 Wanton look
108 Title of respect
109 Gluts
110 Yeltsin denial

DOWN

1 Cudgel
2 Residue
3 Map abbr.
4 "— Loves Me" (Gershwin)
5 Severe discomfort
6 Oleaginous
7 U.N. agcy.
8 Mo.
9 Framework
10 Bid
11 Obstreperous
12 Sea bird
13 Ness' target
14 "— as a daisy"
15 Tibet's capital
16 Part of BLT
17 Prayer word
19 Night sound
23 Walter and Frederick
25 Meryl Streep's alma mater
28 Equal
30 Notable acts
31 Gershwin tune
32 Young lover
33 Aspire
34 Actress Anouk
35 Baseball stats
36 Rotates
37 Singer Ginny
39 Position
40 Bakery items
42 Gershwin's Pulitzer musical
43 Greek physician
44 Derisive sound
46 Liquefies
50 Soft cheese
51 Rubbish
52 Instruments under seal, in law
53 — a time (singly)
54 Petty thief, in England
56 "— Fair" (Matalin-Carville memoir)
58 Largest Italian lake
59 Potpourri
60 Fancy balls
61 Gershwin's "Porgy and Bess," e.g.
62 Bird
63 — und Drang
65 French painter
66 Some students, briefly
68 "At the Races" painter
69 Actress Cassie
71 Confronts
72 Agatha et Jeanne: abbr.
74 "...is — wormwood" (Bible)
76 Tropical fruit
78 "A dillar, —..."
80 Crowd response
81 Kin of tethers
82 Famed designer letters
83 Glow
85 Author Ambler
87 Train
88 Nat Cole hit
89 Ah Sin's creator
90 John of old movies
91 Name in clothing
92 "...a peculiar sort of —"
93 Autocrat
94 — -dieu (prayer bench)
96 — Baba
98 — culpa
99 Eatery order, briefly
100 Ace reporter, Nellie
101 Fib
102 Consume

14

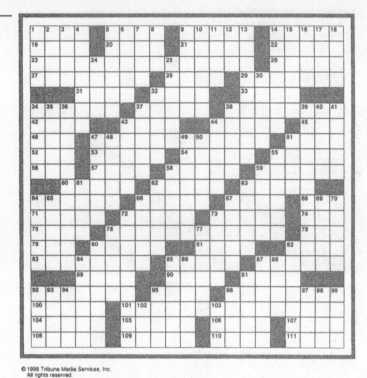

ACROSS

1 Distort
5 Embellishment
9 Venerated
14 Disney deer
19 Logical start
20 Healthy
21 Planet
22 "Better is the — a thing..." (Bible)
23 Old Glory
26 MN city
27 Made beloved
28 Lily family member
29 Paul Revere, e.g.
31 Relieves of a burden
32 Item on a flag
33 Nettle
34 Lumberjacks
37 Astringents
38 Fruit drinks
42 Mild oath
43 Time, to wine
44 Hereditary units
45 Deserter
46 14
47 — Day
51 Tax
52 Whitney or Wallach
53 Corrupt morally
54 Baseball's Banks
55 Desert transportation
56 VIP in D.C.
57 "Pease porridge in — ..."
58 Englishmen, informally
59 New Orleans university
60 Storms
62 Hangs onto
63 Of early morning
64 Capital of the Georgian Republic
66 Jim-dandies
67 Actress Lynn
68 "Major —" (TV show)
71 MO city
72 Much bigger
73 Throng
74 Ziegfeld, familiarly
75 Collections of anecdotes
76 Celebratory courses
78 Japanese admiral
79 Russian fighter plane
80 Less defiled
81 Against
82 At a distance
83 Parts of a horse's hoofs
85 Titled ladies
87 Gaffes
89 Impel
90 Son of Aphrodite
91 Thrill
92 Sousa's compositions
95 — in the neck
96 Negligent
100 Violinist Morini
101 US flag
104 Precipitous
105 Uncanny
106 Art deco name
107 In apple-pie order
108 Dispatches
109 Dutch painter
110 River to the North Sea
111 Sets

DOWN

1 Send a message
2 Former British colony
3 — Foxx
4 Gave impetus to
5 Certain portions
6 Ranks
7 "— Three Lives"
8 — culpa
9 Uncontrolled action
10 Works hard
11 First name in whodunits
12 Alphabet run
13 "— and the Pauper"
14 Scarabs
15 — del Sarto (Florentine painter)
16 1502
17 Pro — publico
18 "— first you don't..."
24 Head covering
25 Temperament
30 Actress Anouk
32 Slumbered
34 Genders
35 Spry
36 Sight on 76A
37 Go-between
38 Certain consonant
39 Marching band complements
40 Corroded
41 Fashion
43 So long, Pedro
44 Men
47 Roma's land
48 Nuchae
49 Leaf ridge
50 Removes the moisture
51 Surrealist painter
55 Attractive ones
58 Packaged
59 French sociologist
61 "— Well That..."
62 Sweetheart
63 Cuban patriot
64 Heavy footfall
65 Ancient region of Asia Minor
66 Attracts
67 Contests
69 Sacred table
70 Some of them are French
72 Ties together
73 Sharpens
76 Remove the undesirable
77 Old film with Loretta Young
80 Possibly
82 Fishing
84 Put in a snug place
85 Darling
86 Gotten up
87 Trade
88 Remarkable thing
91 Sew loosely
92 Muddle
93 Commedia dell' —
94 Nothing: Fr.
95 Curtail
96 Navy bigwigs: abbr.
97 Fencing foil
98 Apply Scotch tape
99 Fast planes
102 Asian holiday
103 Marshal of France

15

ACROSS

1 Grip firmly
6 Large mammal, briefly
11 Speaks with a mannerism
16 Seaman
17 Nautical rope: var.
19 Draw in
21 Jessica in "Murder She Wrote"
22 Hall of fame?
23 Fixed part of a machine
24 Depot: abbr.
25 Bull
27 Related to a king
29 Chestnut sprinkled with white
30 Person of impressive skill
32 Fish once featured in wildlife series?
35 Mountain ridge
36 Balance
38 After deductions
39 Positive attribute
40 It's number one in Berlin
42 Sturm — Drang
43 Unsatisfactory
44 Pose
45 Dry reds of Bordeaux
48 Nobleman
50 Break
53 Meager
54 OR city
56 Unclose, to poets
57 Sign gas
59 Fish talk?
61 Focused on number one
64 Inner: pref.
65 Domingo's field
66 Allowance for waste
68 Yegg's target
69 Exhilarating experience
71 Choose
72 Improper distribution
75 Underweight fish?
77 UT town
79 — Moines
80 Perfect remedy
82 Pointed arch
83 Transfers
85 Greek cheese
86 Impolite
88 English cathedral town
89 Fishy cape?
90 Bikini part
92 US org.
93 Scrape away
96 Golf term
97 Outfits with machinery
99 Tries
103 Cat fish?
106 Violent attack
108 Aquatic predator
109 Portuguese monetary unit
110 Said further
112 Measure, in music
113 German
115 Vacuously
117 Emotional shock
119 Ancient Jewish ascetic
120 Bonds
121 Illustrator Beardsley
122 Trials
123 Overly diffident one
124 Improve

DOWN

1 One who sings religiously
2 Bind
3 Tavern drink
4 Fish receiving everything?
5 Madrid museum
6 Lisa or Paul of TV
7 Election winners
8 SD city
9 Discussion group
10 Genuine article
11 Fine thread
12 Opp. of ext.
13 Fish's relative?
14 Vernacular
15 Everett of "Citizen Kane"
16 Bird in "Peter and the Wolf"
17 Fon du —
18 Put on
20 Artist Max
26 "— in the bag!"
28 Fitting
31 Soft-shell clam
33 Birch family tree
34 Precipitous
37 Baked desserts
41 Tide type
43 Slopes in Scotland
44 Experts
45 Trimmed
46 "— petal of a flower" (Tennyson)
47 Flies
49 Three-toed sloths
50 "Der —" (German magazine)
51 Trickle
52 Sauntered
53 Thread holder
55 Evil Indian spirit
56 Sanctioned
58 Scandinavians
60 Certain missile
62 Tra —
63 Cabin
67 Recorded
70 Calculated according to shares
73 Passively
74 Opp. of long.
76 "— a league onward..." (Tennyson)
78 Frozen fish?
81 Indian bigwig
84 On the sheltered side
85 Destinies
87 Tattooed fish?
89 Derived from lime
91 Creator's reward
93 Ham it up
94 Thinnest
95 Indict
96 Footlike part
97 Steaks
98 Melancholy
100 Brown
101 Held responsible
102 Go wrong
104 Magritte and Descartes
105 Edward Fenech — (Maltese prime minister)
107 Bristles
111 Faulty: pref.
114 Can. prov.
116 Naval off.
118 Justice Fortas

16

ACROSS

1 Too bad!
5 Hostess Perle
10 Morse code signs
16 Markdown
17 Music hall
18 Letter holder
21 Martha and Lloyd's solution to lowering the river?
24 Karen and Lucille vote no?
26 Intensify
27 Bristles
29 Palm tree
30 Ever ready
32 Deep-sea fish
35 Ship hangout: abbr.
36 Perfumed
40 Musical treat
42 Containing animal fat
44 Window part
45 Gem weights
46 Saves
47 Turns over
50 Atop
51 Tropical snake
52 Aves.
53 Reagan or Howard
54 Incline
56 — one's breast (hug)
60 Spanish city
62 — Fein
63 Pliny the —
67 Like some seals
68 Pavilion
72 Artistic movement
74 Social engagements
76 Foot pedal
78 Columnist Barrett
80 Violent storm
82 Move back
85 Hemingway epithet
86 Atlas abbr.
87 Letter add-ons
90 — -fi
91 Unemployed
93 "— a word from our sponsor"
95 Author of "The Canterbury Tales"
97 Certain Italian
99 Concern
100 Siren
101 Precise
102 Sprang back
105 Once — blue moon
106 Had a high opinion of
108 Roman magistrate of old
110 Skirts
112 Some paintings
114 Teaches
119 Orson and Annie serve legumes
122 TV's Della and Maxwell know the ropes
124 Without having to pay
125 Mountaintop nest
126 Acting award
127 They make memoranda
128 Valleys
129 Member of a litter

DOWN

1 Tennis great
2 Ballads
3 Author Waugh
4 Antitoxins
5 High spirits
6 Checked copy
7 Passover dinner
8 Pull
9 Singing brothers
10 Arguments
11 Cove
12 Govt. org.
13 Santa's time: abbr.
14 Acids' opposite
15 Fireplace shelves
19 Faint
20 Slips by
22 Utter without thinking
23 Helping hands
25 Minerals: suff.
28 Tense
31 Springe
33 Hank of baseball
34 Think about
36 Plant with milky juice
37 Strong tobacco
38 Catch
39 Once was
41 God of love
43 Office-at-home necessities: abbr.
45 Ryder or Stanley
48 Merchant
49 Woebegone
51 Tie up
55 Welcome sign
57 Free from
58 Collection of anecdotes
59 "The — and the Sea"
61 Western state: abbr.
64 Bathe like a bird
65 Everlasting
66 Bring back to snuff
69 "... — saw Elba"
70 Negative
71 Explosive letters
73 One — time
75 Intoxicated
77 Sow again
79 Surveying instruments
81 Govt. org.
83 Curtain fabric
84 Instruction: abbr.
85 Sty
87 Shifty persons
88 Group of three lakes
89 Haul to court
92 Not on time
94 601
95 Shinny up
96 — one's bosom (embraces)
97 Reads
98 Fired
102 "— triumph over all mischance" (Shakespeare)
103 Extracts by means of solvent
104 Trices: abbr.
107 Between: pref.
109 Farm machine inventor
111 Privy to
113 Party for men
115 Cupid
116 Forbidden
117 Ireland
118 Leave it alone
120 Frequently
121 Three: It.
123 Kinsman: abbr.

17

© 1996 Tribune Media Services, Inc.

ACROSS

1 A — of thousands
5 Use a rudder
10 Yours truly
14 Seasoning
18 Tennis's Arthur
19 Analyze grammatically
20 Bay window
22 — da capo
23 River in Hades
24 Ram
25 Gaucho's item
26 Wanton look
27 Like slugging fighters
29 From one end of the country to the other
32 Go wrong
33 Horse MD
34 Recoil in pain
35 — instant (immediately)
36 — -relief
37 Saree wearer
38 State strongly
39 Small child
42 Push back
45 Accommodates
46 Ballad
47 Skirt style
48 — podrida
49 Surveys
50 Object of worship
52 Philippines island
53 Pie — mode
54 Thesaurus author
55 Winter white
56 Unruffled
57 — Beach, FL
59 Maine college town
61 Teacher's aide
62 UCLA player
63 Crisp cake
64 Kind of acid
65 Prairie wolves
67 Divorced
68 Expunged
71 Jonathans
72 Whitney and Wallach
73 Chicago airport
75 One — million
76 With — on
77 Narrated
78 John Quincy —
79 Biographer Ludwig
80 Geologic divisions
81 Injunction
82 Love, in Rome
83 Thin in tone
84 Gleam
85 Atlas entries
86 Racing boat
87 Triangle side
88 Singer Tennille
89 A Beatle
90 Swindle
91 "— Done Him Wrong"
94 Police search type
98 Personal discussion type
100 City on the Jumna
101 Future nut tree
102 Exchange
104 Gossip
105 — East
106 Painter Edouard
107 Spud
108 Major end
109 Solidifies
110 Meeting: abbr.
111 "Golden Boy" author
112 Visionary

DOWN

1 Society division
2 Fur trader of old
3 More diffident
4 Printed version
5 Torrents
6 Fortune-telling card
7 Toledo's waterfront
8 Natives of: suff.
9 Countermands
10 Consolation
11 Wipe the board
12 Catalogue
13 Jamboree
14 Beauty shop
15 Quarter
16 Is situated
17 Pastry product
21 Foolish: var.
28 White House office
30 Smallest bills
31 Traffic jam item
34 Crowded
36 Arthur
37 Starlet's dream
38 Near the deck
39 From — (occasionally)
40 "A Bell for —"
41 More terrible
42 Way
43 Ms. Fitzgerald
44 Like sports announcing
45 "— Heroes" (TV sitcom)
47 Seadog
49 Shetlands
50 Circle or sanctum start
51 Kind of salesman
52 Aged
54 Highways
55 Couches
56 Actress Suzanne
58 Gnomes' kin
60 Very fast
61 "— Bovary"
65 Log used in a Scottish sport
66 "Turandot," e.g.
69 OK city
70 Golfer John
72 Eternity
74 Angel's instrument
77 Puddings
78 Little cupid
79 Brain scan letters
81 Diminutive
82 Word of woe
83 Flat rate
85 Stooge name
86 Feats
87 Solitary fellows
88 Deposed rulers
89 Painful spots
90 West Point student
91 Hit, old style
92 Writer Bret
93 Join up
94 Suspend
95 Molding
96 — Mountains, Russia
97 Put an edge on
98 Win, in chess
99 Poems
103 Wonderful, slangily

18

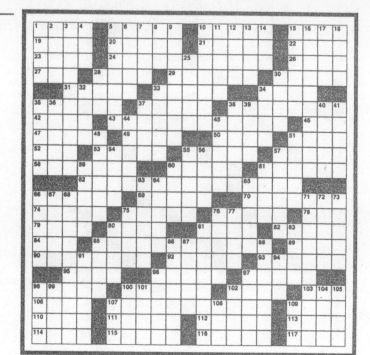

© 1996 Tribune Media Services, Inc.
All rights reserved.

ACROSS

1 Author of "Les Miserables"
5 Mrs. Gorbachev
10 Malicious
15 1054
19 Smell —
20 Bean of comedy
21 New England college town
22 Superior
23 "If This — Love"
24 Heater
26 Urdar or Skuld
27 Tease
28 Internet rider
29 Cass of song
30 Bewildered
31 "— a reasoning animal" (Seneca)
33 Runs away
34 Hint from Christie
35 Minos, e.g.
37 Zodiac sign
38 Decapitated
42 Cronyn
43 Trunk
46 Sunbeam
47 Fix in the mind
49 Musical James
50 "Iliad" or "Odyssey"
51 Blackbird: var.
52 Vigoda
53 Plane surfaces
55 Fresh-water fishes
57 "Enough!" at La Scala
58 Showed off
60 Train
61 Robert Guillaume hit
62 Gear
66 Bindlestiffs
69 Joyce Carol —
70 River nymphs
74 Some computer pictures
75 Rodrigo Diaz de Vivar
76 Intertwined
78 Wrath
79 Tolled
80 Author Harte
81 Gainsay
82 English county
84 Yasmin's dad
85 Sedan
89 — homo
90 Woman in the New Testament
92 Beethoven's "Fur —"
93 Wiley Post and Amelia Earhart
95 Auberjonois of 61A
96 Stanza
97 Ionian Island
98 Soap plant
100 "That — out!"
102 Ridge
103 Stadium sound
106 Rob or Chad
107 Tire
109 Indian ruler
110 Dole's successor
111 River at Lyons
112 Relevant
113 Seaweed product
114 Tennis great
115 Author of "The Green Hat"
116 Literature Nobelist
117 Social dud

DOWN

1 Locks
2 Major or Minor
3 Hood
4 "Master Melvin"
5 Composer of "La Cenerentola"
6 Where Van Gogh slept
7 Munich's river
8 Absalom, to David
9 Plant with medicinal roots
10 Most laid-back
11 Gallico's "Mrs. — Goes to Paris"
12 Take-out words
13 Type of bolt holder
14 Hither's partner
15 Vergil's birthplace
16 Shift
17 Concerning
18 — cava
25 — Street (British journalism)
28 Actress Merkel
30 Trebek
32 Suit to —
33 Guitar ridges
34 Boz's first name, in brief
35 Miserly
36 Cuban dance
37 Thin Man's dog
38 Shepherdess of rhyme
39 Son of Aphrodite
40 Keep an — the ground
41 Poet Thomas
44 "Nothing can — lie" (Herbert)
45 Hundred: pref.
48 Pedestal midsections
51 "There is — slip..."
54 — up (accelerates)
55 Fooled
56 Affected, superior manners
57 Happen to
59 Included with
60 Bristle: pref.
61 Hillside, in Aberdeen
63 Wife of Henry VIII
64 Milk: pref.
65 Ref. bk.
66 King of Tyre
67 FL city
68 Horn
71 Dash
72 Put up
73 Genders
75 Art deco name
76 Hire
77 First name of 63D
80 Ill humor
81 Car path
83 Personal interest
85 Split rattan
86 Seiners
87 Strong passion
88 People for whom things are named
91 Remove
94 Annoy
96 Justice Harlan Fiske
97 Proof mark
98 — breve
99 Meadow sounds
100 Cordelia's parent
101 Conservationist's sci.
102 "The Vamp"
104 Slightly open
105 Adamant
107 Lad's org.
108 Piano center of the Netherlands
109 Tried for office

ACROSS

1 Apartments, slangily
5 Cut into pieces
9 Agreement
15 Old sailor
19 Many
20 US attorney general
21 Ms. Kitt
22 Over again
23 Portico
24 Author Haley
25 Noted football coach
27 Violent storms
29 Stages in a process
30 Chatter
31 Ninny
32 Librarian's word
33 Kind of club
35 Wooden strip
38 Fatty tissues
39 Cads
43 Stretch one's neck
44 Dashing youth
45 Bizarre
46 — tai (bar drink)
47 River isles
48 Muslim decree
49 Martini order
51 French title: abbr.
52 "— go bragh"
53 Spoiled children
54 Average grades
55 Toothlike projections
58 Be furious
59 Hash house
61 Some votes
62 Norman Vincent —
64 — die
65 Add
68 Pied Piper followers
69 High-kicking line
74 Composer of "Wozzeck"
75 Shore
76 — suit
77 Doctors' gp.
78 What some felons do?
81 Clipped
83 Fortas and Vigoda
84 Golfer Ernie
85 Church areas
86 Fictional Lorna
87 Bitter drug
88 Pirate
90 Torment
91 Like the sky, at times
92 Spouted pitcher
93 British sword
94 Name dropper
95 Nautical term
98 Some are bluefins
99 Flowering vine
103 "To — or bend a knotted oak" (Congreve)
106 Inter —
107 Kind of skirt
108 Rectangular column
109 Admittance
110 Pull
111 Seed cover
112 Loch — monster
113 Certain loom bars
114 Nervous
115 Straight

DOWN

1 History
2 Choir member
3 Knob or mat start
4 Star substitutes
5 Hold protectively
6 Spartan slave
7 Some bills
8 Calamity, old style
9 Round silicate glass bodies
10 Hindu princesses
11 Spew magma
12 Men with briefs: abbr.
13 Common article
14 Babi — (scene of an outrage)
15 Kind of cow?
16 Paul of music
17 Furnished
18 Overly precious, in England
26 Kitchen need
28 Top-notch
29 "Blue — Shoes"
32 Campus feature
33 Early Teutons
34 End of the line item
35 Rip-offs
36 Groom oneself
37 "See you —, alligator"
38 Slope
39 Flat-topped hill
40 Host at a roast
41 Gardener, sometimes
42 Spacek
44 Soft cheeses
45 Wild ass
48 Annoyed
49 Nuncupative
50 Certain group
52 Sch. subj.
53 Impetuous
56 European lake
57 Paddles
59 Sacred image: var.
60 Dill, old style
63 Greek letters
64 Mark with cuts
65 Clichy clerics
66 Hostess Mesta
67 Musical notation
68 Cook's tool
70 Fresh pure air
71 Small drum
72 Arabian prince
73 Impertinent
75 English port
79 "Do you —, my lord?" (Hamlet)
80 Type of review
81 Ascends suddenly
82 Firefighter's need
83 Mobile man
86 Degrades
87 Tiny particle
89 Lariats
90 Certain vessel
91 Surreptitious
93 Bolivian capital
94 Hurl
95 Wise — owl
96 Study hard
97 Newts
98 Youngsters
99 Attired
100 Biblical weed
101 African plant
102 Fertile earth
104 Born
105 Genetic letters
106 Voice vote

CHAPTER 20

DIAGRAMLESSES

The diagramless crossword puzzle adds a bit of extra fun to your puzzling task. Not only do you have to know the answers to the clues, but you have to place them in the proper squares on the grid. Start with 1 across and work in pencil. These puzzles have regular crossword puzzle symmetry. You can learn the location of 1 across for each puzzle by turning the page upside down.

Answers begin on page 333.

Clues

Across

1 Brown in the sun
4 Dined
7 Skin opening
8 Cooking container
9 Rock channel
12 Be silent: Music
14 Uneven
15 Nickel
17 Classified and display, for example
18 Summer month: Abbrev.
20 Hemingway novel, "Across the River and _____ the Trees"
21 Caused to reproduce
23 _____ Fleming
24 How prescription drugs are sold: Abbrev.
27 Command for a turn
28 Brit. network
30 Miles _____ hour
31 College senior's test
33 Festivity
35 Skin art
37 Slow down
41 Engraving product, for short
43 "Beamer"
44 The Way: Chinese
45 Philosopher _____ Rand
46 To and _____
48 Automobile efficiency initials
49 Corn holder
51 Related
53 Iridescent gemstone
55 Corp. head
56 "We're _____ to see the wizard…"
59 Purplish brown
60 Kind of deer
62 Plotters
64 Item of footwear in Aspen
65 Robert E. _____
66 Small bouquet
67 Bold and nontraditional
68 Vietnamese holiday

Down

1 Froglike creature
2 Circle parts
3 Word before maiden name
4 Orbit point farthest from Earth
5 Small boy, informally
6 Conclusion
7 School grp.
9 Long-distance company
10 Keynote
11 Kind of résumé
13 Small newspaper, for short
16 Negative prefix
19 Encourage
22 B.A., e.g.
24 Choose
25 British drink
26 Major component of computer terminal: Abbrev.
28 He huffed and he puffed and he _____ the house down.
29 Ballpark utensil
31 Thug
32 Decay
34 Branch
36 Make an effort
38 Banking machine: Abbrev.
39 Tap
40 Lassie, for one
42 Frequently
43 Tree trunk
45 Taken _____
47 Swayed to and fro
49 Police officer, for short
50 Work: Music
52 M.D.'s tag
54 Hawaiian garland
56 Double-reed instrument
57 Expeditious
58 Outfield ball
60 Certain shade tree
61 Astrological sign
63 Likely

1 across starts in the 3rd square from the left.

2

Clues

Across

1 "_____ and the King of Siam"
5 Washcloth
8 Sleeping
12 Smear on
13 Brer Bear in later years
14 Cook a pie
15 Auld Lang _____
16 Loud, continuous noise
17 Masticate
18 Video material
21 Time periods
24 Labor org.
25 Famous uncle
26 Packing box
29 Indian viceroy
33 Apprehend
34 _____ de cologne
35 Young woman, playfully
38 Shoal
40 Aviation body: Abbrev.
42 Knightly honorific

43 Apex
44 Matures
46 Pierce with a knife
49 Eight: Prefix
51 Spheres
55 Fishhook tip
56 Maiden name preceder
57 Traditional knowledge
58 Poker stake
59 Turf
60 Chair part

Down

1 Description of salable goods
2 Negative vote
3 Sister
4 Assist
5 Western competition
6 Muhammad _____
7 Identity determinants
8 Fundamentals
9 Expression of scorn
10 To manage, but barely: "_____ out"
11 Condensed moisture
19 Emote

20 Cherry or cream, for example
22 Operated
23 Med. grp.
26 24-hour news network
27 Beam of light
28 Certain missile: Abbrev.
30 Buzzer
31 Lout
32 Mass transit vehicle
36 Military rank: Abbrev.
37 Noah's second son
38 Oil derrick
39 Before, poetically
41 Thousands and thousands of years
42 Satisfied
43 Priest's title: French
45 Hurok and Roman sun god
46 Gov't. agency concerned with small business
47 Khaki
48 _____ Carney
50 Corporate bigwig: Abbrev.
52 Fish eggs
53 Swimsuit top
54 Ready to go

1 across starts in the 1st square, second row.

12 Automatic advance in tournament
13 Slippery as an _____
14 Mineral
15 Go quickly
16 Cologne
18 Not his
19 Doctors' group
21 AFL partner
24 Boy
27 Primate
28 Disk that converts circular into linear motion
29 Rack up points
30 Established custom or practice
32 Protects from weather
33 Medicines
34 Color
35 Applies lightly
36 Reverence
37 A simpleton
38 Drive
39 Alias
41 Sink quickly
42 The seed of an Asiatic legume
47 Start of a trick in bridge
48 Clairvoyance, e.g.
50 Smoking residue
51 Fifth sign of the Zodiac
52 Take to one's heels
53 Fed
54 Layer of turf

Clues

Across

1 Value
4 An athlete who plays for pay
7 Head covering
8 Legislator's concern
9 A French abbot
10 Matures
12 Stakes
15 Adult female bird
17 Satisfaction
20 Affirmative
21 Former OSS
22 Surround
23 Building annex
24 Exchange
25 Anger
26 Chocolate source
29 The center of a city
31 Temporary living quarters
32 Towel letters
33 Pol. affiliation
34 Despised
36 Rapid bustling movement

38 Stretched tight
40 Dates
43 No longer is
44 Supplement with difficulty
45 Word element meaning life
46 Female sheep
47 Linear unit
48 Catch sight of
49 Auction, e.g.
52 Laddie's companion
55 Large body of water
56 At the peak
57 Mortar trough
58 Kind of school, for short

Down

1 Talk
2 Horny projecting jaws of a bird
3 Pakistani rupee
4 Strategy
5 Annoy
6 Be obliged to repay
7 Consumes
11 Indian term of respect

1 across starts in the 5th square from the left.

Clues

Across

1 Common cereal grass
4 Nickname for some Scots
7 Weep
10 In the style of
11 Volcano product
12 Cry of discovery
13 Relative
14 Mountain lift
15 Familiar saying
19 Droop
20 Symbol of silence
22 Espionage org.
23 Bribe
25 Rapidly fermented drink
26 Actor Hanks
27 Stair gradients
31 "_____ from the Crypt"
32 Ordinary
36 Subject
38 Give voice to
39 School grp.
42 Offbeat
44 Kind of sweet potato

47 _____ mot (good word): French
48 Golfing necessities
50 Marsh
52 Musical composition
54 Palestinian grp.
57 Hail; farewell: Latin
58 _____ canto (beautiful song): Latin
59 Debtor's note: Abbrev.
60 Title of address for a knight
61 Mistress: Abbrev.
62 Acorn, e.g.
63 Garment border

Down

1 Sturdy trees
2 Pseudonym
3 South American dance
4 Glutton's order: Span.
5 Inquire
6 Elegantly fashionable
7 Plotters
8 Quality of some poetry
9 Ship's lateral drift
16 Fall mo.
17 Brazilian metropolis

18 Dike
21 Fatigue; listlessness
24 Western time zone: Abbrev.
28 Make lace
29 Easterly: Abbrev.
30 Vim
33 Feline
34 Liable
35 Confederate general
37 Arid
39 Television network
40 Also
41 _____ Arbor, Mich.
42 Weasel's relative
43 Distributes cards
45 Disconcert
46 Film
49 Make thread
51 Certain bacterium
53 Missile variety
55 Actor Gossett
56 Retired batter

1 across starts in the 1st square on the left.

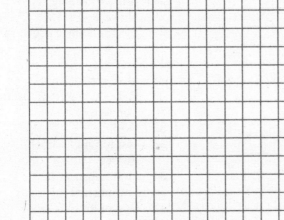

Clues

No. 5: This puzzle is 15 squares wide by 15 squares deep

Across

1 Pair of singers
4 Not activated
5 Wrestler's pad
8 "The Longest _____"
11 Small children
13 Adam's significant other
14 Republican presidential candidate
15 Keenness in understanding
17 Chills
18 Certain Scandinavian
20 Pouch
22 Kind of tape
23 Word-and-picture puzzle
27 Cigar dropping
28 Mild oath
31 Kind of farm
32 Authoritative others (_____ say)
34 Nope
35 Beloved
37 Before: Poetic
38 _____ Ruth
39 By way of
40 Mister: Span.
42 Warn
44 Pop
46 Browns
47 "Pre-owned" car
50 Rouse
53 Ultraviolet, for example
54 Restaurant bill
55 "To _____ His Own"
59 Direction: Abbrev.
60 Circle segment
61 Grackle
62 Cunning

Down

1 Gov't. dept.
2 Alien craft (?)
3 Frequently
5 Reminder, for short
6 Street designation: Abbrev.
7 Bo Derrick et al.
8 M.D.'s nickname
9 Tavern order
10 Affirmative
12 Rational
14 Roll the _____
16 Corp. No. 1
18 Plates
19 Stick
21 Carney or Garfunkel
22 Tank
24 "I Got It _____ and That Ain't Good"
25 Of varying lengths
26 Steps
28 Deoxyribonucleic acid, familiarly
29 Umbrella component
30 Have an _____ to grind
33 Yearning
36 I smell a _____!
38 Undergarment
41 Probability
42 Lunched
43 Kent's companion
45 Facts
47 Large coffee container
48 _____ Fernando
49 Ogle
51 Kind of clouds or correspondent
52 TV network
56 Sale promotions
57 Silent _____
58 Public road: Abbrev.

5

1 across starts in the 1st square on the left.

Clues

Across

1 Browning's "_____ Lippo Lippi"
4 Circuit
5 Rear of a boat
8 Opp. of Rev.
11 Selects
13 School dance
15 Burn
17 Deep gully
19 In a frigid manner
20 Object in the sky: Abbrev.
21 Madre _____!
23 Golfing necessity
24 Caress
25 Whole
27 Marriage title
28 _____ Alda
31 Letters rel. to automobile efficiency
34 Former Chinese leader
35 Some males
36 Tire necessity
37 Alias initials
38 Hotel employee
39 Maiden name preceder
40 Tranquil
43 Block
44 Mild oath
46 Drunkard
47 Journalist's exclusive
50 Secretary of Defense et al.
54 Hovels
55 Dry
56 Soggy
59 Up to now
60 Blend
61 Enemy
62 "_____ Little Indians"

Down

1 Florence, for short
2 Style of popular music
3 Liable
5 Spring mo.
6 To and _____
7 Plaything
8 Broadcast overseer: Abbrev.
9 The least bit
10 Valley
12 Vaults
14 Pop's companion
16 "Catcher in the _____"
18 Decay
19 Author Fleming
20 Hullabaloo
22 Electronically charged atom
26 Sent forth
27 Car type
28 Med. grp.
29 Welcoming gift on Oahu
30 Connector
32 Dock
33 Test for grad school: Abbrev.
34 More: Spanish
38 Encountered
41 God of love
42 Snooze
43 _____ appétit
45 Fraudulent scheme
46 Caesar, for example
47 Bashful
48 Actor's signal
49 Baseball legend Mel
51 Onassis
52 Jazz trumpeter Beiderbecke
53 _____-Hartley Act
57 Stooge
58 Prison, slangily

1 across starts in the 1st square on the left.

25 Cards used in fortunetelling
28 Shoe bottoms
30 Cover with concrete, for example
32 Time zone: Abbrev.
33 Life: Prefix
34 Collection of anecdotes
35 Sort
37 Complete
38 Fish eggs
39 Attempt

Clues

40 Narrow stream extending from a river or lake
41 Saxophone
42 Sturdy trees
43 Actress Susan _____

Across

1 Vat
4 Person as individual
8 In progress
11 Drilled
12 Telephone place
13 Mistake
14 Hackneyed
16 Monkey relative
19 Pierce
23 Campus vine
24 On the other hand
26 In the style of
27 Nectar-gathering insects
29 Knocked
31 Kind of play
33 Dumps water overboard
36 Not covert

Down

1 Small projecting flap
2 Alien craft (?)
3 Frightening word
4 Painful places
5 Make a mistake
6 Zodiac sign
7 WWII pres.
9 Director Preminger
10 Pulsate
11 Put money on, so to speak
15 Harden
16 Child's dining apparel
17 Street designation: Abbrev.
18 See ya, e.g.
20 Rap
21 Fermented beverage
22 Spoiled

1 across starts in the 1st square on the left.

8

Clues

Across

1 Deprive of unlawfully
4 Evidence of fire
7 Bird of prey
8 Make love to
9 Gas used in some signs
11 Blend
12 Half-size newspaper, for short
14 Iniquitous
15 Director's stick
17 Jailbird
18 Carries
20 N. Amer. nation
21 Pouch
23 Four of spades, for example
25 Yaks
28 In the style of
29 Lad
30 Spider milieu
31 _____ Diego

Down

1 Director Howard
2 Be in debt
3 Rorschach image
4 Overcome
5 Old _____
6 Trough for mortar
10 Apprehend
11 Painter Ray
13 Francis _____
14 Skeletal parts
16 Add up
18 Small boy
19 Droop
20 Zodiac sign
22 Taxis
23 Crow call
24 Tavern order
26 Snuggly snake
27 Opp. of ant.

9

21 Stuck together
22 Egg-shaped ornament: Archit.
24 Timid
26 Dine
27 What to do in Vail
28 Milky gemstone
29 Large container for tea or coffee
33 Cow's offspring
36 Spelling competition
37 Scoundrel
38 What some amateurs turn
39 Paddle
40 Strong alkaline solution

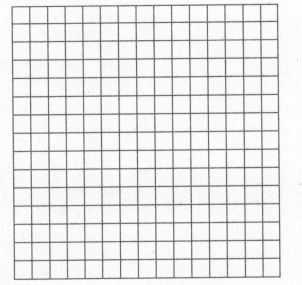

Clues

Across

1 Enemy
4 _____ relief
7 Annoy
8 Tool for punching holes
9 French priest
10 Negative vote
11 Circle part
13 Offensive implement in baseball
16 Expression of contempt
17 I smell a _____!
19 Be in debt
20 Three-footed stand
23 Main parts of churches
25 Obis, for example
28 Three strikes
30 Gab
31 Before: Prefix

32 Twitch
34 Linking word
35 Alphabetical beginning
38 Survey
41 Meadow
42 Actor Liotta
43 Gov't.
44 Lead or silver

Down

1 Lie
2 Globe
3 Make sufficient by adding to (with out)
4 Inlet
5 Reverence
6 Thick, flat piece of something
9 Dull, steady pain
11 Dwellings
12 Uncooked
14 Painting, for example
15 Sailor, slangily
18 One of Dorothy's companions: _____ Man

1 across starts in the 12th square from the left.

10

Clues

Across

1 Football org.
4 Alternative to coffee
7 Causes to reproduce
11 What certain bandits have one of
12 Chocolate chip or oatmeal, for example
13 Naval jail
15 European trade org.
16 Kind of snake
17 Before: Poetic
20 Cow's alternative to gum
22 Term of endearment, for short
23 Deface
24 Existed
25 Time zone: Abbrev.
26 Roof of the mouth
28 Weekend day: Abbrev.
29 Planted
32 Rear of a ship
35 Evil
36 "Adam's _____"

38 Board pieces
39 Wrestler's pad
40 Kind of resort
41 Sandwich favorite: Abbrev.
42 Hawaiian specialty
44 Plea: _____ contendere
46 Settle for the night
50 Bear's cave
51 Cotton menace
52 Arid
53 Britain's Isle of _____

Down

1 TV network
2 To and _____
3 Zodiac sign
4 No-no's
5 Wandering
6 Friend: French
8 Managed by adding to: _____ out
9 Expire
10 Not sweet (said of wine)
14 Precious stone
16 Brake horsepower: Abbrev.
18 Kind of popular music
19 Effaced

20 Feline
21 Employ
24 Irrigates plants
27 Lad
29 Gov't. agency serving small businesses: Abbrev.
30 Sup
31 Low place in road
32 Writer Eric
33 Serious crime
34 Explosive
37 Prohibit
39 Rodents
42 Church seat
43 Undivided
45 Eccentric
47 Hail: Latin
48 1/1,000th of an inch
49 A single thickness or layer of something

1 across starts in the 9th square from the left.

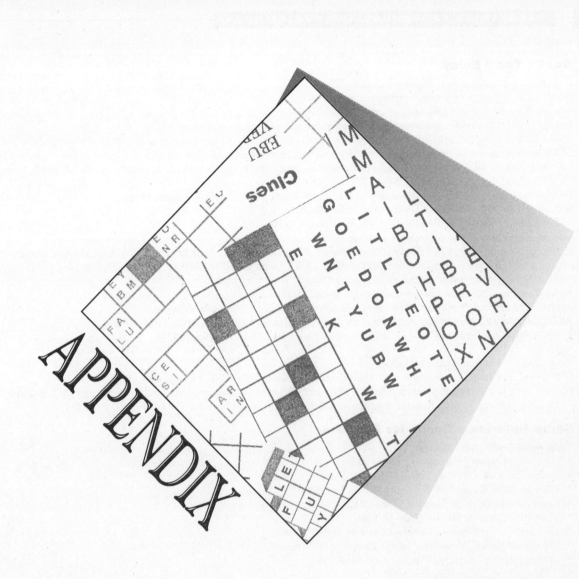

APPENDIX

Books You'll Enjoy

J. G. Barton, *Ultimate Word Challenges* (Cardoza, 1994).

John Ciardi, *A Browser's Dictionary* (Harper & Row, 1980).

———, *A Second Browser's Dictionary* (Harper & Row, 1983).

David Crystal, *The Cambridge Encyclopedia of Language* (Cambridge University Press, 1987).

Ross Eckler, *Making the Alphabet Dance* (St. Martin's Press, 1996). This is heavy going here and there—the author has a Ph.D. in mathematics from Princeton—but it's a fascinating collection of curiosities.

———, ed., *Word Ways*. A quarterly magazine devoted to wordplay. The subscription price is $20, and the address is Spring Valley Road, Morristown, NJ 07960.

Sterling Eisiminger, *Wordspinner: Mind-Boggling Games for Word Lovers* (Littlefield Adams, 1991).

Willard R. Espy, *The Almanac of Words at Play* (Clarkson Potter, 1975).

———, *Another Almanac of Words at Play* (Clarkson Potter, 1980).

———, *The Game of Words* (Grossett & Dunlap, 1972).

Helene Hovanec, *Creative Cruciverbalists: Those Curious Crossword Creators and Their Best Puzzles* (William Morrow, 1988). Thirty-one puzzling people are the subjects of this book filled with thumbnail sketches, anecdotes, and puzzles.

———, *The Puzzler's Paradise* (Paddington Press, 1978).

Richard Lederer, *Adventures of a Verbivore* (Pocket Books, 1994).

Eugene T. Maleska, *A Pleasure in Words* (Simon & Schuster, 1981). A word-lover's delight.

Tom McArthur, ed., *The Oxford Companion to the English Language* (Oxford University Press, 1992).

Roger Millington, *Crossword Puzzles: Their History and Their Cult* (Thomas Nelson, 1974).

Mel Rosen and Stan Kurzban, *Random House Puzzle Maker's Handbook* (Times Books, 1981). The best source for practical advice on constructing and freelancing.

Will Shortz, *The Puzzlemaster Presents 200 Mind-Bending Challenges from NPR* (Times Books, 1996).

William Steig, *CDC?* (Farrar, Straus & Giroux, 1984). A collection of cartoons by a long-time contributor to *The New Yorker*. One, for example, shows a ballerina complaining about the condition of her tutu. The caption: "D 2-2 S C-D."

Some Reference Books for Puzzlers

- *Anagram Finder* (John Daintith)
- *The A to Z Crossword Puzzle Solver* (Brian Padol)
- *Brewer's Dictionary of Phrase & Fable* (Ivor H. Evans)
- *The Cambridge Biographical Dictionary* (David Crystal)
- *Cassell Cluefinder: A Dictionary of Crossword Clues* (J. A. Coleman).
- *The Cassell Crossword Finisher* (John Griffiths)
- *The Complete Word-Finder Crossword Dictionary* (Bruce Wetterau)
- *The Concise Oxford Dictionary of English Etymology* (T. F. Hoad)
- *Crossword Puzzle Dictionary* (Andrew Swanfeldt)
- *A Dictionary of Clichés* (Eric Partridge)
- *Dictionary of Gods and Goddesses, Devils and Demons* (Manfred Lurker)
- *The Merriam-Webster Pocket Dictionary of Proper Names* (Geoffrey Payton, ed.)
- *Movie and Video Guide* (Leonard Maltin)
- *The Multicultural Dictionary of Proverbs: Over 20,000 Adages from More Than 120 Languages, Nationalities and Ethnic Groups* (Harold V. Cordry)
- *A New Dictionary of Music* (Arthur Jacobs)
- *The Oxford Dictionary of Quotations*
- *A Pocket History of the United States* (Allan Nevins and Henry Steele Commager)
- *Portmanteau Dictionary: Blend Words in the English Language, Including Trademarks and Brand Names* (Dick Thurner)
- *Webster's New International Dictionary*, Second Ed. (William A. Neilson *et al.*)
- *Webster's New World Crossword Puzzle Dictionary* (Jane Shaw Whitfield)
- *Webster's New World Pocket Biographical Dictionary* (Donald Stewart and Laura Borovac, eds.)
- *Webster's New World Pocket Geographical Dictionary* (Donald Stewart and Laura Borovac, eds.)
- *The Wordsworth Dictionary of Eponyms* (Martin H. Manser)
- *The World Almanac and Book of Facts* (Robert Famighetti, ed.)
- *Webster's New World Companion to English and American Literature* (Arthur Pollard, gen. ed.)

ANSWERS

Preface

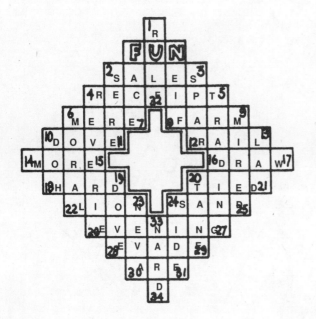

Acrostics

1

AUTHOR: (Bob) Uecker

TITLE: Catcher in the Wry

QUOTATION: People asked me what was the best way to catch a knuckle ball. I told them that what worked for me was to wait for the ball to stop rolling, then just pick it up.

A. Umps
B. Ethel
C. Cajoled
D. Kowtow
E. Emphasis
F. Roth
G. Cakewalk
H. Appetite
I. Tattled
J. Cuffs
K. Hawk
L. Estop
M. Rowboat
N. Inkwell
O. Nothing
P. Tarts
Q. Habit
R. Embattled
S. Watch
T. Roll
U. Youth

2

AUTHOR: S(tephen) King

TITLE: Skeleton Crew

QUOTATION: A short story is like a quick kiss in the dark from a stranger. That is not the same thing as an affair or a marriage, but kisses can be sweet, and their very brevity forms their own attraction.

A. Softest
B. Kentucky Derby
C. Inherit the Wind
D. Natasha
E. Grass skirt
F. Savoir-faire
G. Kashmir
H. Embarrass
I. Lion tamer
J. Earthquake
K. Tacit
L. Observation
M. North Star
N. Creationism
O. Rotate
P. Effigy
Q. Washing

Acrostics

AUTHOR: John Crosbie

TITLE: Dictionary (of Puns)

QUOTATION: When Sam Goldwyn was at his height as a motion-picture producer, it is said that he rejected the script for a movie called "The Optimist" because he didn't think that a story about an eye doctor would sell.

A. Jots
B. Othello
C. Hawaii
D. Nestled
E. Cow town
F. Rapped
G. Omitted
H. Shatters
I. Backlash
J. I Love You to Death
K. Elicits
L. Sorghum
M. Depth charge
N. Initiated
O. Chided
P. Tempestuous
Q. Iberian
R. Onward
S. Nastiest
T. After
U. Rhythm
V. Yucca

AUTHOR: C(edric) Belfrage

TITLE: Away from It All

QUOTATION: [Tangier] was the nearest thing to the Glamorous East I had seen outside of the Fox Westwood Hills lot. You wonder whether in such a case the movies were any longer borrowing from life, or it was life now that took its cue from Hollywood.

A. Cowered
B. Boohoo
C. Emory
D. Loft
E. Foghorns
F. Reviewed
G. Achilles
H. Gone with the Wind
I. Emotions
J. Assortment
K. White wines
L. Anguishes
M. Yellow
N. Foxholes
O. Roosts
P. On the Waterfront
Q. Mariah Carey
R. It Takes Two
S. Thoroughfares
T. Awful
U. Latitude
V. Longitude

AUTHOR: Martin M. Goldwyn

TITLE: (How a Fly Walks) Upside Down

QUOTATION: The flapping wings of the hummingbird are so rapid that...only a misty outline can be seen....Its wings flap forty to fifty times each second, and it has been estimated that its speed in flight reaches about seven hundred miles per hour.

A. Memorable
B. Avalanche
C. Rapport
D. Thereby
E. Iterated
F. Necessary
G. Metaphors
H. Go-ahead
I. Outhit
J. Lashings
K. Definite
L. Whipping
M. Youngsters
N. Night table
O. Unfasten
P. Pent
Q. Shimmed
R. Institutes
S. Deftly
T. Efficient
U. Demands
V. Officious
W. Withholds
X. Nibs

AUTHOR: (Carolyn) Wells

TITLE: (A) Nonsense Anthology

QUOTATION: The sense of nonsense will enable us not only to discern pure nonsense, but to consider intelligently nonsense of various degrees of purity. Absence of sense is not necessarily nonsense, any more than absence of justice is injustice.

A. Winnebago
B. Enunciation
C. Lennon
D. Leafiness
E. Sayers
F. Nonentity
G. Opportune
H. Necessities
I. Suddenness
J. Efficiency
K. Nelson
L. Seventies
M. Ebullient
N. Adjourns
O. Nocturnes
P. Troubles
Q. Horse Feathers
R. Objections
S. Looseness
T. Olfactory
U. Gneiss
V. Yes-men

Acrostics

7

AUTHOR: S(arah) Ballard

TITLE: Golf in America

QUOTATION: American women golfers were...hampered by...fashions. Wide-brimmed straw hats, starched leg-of-mutton sleeves, corseted waistlines, and...ankle-length skirts...were enchanting subjects for the illustrators...but...infuriating to their victims.

A. Swatters
B. Buckwheat
C. Arrows
D. Lubricants
E. Lowish
F. Attends
G. Reassessing
H. Demented
I. Grandmother
J. Outfielders
K. Lightweight
L. Favorites
M. Injunctive
N. Nightly
O. Ammunition
P. Mews
Q. Establishment
R. Ricochets
S. Interferes
T. Coffee breaks
U. Arnold Palmer

8

AUTHOR: (Dave) Bryant

TITLE: Reader's Digest

QUOTATION: A woman borrowed a video of "The King and I" from the library. The next day she returned it, huffily slammed it down, and exclaimed, "There's nothing about Elvis in here!"

A. Behind
B. Rush
C. Yield
D. Andromeda
E. Nibble
F. Thief
G. Rewind
H. Extortion
I. Avoid
J. Damn
K. Everywhere
L. Retain
M. South Dakota
N. Do the
O. Income tax
P. Guffaw
Q. Elmer Gantry
R. Shellfish
S. Timon

9

AUTHOR: Woody Allen

TITLE: The UFO Menace

QUOTATION: To us a century seems quite long, particularly if you are holding an IOU, but by astronomical standards it is over in a second. For that reason, it is always best to carry a toothbrush and be ready to leave on a moment's notice.

A. Warranty
B. Ornate
C. Oasis
D. Day of Atonement
E. Youngsters
F. Active
G. Loquacious
H. Lumbago
I. Ethelred the Unready
J. Nasal
K. Toady
L. Honorably
M. Eras
N. Unbuttons
O. Fobbed
P. Optimistic
Q. Mortars
R. Early
S. Noised
T. Altruistic
U. Christians
V. Evocation

10

AUTHOR: (Judy Jones and William) Wilson

TITLE: (An) Incomplete Education

QUOTATION: The French have them, the Germans have them, even the Russians have them...why shouldn't we? Admittedly, in a country that defines "scholarship" as free tuition for quarterbacks, intellectuals tend to be a marginal lot.

A. Wombat
B. Inky
C. Lufthansa
D. Shill
E. Owners
F. Number
G. Infirm
H. Niggardly
I. Chatters
J. Other
K. Mather
L. Pharaoh
M. Lithe
N. Enervate
O. Thatched
P. Evacuates
Q. Equivocated
R. Deems
S. Unhealthful
T. Chevy
U. Anthem
V. Taft
W. Insisted
X. Otters
Y. Nonetheless

Acrostics

AUTHOR: S(cott) Rice

TITLE: (Dark and Stormy:) The Final Conflict

QUOTATION: Neutral sources are over-rated. They usually lack the emotional involvement to be interesting. You will get much more colorful data, the kind that sells books, from partisans, those with an ox to grind or whose ax has been gored.

A. Shake, Rattle and Roll
B. Revolution
C. Inge
D. Camus
E. Exposure
F. Toolboxes
G. Hot Shots
H. Egged on
I. Freshest
J. Isthmuses
K. No-hitter
L. Authority
M. Lawyers
N. Contaminate
O. Omaha
P. Null and void
Q. Foreknowledge
R. Lowball
S. Invertebrate
T. Chromatic
U. Turkey

AUTHOR: E.M. Forster

TITLE: Howard's End

QUOTATION: Take my word for it, that smile was simply stunning, and it is only you and I who will be fastidious, and complain that true joy begins in the eyes, and that the eyes of Jacky did not accord with her smile, but were anxious and hungry.

A. Exhausted
B. Memories of Midnight
C. Fisk
D. Outwitting
E. Rubaiyat
F. Sidney Sheldon
G. Three Men and a Baby
H. Eric Clapton
I. Raisins
J. Howdy
K. Out of harm's way
L. Willy-nilly
M. Attitudes
N. Rejoicing
O. Dynasty
P. Saudi
Q. Elephant jokes
R. Nuthatch
S. Downtown

AUTHOR: Gloria Buckner

TITLE: Vile Puns

QUOTATION: Due to your excessive consumption of egg and lemon sauces, Mr. Pigout, we must pull all your teeth and replace them with a chrome plate, but you'll soon find there's no plate like chrome for the hollandaise.

A. Galleys
B. Little
C. Off the Wall
D. Rommel
E. Impetuous
F. Autographed
G. Box lunch
H. Unhurried
I. Couch potato
J. Knights of Malta
K. Nuance
L. Elysium
M. Rehearse
N. Vowel
O. I met a
P. Leprosy
Q. Edict
R. Phoneme
S. Unscorned
T. Needle
U. Stoops to

AUTHOR: Richard Lederer

TITLE: (The Miracle of) Language

QUOTATION: Sunday supplement jeremiads tell us of the decline of language....But whatever you may be hearing about the closing of the American mind, there has never been a more passionate moment in the history of the American love affair with language.

A. Rhone
B. In a jiffy
C. Cash
D. Helen Hayes
E. About Last Night
F. Remove
G. Deep Space Nine
H. Laugh-In
I. Eleanor Rigby
J. Detente
K. Emulation
L. Run the gamut
M. Empire of the Sun
N. Ruth
O. Left off
P. Abrasive
Q. Nadia Comaneci
R. Gamma rays
S. Utmost
T. Above the Law
U. Gordie Howe
V. Elements

Acrostics

15

AUTHOR: T(homas) E(dward) Lawrence

TITLE: Seven Pillars (of Wisdom)

QUOTATION: All men dream but not equally. Those who dream by night in the dusty recesses of their minds wake in the day to find that it was vanity. But the dreamers of the day are dangerous men for they may act their dream with open eyes to make it possible.

A. Thwarted
B. Employed
C. Loathsome
D. Affray
E. W.B. Yeats
F. Rubbery
G. Edith Head
H. Nostradamus
I. Chastity
J. Equanimity
K. Sweet tooth

L. Embody
M. Venerate
N. Earth Day
O. Notwithstanding
P. Pumice stone
Q. Immensely
R. Leif Erikson
S. Laminated
T. Afterthought
U. Renders
V. Sheikh

Connectors

1

O	B	T	U	S	E	A	W	O	R	T	H	Y	M	E	A	N	D	E	R
E	L	I	C	T	A	N	G	E	N	T	I	L	E	T	H	A	R	G	Y
R	A	T	E	L	I	E	R	A	D	I	C	A	T	E	C	H	I	S	M
U	G	G	L	E	A	N	A	L	O	G	U	E	R	R	I	L	L	A	M
A	N	U	E	N	S	I	S	T	H	M	U	S	E	D	A	T	E	D	I
O	D	S	U	R	E	R	R	A	N	T	I	P	A	T	H	Y	M	E	N
E	A	L	F	R	E	S	C	O	U	R	G	E	L	I	D	E	O	L	O
G	U	E	R	N	S	E	Y	E	S	H	I	V	A	P	I	D	I	T	Y

Connectors

```
E X O D U S U F R U C T I F Y A W L U C
I D E C R Y P T I C L A N D E S T I N E
O P H Y T E N A B L E I T M O T I F A C
T I T I O U S U R P O L Y G L O T I O S
E R A P H I C O N O C L A S T R A L O O
F F I C I O U S U P E R C I L I O U S U
F F I C E D E R U C T R I F L E N I E N
T U M I D I O M A T I C A R A F E R A L
```

```
C O R R U G A T E D U C E N T R I P E T
A L I S M A N N U L I A I S O N O R O U
S T R I D E N T A I L L I C I T A D E L
U D E M E A N T I P O D A L I R R U P T
A B L E A U T O N O M Y R M I D O N J O
N U S C I N T I L L A G E N I A L A C U
N A R C I S S I S M U T C H I C A N E R
Y A R M U L K E N D E M I C A N V A S S
```

```
C O N T R I T E R S E R R I E D I F I C
E L E R I T Y C O O N T O L O G Y N A R
C H Y P O T H E S I S Y P H U S T I N G
S U M M A R Y E A R N I B L I C K I B B
U T Z E P H Y R I S I B L E N C H A F F
L A T T E R I S T I C O N D E R O G A T
E N E B R O U S I N G U L A R U B R I C
K E T Y M P A N I C H O L A S P H A L T
```

```
M E T E O R I E L I G I B L E V I T Y A
C H T R O G L O D Y T E M P O R A L T R
U I S M O R O S E N T E N T I O U S E A
S O N A B L E S S E D U L O U S E C L U
D E X P L I C A T E X P E D I T E X P I
A T I O N O V I C E N T A U R U S U F F
E R O S T E R T I A R Y A N G E S T A P
O S T A T E L Y C E U M B R A N D I S H
```

Connectors

6

```
P R O D I G I O U S P O R A D I C O N S
T R U E L I C I T E R A T E M E R I T Y
O K E Q U I V O C A L L O W A T E R S H
E D O N I S M U L T I F A R I O U S A L
I E N T O U R A G E N D A I S Y N O P S
I S H I B B O L E T H O R O U G H G O I
N G R A T U I T O U S U S C E P T I B L
E O N I N E B U L O U S O C I O P A T H
```

7

```
P A T H E T I C U S P E C I O U S O P O
R I F I C E R B E R U S E Q U A C I O U
S T R I C T U R E E N E R V A T E N A C
I O U S T I G M A L A D R O I T A N T A
M O U N T E B A N K E Y S T O N E X U S
U R F E I T H E R M E T I C O N E R O U
S A N G U I N E O L O G I S M A R T L E
S S O M N A M B U L A T E N T O R P I D
```

8

```
V I N D I C A T E G O R I C A L A B A S
H R A M O I E T Y M O L O G Y N E P H O
B I A S P E C U L A T E R M I N U S C U
L E G A T E N T A T I V E R A C I O U S
L A K E S C R I T O I R E S U R G E N U
F L E C T I R A D E V O I D I C H O T O
M Y T H O M A N I A U G U R Y E X T E N
U A T E P I D R O O L A M E N T A R R Y
```

9

```
A P P R O B A T I O N G O I N G L O R I
O U S T U L T I F Y A M A L G A M B I T
I N E R A R Y A S H M A K I N D L E A V
E N E E R R A T I C O N T R A V E N E R
A T E E M P A T H Y S T E R I A U S P I
C I O U S U P E R F L U O U S U R C E A
S E C L U S I V E N I A L I E N J O I N
V E T E R A T E M P O R I Z E F F A C E
```

Connectors

```
P R U R I E N T A N G I B L E X C U L P
A T E X I G E N T H E O C E N T R I C U
L P A B L E N M E S H Y P E R B O L E V
I N C E N O T A P H O E B U S I N E C U
R E T R O S P E C T R A N S C E N D E N
T A L M U D I S P A R A T E X T R A P O
L A T E R G I V E R S A T I O N T O L O
G I C A L L O U S E D U C E L I B A T E
```

```
E L L I P S I S U B J A C E N T E N A R
I A N I H I L I S M U G L O W E R I S T
I C K L E P T O M A N I A Q U I L I N E
R A S M U S T E R P S I C H O R E A N N
E A L T E R N A T E P I C E N T E R M A
G A N T I G O N E R I L L I Q U E S C E
N T R E S O L I D U S K I T T I S H E A
F U L C R U M U T A T I O N A S C E N T
```

```
N O X I O U S P O R T I V E X A T I O U
S P U R I O U S T O L I D E L E G A T E
Q U I T A B L E G R E S S A C R A L I E
N A T E N O R A T O R I O B D U R A T E
M A N A T E N D U E X P O U N D O M I N
E E R E D O L E N T R A C T A B L E M U
L A T E R A L B E I T O M E A N D E R E
I F Y I D D I S H A M I E N C O M I U M
```

```
H A C K N E Y E D I V E R S I O N O N D
E S C R I P T I T U L A R D U O U S C U
R R I L O U S E M B L A N C E L O T R A
V E R S E Q U E N T I A L L O C A T E M
B L O R G N E T T E S S E L L A T E D I
S C O M F I T A C T I L E T H A L C Y O
N U L L A C O N I C A E S U R A N U S U
R R O G A T E D I C T A C I T E M P E R
```

Connectors

14

```
A D E P T H E S I S P A R T A N T A L I
Z E N I T H W A R T R I P T Y C H R O N
I C O E V A L I D A T E T R A D I X E N
O P H O B I A S P E R S E R P E N T I N
E X O R A B L E X I G U O U S U B L I M
I N A L L U D E V O L V E R T I G I N O
U S T I P U L A T E N U R E T A I N V O
K E P I T H E T R A N S F U S E C E D E
```

15

```
S E R E P E L U C I D E M O T I C O R P
O R A L L E V I A T E F F L U E N T O R
T U O U S A C R I L E G E R M A N E N C
I P H E R G O U R M A N D A T E X C U R
S I V E X E C R A T E X T R O V E R T R
A V A I L I T I G A T E N U N C I A T E
L U C I D A T E N T H R A L L U G U B R
I O U S A R D O N I C L E M E N T I T Y
```

Directional Puzzles

1

```
    L S E   D A R G I
F A   E M E       T
T   I T   T I C E N
E R M   E N   I
    I L M   E L
T E R   E S I   I C I
N     I D   S A C
I O   S   R T L E M
  P P A P A   T A   A
  A     I M E   A R
Q U E I L   D A C
```

2

```
O S S   B L E   E N T
R A   A M E   R
C A L A C I M A R S Y
  B P     V T
S A L L A S H I E N A
H P H O L D
A M S A L A V E D U N
  E N     R T
E D E C E L A T S O R
I R N B U T
F I T T U O O R U
```

Directional Puzzles

Puzzle 3

```
S   D E C   A C H C
T N E   E S E   R A
A   D P R   L E D   V
M P E   D A B   A R E
    P E N   A G     D
D N E         I V E
E     D E   D E L
N C E   M U R   I V E
U   N S O   O I S   R
D E   R E N   O P P
  T A S E   U T R   O
```

Puzzle 4

```
R S H C U   M M O C E
A   E   O   I G   T
M O R E T   N G I T A
  O   G   E   L   T
S T R A N G D E R E P
  E   Y   O   O   E R
C U L A M E L G V E I
  C   R   N   G   R
E R Q O S T R A I T O
V N   U   A   T   R
E L E R O C N M U L A
```

Puzzle 5

```
A C I L E D A L E K C
N   N   P   M   R   I
G I S I T U A T T T H
  P   D     E   O
D I N E M R E G A L S
O   A   A   L   C   N
R M C E N A M E K R O
  A   U       N   K
I R I V E R A I L E R
D   L   C   N   E   N
A N E V O U T U R L E
```

Puzzle 6

```
D U R G E B A C C U S
G   E   R   T   H   T
E S T Y A T E N A M O
N   A   B   G   N   N
M A T E D A E L A G E
P   E   E   R   M   V
E R R A N T H T B E N
N   A   I   E   B   T
T A M A T S I V E G O
O   E   A   R   N   P
R Y N O G G E L A C I
```

Double Trouble

Puzzle 1

```
E V I C T
P R O U D
O V E R T
C U P I D
```

Puzzle 2

```
T O P I C
B R A V E
P I V O T
B R A C E
```

Puzzle 3

```
P R O B E
M U S T Y
B U M P Y
S T O R E
```

Double Trouble

B	I	G	O	T
S	P	U	R	N
B	O	G	U	S
P	R	I	N	T

F	E	L	O	N
S	T	A	M	P
O	F	T	E	N
P	S	A	L	M

G	U	I	L	E
S	M	A	R	T
M	A	G	U	S
L	I	T	E	R

B	R	O	A	D
I	S	L	E	T
S	T	O	L	E
B	R	A	I	D

A	L	O	N	E
B	U	R	S	T
B	L	A	R	E
S	N	O	U	T

G	U	A	R	D
P	L	I	E	S
G	R	U	E	L
S	A	P	I	D

L	A	P	S	E
C	U	R	I	O
P	I	O	U	S
C	L	E	A	R

C	R	U	D	E
B	L	A	S	T
S	C	A	L	D
B	R	U	T	E

P	L	A	C	E
S	H	I	R	T
C	R	I	S	P
L	A	T	H	E

Dropouts

1

W	E		K	N	O	W		A	C	C	U	R	A	T	E	L	Y
O	N	L	Y		W	H	E	N		W	E		K	N	O	W	
L	I	T	T	L	E		W	I	T	H		K	N	O	W	L	E	D
G	E		D	O	U	B	T		I	N	C	R	E	A	S	E	S	

GOETHE

2

T	O		S	P	E	A	K		A	N	D		T	O		S	P	E	A
K		W	E	L	L		A	R	E		T	W	O		T	H	I	N	G
S		A		F	O	O	L		M	A	Y		T	A	L	K		B	U
T		A		W	I	S	E		M	A	N		S	P	E	A	K	S	

BEN JONSON

Dropouts

THE LIE INDIRECT
IS OFTEN AS BAD AN
D ALWAYS MEANER AN
D MORE COWARDLY TH
AN THE LIE DIRECT

ANON.

IT IS NOT THE CRY
OF THE WILD DUCK
BUT ITS FLIGHT THA
T LEADS THE FLOCK
TO FLY AND FOLLOW

CHINESE PROVERB

THERE IS IN HUMAN
NATURE GENERALLY
MORE OF THE FOOL
THAN OF THE WISE

BACON

YOUTH IS A MALA
DY OF WHICH ONE
BECOMES CURED A
LITTLE EVERY DAY

MUSSOLINI

NONE ARE MORE HOPEL
ESSLY ENSLAVED THAN
THOSE WHO FALSELY BE
LIEVE THEY ARE FREE

GOETHE

IF THERE ARE OBSTACL
ES THE SHORTEST LINE
BETWEEN TWO POINTS MA
Y BE THE CROOKED ONE

BRECHT

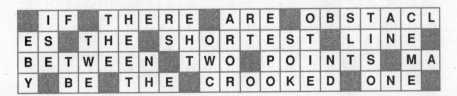

Dropouts

9

	H	E		W	H	O		L	O	V	E	S		W	I	T	H		P	U	R
I	T	Y		C	O	N	S	I	D	E	R	S		N	O	T		T	H	E	
G	I	F	T		O	F		T	H	E		L	O	V	E	R		B	U	T	
T	H	E		L	O	V	E		O	F		T	H	E		G	I	V	E	R	

ANON.

10

Y	O	U		A	R	E		N	O	T		V	E	R	Y		G	O	O	D
	I	F		Y	O	U		A	R	E		N	O	T		B	E	T	T	E
R		T	H	A	N		Y	O	U	R		B	E	S	T		F	R	I	E
N	D	S		I	M	A	G	I	N	E		Y	O	U		T	O		B	E

LAVATER

11

	H	A	D		W	E		N	O	T		F	A	U	L	T	S		O	F
O	U	R		O	W	N		W	E		S	H	O	U	L	D		T	A	K
E		L	E	S	S		P	L	E	A	S	U	R	E		I	N		C	O
M	P	L	A	I	N	I	N	G		O	F		O	T	H	E	R	S		

FÉNELON

12

T	H	E		H	A	P	P	I	E	S	T		L	I	F	E		I	S	
T	H	A	T		W	H	I	C	H		C	O	N	S	T	A	N	T	L	Y
	E	X	E	R	C	I	S	E	S		A	N	D		E	D	U	C	A	T
E	S		W	H	A	T		I	S		B	E	S	T		I	N		U	S

HAMERTON

13

	T	H	E		S	A	F	E	S	T		W	A	Y		T	O		D	O	U
B	L	E		Y	O	U	R		M	O	N	E	Y		I	S		T	O		F
O	L	D		I	T		O	V	E	R		O	N	C	E		A	N	D		P
U	T		I	T		I	N		Y	O	U	R		P	O	C	K	E	T	

ANON.

14

	W	H	A	T		I	S		D	E	F	E	A	T		N	O	T	H	I
N	G		B	U	T		E	D	U	C	A	T	I	O	N		N	O	T	H
I	N	G		B	U	T		T	H	E		F	I	R	S	T		S	T	E
P		T	O		S	O	M	E	T	H	I	N	G		B	E	T	T	E	R

WENDELL PHILLIPS

Dropouts

T	H	O	U	G	H	T		M	U	S	T		B	E		D	I	V	I	D
E	D		A	G	A	I	N	S	T		I	T	S	E	L	F		B	E	F
O	R	E		I	T		C	A	N		C	O	M	E		T	O		A	N
Y		K	N	O	W	L	E	D	G	E		O	F		I	T	S	E	L	F

ALDOUS HUXLEY

	T	O		T	R	A	V	E	L		H	O	P	E	F	U	L	L	Y		I
S		A		B	E	T	T	E	R		T	H	I	N	G		T	H	A	N	
T	O		A	R	R	I	V	E		A	N	D		T	H	E		T	R	U	E
	S	U	C	C	E	S	S		I	S		T	O		L	A	B	O	R		

ROBERT LOUIS STEVENSON

Fill-ins

Fill-ins

3

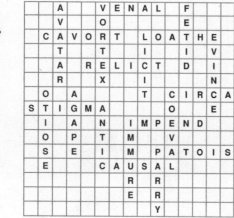

```
  A     V E N A L   F
  V     O         E
C A V O R T   L O A T H E
  T     T   I     I   V
  A   R E L I C T   D   I
  R     X   I         N
O   A       T   C I R C A
S T I G M A       O   E
I   A N   I M P E N D
O   P T   M   V
S E   I M   P A T O I S
E     C A U S A L
        R   R
        E   R
        Y
```

4

```
      A
D E A R T H       D
    C   I     A V I A N
  F A C A D E     C     O
    N   T   S   A T T E S T
    E   U   C     U   T   O
        S C H I S M   I   R
  M       E         C   P
  A       W       A     I
A X I O M       I M P E N D
I       I   D       A
M   P A T H O S     T
    S     G       H
    M   A M I T Y
M A N I A     A
```

5

```
  E X H O R T     R
  V         A E G I S
  O   D E I G N   P   A
  L   E         O   P
D I V E R T   L A P S E   I
E   E   I   U   E     D
M   E V I N C E       R
E   E   E   E A     E
A     P E N U R Y   B
N   A   E T   G   U
  R E V E R T   P O S I T
  E   A   U       T
  I   T   S
E F F A C E
  Y   R
```

6

```
          C
      B A N A L
  B       V   S
R E L I C T   M I L I E U
  M       L   B     V
Q U O R U M     M Y R I A D
  S     O     L     P
  E   G U I L E   O   I
    G   E   N   S A P I D
    A   A T O N E   P
H O M I L Y   U   E   U
E   B   L   I M P U G N
N   I   U     O   N
C   T E D I U M   C
E     E       H
```

7

```
    C I R C A
        N     G
L I C I T   V I A B L E
O       M     O
A   D I C T U M   W
T   E     S E C E D E
H U B R I S   N   R
    I   O   T   D
  A D V E R T   O   E
  V   E   D   R E M A N D
  A     I     R   I
S T O L I D     S T A V E
  A           H   E
  R U B R I C       S
        E V E R T
```

8

```
        U M L A U T
              E
    A   E     U M B R A
    B   F   H   S     S
B E R E F T   I   U   E
    U   E   M A T R I X
I M P U T E   T   P
M   T   E N D U E   O
P   Z   N   S   B
U   N E X U S   D O Y E N
G   N   I   E   S
N A D I R   E F F A C E
    T       E
    H E C T O R
```

Fill-ins

Puzzle 9:

```
    S  E                       V
 A  D  H  E  R  E              E
 R  E  U                    E  N
 R  A  C                 A  M  B  I  T
 A  F  T  S                 E  A
 N     D     T     V  E  N  A  L
 T  O  K  E  N     E        D
       C     C  A  V  O  R  T        D
    M  Y  R  I  A  D        T        I
    E     Y     N     S  E           C
    L        V  O  R  T  E  X     W  T
 D  E  M  E  A  N     I           A  U
    E     P     G           A  X  I  O  M
          I     M                 V
 S  A  P  I  D        A  D  D  U  C  E
```

Puzzle 10:

```
 O  E  U  V  R  E     B  A  T  H  O  S
             T        E              L
    A     S  P  H  E  R  E     D  R  O  S  S
    B     P     O     A           R     T
 P  A  T  H  O  S     T           O     H
    S     I        E  V  E  N  T        A
    E  N  N  U  I              E  R  A  S  E
          X     N     T           I     S
          I     I  N  D  U  C  E  T     A
          N        A     M        E     Y
          E     A  T  T  I  R  E
 P  R  O  S  E        D     P
    T     T              L  O  C  U  S
          R  I  G  O  R     C
          R                 H
```

Four Corners

Puzzle 1:

```
L A V A L A M P
O W E N A G I O
N O T E B E E R
G L O W S E N T
S L O W H A S H
H A R E O L E O
O V A L S T A N
T E L L T A L E
```

Puzzle 2:

```
G L E E C L U B
A E R Y R O S A
M A I A A G E S
E K E S M E R E
S C A B S T U B
H O B O L A R A
O D E S O R A L
W A L K T A L L
```

Four Corners

3

H	A	R	D	H	E	A	D
E	L	I	A	A	L	L	O
A	T	O	M	F	L	E	W
D	O	T	E	T	E	E	N
R	A	M	P	M	E	S	H
E	S	A	U	O	L	E	O
S	I	L	L	S	I	A	M
T	A	L	L	T	A	L	E

4

L	A	M	E	D	U	C	K
I	B	E	X	A	L	A	N
M	E	T	E	D	A	N	E
A	L	A	S	A	N	T	E
B	U	F	F	H	E	L	D
E	R	L	E	E	D	I	E
A	G	E	S	R	I	M	E
N	E	X	T	S	T	O	P

Groupies

1

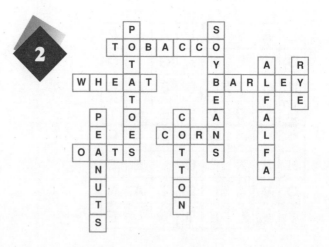

2

Groupies

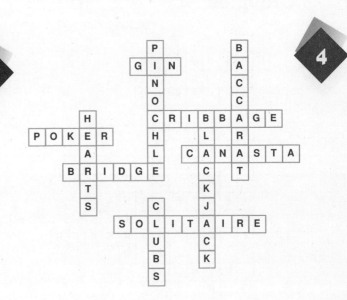

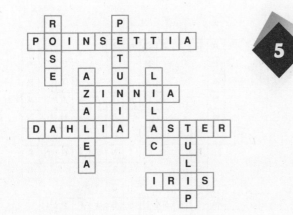

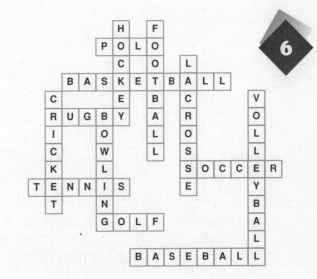

Groupies

7

```
      P
  C A S H M E R E
  R     U
S H A R K S K I N
  M     L
  A   S I L K
S A T E E N
  T   E     F
  A   R     L   C
    A S T R A K H A N
  D   U     N   I
F L E E C E   N A N K E E N
  N   K     E   O
  L I N E N   L
  M   R
```

8

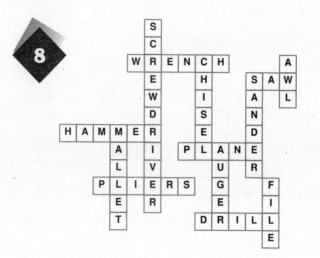

```
        S
        C
    W R E N C H         A
        W     H     S A W
        D     I     A   L
H A M M E R   S     N
        A     E P L A N E R
        L       U     R
    P L I E R S  G     F
        E        E     I
        T     D R I L L
                      E
```

9

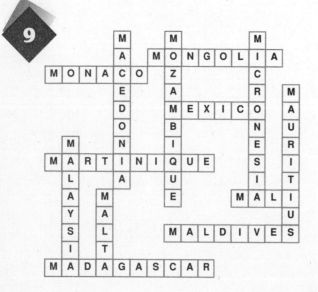

```
        M       M           M
            M O N G O L I A
M O N A C O   Z           C
          E   A           R
          D   M E X I C O  O
      M   O   B           N   M
M A R T I N I Q U E        E   A
      L   N   A           S   U
      A       U           I   R
      Y   M   E           I   I
      S   A         M A L I   T
      I   L                   I
        M A L D I V E S
M A D A G A S C A R
```

10

```
A R I Z O N A               A
L         H         U T     R
A         I               K
S     M O N T A N A H     A
K         E       H       N
H A W A I I               S
  A         I N D I A N A  S
  S         E
  H         S
M I S S I S S I P P I
  N         E         D
  G     I   N E V A D A
  T     O             H
  O     W   O R E G O N
K A N S A S
```

Groupies

11

Across/Down answers:
- RAMADAN
- HANUKAH
- TET
- EASTER
- CHRISTMAS
- LENT
- PASSOVER
- ADVENT

12

- MOSCOW
- SOFIA
- MANILA
- VIENNA
- SHANGHAI
- HANOI
- NAIROBI
- WASHINGTON
- OSLO
- LIMA
- LAHORE
- SEOUL
- MELBOURNE
- NAPLES
- ROME
- KABUL

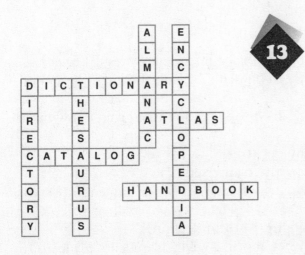

13

- DICTIONARY
- ALMANAC
- ENCYCLOPEDIA
- ATLAS
- THESAURUS
- CATALOG
- DIRECTORY
- HANDBOOK

Hidden Meanings

1. **peruse** To read (4) or examine (7), esp. with great (5) care (4).
2. **obfuscate** To make (4) obscure (7); to confuse (7).
3. **peremptory** Imperious (9); dictatorial (11); expressed (9) so decisively (10) and conclusively (12) as to admit (5) of no further (7) delay (5), discussion (10), or contradiction (13).
4. **nominal** In name (4) only (4); so small (5) as to be unimportant (11) or insignificant (13).
5. **propinquity** Nearness (8) in time (4) or place (5); closeness (9) of relationship (12); kinship (7).
6. **recidivism** Habitual (8) or chronic (7) relapse (7) into a former (6) pattern (7) of behavior (8), esp. criminal (8).
7. **extrapolate** To infer (5) or estimate (8) by projecting (10) known (5) facts (5) or figures (7).
8. **misprision** Misconduct (10) in public (6) office (6); failure (7) to prevent (7) or report (6) a crime (5).
9. **sciamachy** A fighting (8) with shadows (7) or imaginary (9) enemies (7). Shadowboxing?
10. **umbrage** Offense (7) or resentment (10).

1. **efficacious** Being capable (7) of producing (9) the intended (8) result (6).
2. **natter** To talk (4) naggingly (9), mostly to oneself (7), with the intention (9) of being overheard (9).
3. **gratuitous** Granted (7) without charge (6) or obligation (10); given (5) without cause (5) or justification (13).
4. **mitigate** To make (4) or become (6) milder (6) or less (4) severe (6).
5. **dishabille** State (5) of being only (4) partly (6) dressed (7).
6. **asperse** To spread (6) false (5) or damaging (8) charges (7) or innuendo (8); to besmirch (8) (one's) reputation (10).
7. **expatiate** To discuss (7) at great (5) length (6) or in detail (6).
8. **heuristic** Applied to a method (6) of teaching (8) by which students (8) learn (5) through investigation (13) and discovery (9).
9. **caveat** A warning (7) enjoining (9) (someone) from specific (8) acts (4) or practices (9).
10. **exigency** An emergency (9) or critical (8) situation (9) calling (7) for immediate (9) action (6) or attention (9).

Hidden Meanings

1. **flout** To <u>scoff</u> (5) at or <u>show</u> (4) <u>contempt</u> (8) for.
2. **fastidious** <u>Careful</u> (7) and <u>exacting</u> (9); <u>difficult</u> (9) to <u>please</u> (6); having <u>high</u> (4) and often <u>capricious</u> (10) <u>standards</u> (9); <u>refined</u> (7) in an <u>oversensitive</u> (13) <u>way</u> (3); showing <u>excessive</u> (9) <u>delicacy</u> (8).
3. **perspicacious** <u>Highly</u> (6) <u>perceptive</u> (10); having <u>keen</u> (4) <u>judgment</u> (8) or <u>understanding</u> (13).
4. **didactic** <u>Intended</u> (8) for <u>teaching</u> (8); <u>morally</u> (7) <u>instructive</u> (11); <u>boringly</u> (8) <u>pedantic</u> (8) or <u>moralistic</u> (10).
5. **inexorable** <u>Not</u> (3) to be <u>persuaded</u> (9) or <u>influenced</u> (10) by <u>entreaty</u> (8); <u>adamant</u> (7); <u>relentless</u> (10).
6. **maieutic** Pertaining to or resembling the <u>Socratic</u> (8) <u>process</u> (7) of <u>helping</u> (7) (a person) to <u>bring</u> (5) <u>forth</u> (5) and <u>become</u> (6) <u>aware</u> (5) of <u>latent</u> (6) <u>ideas</u> (5).
7. **discomfit** To <u>frustrate</u> (9) the <u>plans</u> (5) or <u>expectations</u> (12) of; to <u>disconcert</u> (10) or <u>distress</u> (8).
8. **fatuous** <u>Complacently</u> (12) <u>foolish</u> (7) or <u>stupid</u> (6).
9. **distrait** <u>Absent</u> (6) - <u>minded</u> (6); <u>inattentive</u> (11).
10. **reify** To <u>think</u> (5) of or <u>treat</u> (5) an <u>abstraction</u> (11) as if it were <u>concrete</u> (8).

1. **expeditious** <u>Done</u> (4) <u>speedily</u> (8) or with great <u>efficiency</u> (10).
2. **florescence** A <u>flowering</u> (9); a <u>period</u> (6) <u>marked</u> (6) by <u>success</u> (7) or <u>achievement</u> (11).
3. **apocryphal** Of <u>doubtful</u> (8) <u>authorship</u> (10) or <u>authenticity</u> (12); not <u>genuine</u> (7).
4. **credulity** An <u>inclination</u> (11) to <u>believe</u> (7) too <u>readily</u> (7); <u>easily</u> (6) <u>persuaded</u> (9).
5. **evince** <u>Show</u> (4) <u>plainly</u> (7); <u>demonstrate</u> (11) <u>clearly</u> (7) or <u>convincingly</u> (12).
6. **sciolism** <u>Superficial</u> (11) <u>knowledge</u> (9) or <u>learning</u> (8).
7. **callipygian** <u>Having</u> (6) <u>shapely</u> (7) <u>buttocks</u> (8).
8. **exonerate** To <u>free</u> (4) from <u>blame</u> (5); <u>exculpate</u> (9).
9. **propitiate** To <u>cause</u> (5) to be <u>favorably</u> (9) <u>inclined</u> (8); to <u>win</u> (3) or <u>regain</u> (6) the <u>good</u> (4) <u>will</u> (4) of.
10. **extant** <u>Still</u> (5) <u>existing</u> (8); <u>not</u> (3) <u>defunct</u> (7) or <u>destroyed</u> (9).

Hidden Meanings

1. **meticulous** Extremely (9) or excessively (11) careful (7).
2. **inveterate** Firmly (6) established (11) over an extended (8) duration (8) as a habit (5); persisting (10) in habitual (8) behavior (9) of long (4) standing (8).
3. **inure** To make (4) (one) accustomed (10) to something (9) undesirable (11); to habituate (9).
4. **extenuate** To lessen (6) or downplay (8) the seriousness (11) of an offense (7), error (5), etc., by giving (6) an excuse (6).
5. **vitiate** To diminish (8) the value (5) of; to corrupt (7); to render (6) legally (7) ineffective (11).
6. **fulsome** Offensively (11) excessive (9) or insincere (9).
7. **Zeitgeist** The spirit (6) of the time (4); the thinking (8) and feeling (7) identified (10) with a period (6).
8. **hebetude** The quality (7) or condition (9) of being dull (4) or lethargic (9).
9. **mores** Folkways (8) and customs (7) that are considered (10) conducive (9) to the welfare (7) of society (7) and through observance (10) have become morally (7) binding (7).
10. **troglodyte** Prehistoric (11) cave (4) dweller (7); a person (6) who chooses (7) to live (4) in seclusion (9); (anyone) having outmoded (8) habits (6) or opinions (8).

Hidden Names

American Authors

1. Ernest Hemingway
2. Emily Dickinson
3. Thomas Wolfe
4. John Steinbeck
5. Nathaniel Hawthorne
6. Robert Frost
7. Sylvia Plath
8. Toni Morrison
9. James Baldwin

Rock 'n' Roll Stars

1. Chuck Berry
2. Little Richard
3. Fats Domino
4. James Brown
5. Jackie Wilson
6. Aretha Franklin
7. Gloria Estefan
8. Alanis Morissette
9. Kurt Cobain

Film Stars

1. Laurence Olivier
2. Brad Pitt
3. Alec Baldwin
4. Molly Ringwald
5. Sylvester Stallone
6. Meryl Streep
7. Whoopi Goldberg

Hidden Names

U.S. Presidents

1. Rutherford B. Hayes
2. Grover Cleveland
3. Benjamin Harrison
4. Dwight Eisenhower
5. Ronald Reagan
6. Andrew Johnson

U.S. Artists

1. Winslow Homer
2. Frederic Remington
3. Grandma Moses
4. Norman Rockwell
5. Andy Warhol
6. Jackson Pollock
7. Georgia O'Keefe
8. Jacob Lawrence

Thinkers

1. Isaac Newton
2. René Descartes
3. Immanuel Kant
4. Francis Bacon
5. Albert Einstein
6. Camille Paglia
7. Barbara Jordan

TV's Biggest Stars

1. Milton Berle
2. Walter Cronkite
3. Johnny Carson
4. Captain Kangaroo
5. Lucille Ball
6. Roseanne Barr
7. Ellen Degeneres
8. Jerry Seinfeld

Hidden Words

SOME PHOBIAS

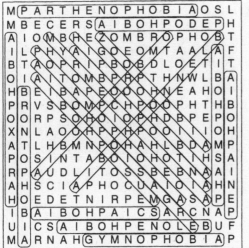

SOME MANIAS

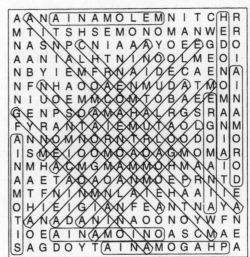

Hidden Words

3   I BEFORE E, EXCEPT...

```
N E B S P S O T H E V E I R T E R D
D E C E N W H H E T E N V T T F L I
F D B E L I E F E I O O E E O E P H
S D G A E S R C O H F W D R I S I C
C R S S R E N R E T I L B Y O E E E
O T R A L E E V E I H C A S A U D I
N O A I I O I A E C G R I E V E C L
T D E C R W E F P V E T E E F D O I
O F S U G G E A E E E I S O H E N N
T T E D E R V V D T R I V T E C C G
T E T I A D I S V R D C L E Y E E P
H E S V C E E E D I L E E E E I I L
I R C H E F C C F H E B F I B O T N
E P I E I R N B E T I C C V V H W S
F E I E O H O S O I W P E A N E E E
F H R E E T C N T T V A N R E V I I
I C D E C E I T S K V E I R G C R Z
E Y I A E E D E N E A T S I N O D E
```

4   OOH, NO!

```
G O O F U C A Y D S E N O O B T I N
C W O D T M W M V P U R R E O N A K
H N D E I G H O O D S O O T I A O T
T O O K I U O E S I R G T R N O R M
E T N E A A U O F E O M O L B N O N
S M S D R D N D D T N O R T H H O B
H N E O I X N L E T P L O O C G W O
W O F P M O O B E N I E C I N O S O
S L X O N R E E O D R A R O E O Y T
L O I K O O R O I W I I O E E E C C
T O I O O T K D C V L G O T K B O E
H W F A S H K O O H O C T O R I M H
N O S D D O J A A T O A O O A E P K
G R F I Y O L W K O N L R M U T O W
T D O O C P G O T D N O N P B O E I
I W G O O E L S O E O F L O C G O D
I S R E B D H O Y I A A E F O O L O
F C D F O O W U E M O O L S A M S T
```

5   SOME LOOKALIKES

```
I H C O A R S N E D O N C D R T E E
N E L I C I T C R S A C E A E I L R
A O I U X C A N O G R S A R M I I A
D C T A R A C A A U S U A P C O M T
T E E R C S I D A E E C O P I O N L
E R B T D I S C R E T E T G O T M A
B U A N A R H T L A I T E M E I O E
B E E A R A R E E C S N P B O R E L
R E M I B R R O T N E M I L P M O C E R
E A I R R E N B C X A T E L L R U O S O
A C H G R A T A O L E N S F E A A A A N
C N R C A D P C I N E G G C R N U O O E
H I O C T S N D U A I G S G E D C R S
I T T M I E S A F A T A U T R U N A
O A P T A A L T E R C R A S E M P R E
L H I D E S E R T N A R G I M M I E
S T O L T H T N E C S A S I C U P I
```

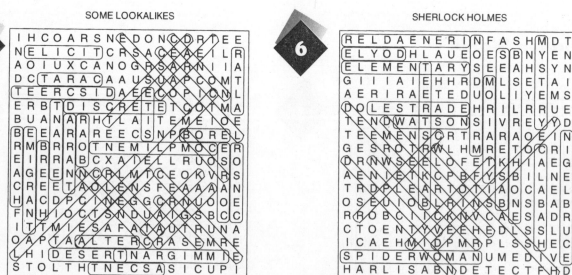

6   SHERLOCK HOLMES

```
R E L D A E N E R I N F A S H M D T
E L Y O D H L A U E O E S B N Y E N
E L E M E N T A R Y S E E A H S E T A N I
G I I I A I E H H R D M L S E T Y A M S
A E R I R A E T E D U O L I L R R U E
D O L E S T R A D E H R I L R E Y Y D
T E N D W A T S O N S I V R E Y I N
T E E M E N S C R T R A R A O E I N
G E S R O T R W L H M R E T O C I R E
D R N W S E E L O F E T K H I E N G
A E N I E T K C P B F Y B I C A E I
T R D P L E A R T O T I A O N S A B L
O S E U I O B L R I N S B L E A D R
R R O B C I C K N V C A E I C A A B U
C T O E N T Y V E E H E D L S S H E C
I C A E H M I D P M R P L S S H E
S P I D E R W O M A N U M E D I V E
H A R L I S A B N D E T E C T F H D
```

Hidden Words

MAGAZINES

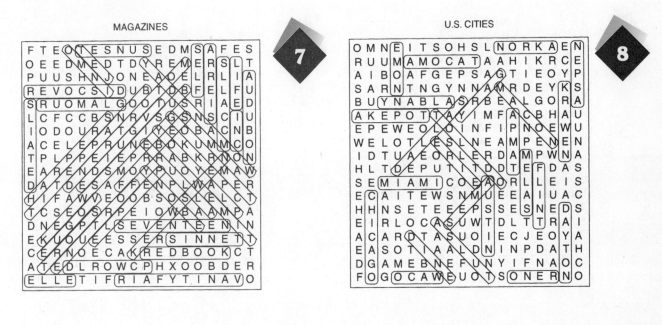

U.S. CITIES

HERBS & SPICES

GOLFSPEAK

Hidden Words

WANNA DANCE?

BRIT LIT 101

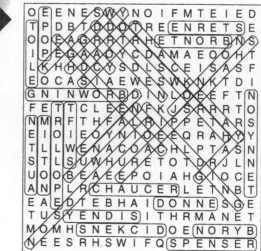

ROUNDABOUT

ANTI & ANTE

Hidden Words

BIG BANDS

Missing Vowels

GET-TOGETHERS

Missing Vowels

MUSICALS

TV WESTERNS

Missing Vowels

HATS

JUST FOR FUN

Missing Words

CLICHES 1

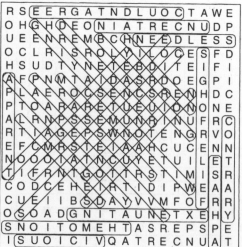

Headlines

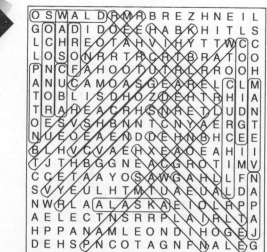

Missing Words

FILMS OF THE FIFTIES

CLICHES 2

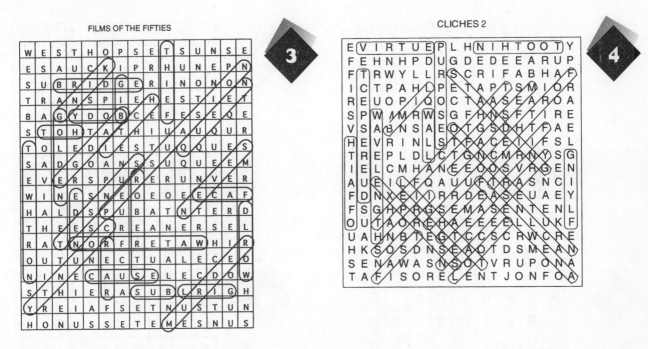

Lost and Found

Lost and Found

3

	J			C	A	S	H	
M	O	U	E		O	L	E	O
I		D		C	H	A	R	T
A		I	N	H	E	R	E	
S	I	C		A	R	M		T
M	I	D	L	E				O
A		A		K		W	A	X
L		R				R		I
	S	Y	Z	Y	G	Y		C

4

	P			J	U	M	B	O
P	A	S	T	A		A		
E	N	C	O	M	I	U	M	
W	E	E				N	O	R
	G	N	A	T		D	O	
R	Y	E			C	E	D	E
	R		Y	O	U	R		A
L	I	M	O		B		S	
	C	A	U	S	E	W	A	Y

5

	A		T	R	U	M	P	S
A	P	P	R	I	S	E		C
	P	R	I	D	E		D	O
C	R	O	P					N
L	A	W		A	D	A	G	E
A	I	L	S		R		E	
U	S		A	R	O	U	N	D
S	E	E	P		V		R	
E			S	K	E	W	E	R

6

B	Y	W	A	Y		G		
U		N		W	R	Y		
S		Y			E		K	
Y		A	W	E		A	C	E
B		Y	A	W		T	O	Y
O		E	Y	E			Y	
D			S	L	Y	L	Y	
Y			Y		Y		Y	
		E	Y	E				

7

	Q		Z		Z		
	Q	U	E	U	E	S		A
Q	U	I	Z		R	E	A	P
	I	N		O	X			
A	N	T		Z	E	U	S	
	C		T		S	A	P	
Y	U	L	E		L	A	X	
	N		X		D			
E	X	I	T		H	E	X	

8

	O		S		S	U	M	S
A	B	S	T	R	U	S	E	
	T		A		M			
B	U	S	Y		M		Q	
U	S		F	O	R	U	M	
B	E	A	C	O	N		A	
B			R		R			
L		P	R	A	Y	E	R	S
E			Y		Y			

Lost and Found

9

A	B	B	O	T		F	E	W
T	E	E		A		A		H
		L		P	A	R	K	A
S		F	O	I	L		A	T
C	A	R	R	O	T			R
A	N	Y		C	A	R	A	T
M	E		C	A	R	E	T	
	N	O				A		
S	T	R	A	P		P	R	Y

10

		C	R	O	P		H	A
	F	E	E		E	P	I	C
C	E	N	S	U	R	E		R
R	U	S	T		U	G	L	Y
A	D	O		U	S			L
D		R		M	E			I
L			B		T	I	C	
E	X	P	I	R	E			
		F	A	M	O	U	S	

11

	I	O	N			B		U
I	N	G	E	N	U	O	U	S
	G	L	E	E		A	P	E
F	E	E	D	S				
O	N			T	R	I	T	E
L	I	T	T	L	E			M
D	O		R	E	M	O	T	E
	U		E		I		O	N
A	S	C	E	N	T			D

12

P	A	G	E		B	A	I	T
A	H	A		T	A	S	T	E
G	A	R	N	I	S	H		A
A		N	A	M	E		A	S
N	A	I	V	E		A	C	E
		S	E	S	A	M	E	
		H			B	R	A	
		E		B	I	B		
S	H	E	R	B	E	T		

13

S	T	E	W		A	S	E	A
	E		R	A	C	K		W
D	A	T	A		C	I	T	E
I		O	C	T	E	T		S
M	I	N	K		N		D	O
P			S	T	E	A	M	
L	A	P		I			M	E
E	D	I	C	T			P	
S	O	N		E	R	A		

14

		T	A	P		S	O	
P	O	R	T	I	O	N		T
I		A			A	D	O	
A		M		B	A	G	E	L
N	A	P		R			W	E
O	N		B	E	A	D		R
	G		R	A	C	E		A
B	R	E	A	T	H	E		T
	Y		T	H	E	M		E

Lost and Found

 15

```
      A B J U R E
L I M P   O     K
  M O P   V A S E
O P P O S I T E
F E E S   A R E
  L   I   L I K E
O   A T E   A   X
F A D E   T   H I
T   D   C O V E T
```

 16

```
A L L A Y   O D D
T O   U   W   I
  A U G U R   S O
A T   E   E T C H
C H O R D S   O
C   U   A T O M S
E A T E N     F
D   E   C A V I L
E E R I E     T
```

 17

```
C   W     A   S
H   S H E R B E T
E X T O L   R   R
S   R   A R O M A
S C A N T   G   I
  H I   E X A L T
S A G E     T
  S H Y     E   O
H E T E R O D O X
```

 18

```
  D I S C R E T E
  I     U     O
A S T E R I S K S
  C     T     E
E R R S   V E N D
B E E P     V   E
B E G I N   E K E
T A N     R   M
  L E A S T
```

 19

```
V I E D   P   A
I N V I D I O U S
O S A G E   D   P
L I D   T R I T E
A D E   R   U   R
S I D E A R M   I
  O     C   A T
A U D I T   W R Y
  S     S E C
```

 20

```
    S L I G H T
    L I N E A R
    P E N A L T Y
  F R I E N D   S
  L A G   E   A T
P A T H     W
W E T   A B E T
E       L       I
I D L Y   B L O C
```

Missing Links

P	H	E	R	O	M	O	N	E
F	U	S	I	L	L	A	D	E
B	R	O	A	D	L	O	O	M
C	U	B	B	Y	H	O	L	E
C	O	N	F	O	U	N	D	S
P	R	O	F	U	S	E	L	Y
N	O	M	I	N	A	T	O	R
I	M	P	U	G	N	I	N	G
S	C	A	L	A	W	A	G	S

O	B	F	U	S	C	A	T	E
N	E	O	L	O	G	I	S	M
B	A	L	A	L	A	I	K	A
P	U	N	C	T	I	L	I	O
S	T	A	N	C	H	I	N	G
H	Y	D	R	O	X	I	D	E
E	S	C	A	P	A	D	E	S
O	B	L	O	Q	U	I	E	S
S	U	B	S	C	R	I	P	T

B	U	L	W	A	R	K	E	D
H	E	A	R	T	F	E	L	T
N	U	T	R	I	M	E	N	T
T	H	E	R	E	U	P	O	N
R	E	F	O	R	E	S	T	S
F	I	R	E	P	O	W	E	R
S	O	U	T	H	W	E	S	T
S	C	I	N	T	I	L	L	A
M	O	T	H	B	A	L	L	S

I	D	E	N	T	I	C	A	L
W	O	E	B	E	G	O	N	E
E	N	U	N	C	I	A	T	E
S	T	O	U	T	N	E	S	S
A	B	D	I	C	A	T	E	S
J	U	X	T	A	P	O	S	E
S	Y	M	P	H	O	N	I	C
M	A	N	N	I	K	I	N	S
S	P	A	G	H	E	T	T	I

D	A	C	H	S	H	U	N	D
T	H	E	O	S	O	P	H	Y
S	H	I	P	M	A	T	E	S
W	A	T	E	R	S	H	E	D
M	A	C	H	I	N	E	R	Y
U	N	C	O	U	T	H	L	Y
E	B	U	L	L	I	E	N	T
V	I	N	D	I	C	A	T	E
D	I	S	S	U	A	D	E	S

P	O	L	Y	G	O	N	A	L
M	E	L	O	D	R	A	M	A
O	M	B	U	D	S	M	A	N
L	I	B	R	A	R	I	A	N
H	O	P	E	F	U	L	L	Y
U	N	P	O	P	U	L	A	R
C	A	R	N	A	T	I	O	N
A	F	T	E	R	N	O	O	N
O	B	E	I	S	A	N	C	E

Missing Links

S	C	A	P	E	G	O	A	T
L	U	C	R	A	T	I	V	E
A	B	S	C	O	N	D	E	D
N	A	R	R	O	W	E	S	T
D	A	L	M	A	T	I	A	N
E	D	E	L	W	E	I	S	S
R	A	T	I	O	N	A	L	E
L	I	T	I	G	I	O	U	S
E	A	R	T	H	W	O	R	M

A	D	E	N	O	I	D	A	L
M	E	L	I	O	R	A	T	E
P	L	A	N	G	E	N	C	Y
H	A	R	B	I	N	G	E	R
D	Y	S	E	N	T	E	R	Y
I	S	O	M	E	T	R	I	C
C	A	S	S	E	R	O	L	E
P	R	E	F	I	G	U	R	E
H	E	I	N	O	U	S	L	Y

I	S	O	M	O	R	P	H	S
A	T	A	V	I	S	T	I	C
D	I	A	P	H	R	A	G	M
F	L	U	C	T	U	A	T	E
A	L	U	M	I	N	I	U	M
S	W	A	N	S	D	O	W	N
M	A	R	Q	U	E	T	R	Y
S	T	A	T	U	E	T	T	E
D	E	C	O	U	P	A	G	E

V	E	N	T	I	L	A	T	E
P	A	R	O	C	H	I	A	L
A	D	V	A	N	T	A	G	E
S	I	N	G	L	E	T	O	N
D	E	C	O	R	A	T	O	R
C	O	L	O	N	N	A	D	E
L	A	U	D	A	T	O	R	Y
D	R	A	C	O	N	I	A	N
C	I	G	A	R	E	T	T	E

Mixers

 1 PEARL, OUTCAST, ADULTERY, MINISTER, THE SCARLET LETTER

 9 TULIP, FLUTE, COUPE, SAUCER, CHAMPAGNE GLASSES

 2 PODIUM, STRINGS, CONDUCTOR, WOODWINDS, SYMPHONY ORCHESTRA

 10 MAPLE, LOCUST, POPLAR, CHESTNUT, DECIDUOUS TREES

3 SAMBA, LAMBADA, CARIOCA, BOSSA NOVA, BRAZILIAN DANCES

 11 TUREEN, CHARGER, COMPOTE, DECANTER, SERVING CONTAINERS

4 TILDE, GRAVE, MACRON, CIRCUMFLEX, DIACRITICAL MARKS

 12 PIPE, SOCKET, MONKEY, CROWFOOT, KINDS OF WRENCHES

 5 COURIER, SENTINEL, OBSERVER, SPECTATOR, NEWSPAPER NAMES

 13 SABRINA, TIFFANYS, CHARADE, MY FAIR LADY, AUDREY HEPBURN

 6 MICE, GRAPES, TORTILLA, DEPRESSION, JOHN STEINBECK

14 JUNO, DIANA, VESTA, FORTUNA, ROMAN GODDESSES

 7 RAIN, GHOSTS, INTERFERENCE, ROLLING PICTURE, TELEVISION PROBLEMS

 15 SONG, SWAMP, VESPER, LINCOLN, KINDS OF SPARROWS

 8 OILER, BRUSH, BROACH, TWEEZERS, WATCHMAKER(')S TOOLS

 16 KEATS, BYRON, SHELLEY, TENNYSON, ENGLISH POETS

Providers

1

T	A	J		T	A	L	C	S		T	E	T
A	L	A		A	D	I	E	U		A	L	E
C	O	D		C	O	B	L	E		U	S	E
T	E	E	T	E	R		E	D	I	T	E	D
			A	T	E		R	E	C			
S	T	A	B		D	A	Y		Y	E	A	S
E	A	T			A				A	M	P	
T	O	M	B		T	H	E		Q	U	A	Y
		E	R	E		C	P	U				
O	R	A	T	O	R		H	E	A	R	T	S
A	I	R		A	R	B	O	R		A	H	A
T	N	T		S	O	R	E	S		C	A	N
S	K	Y		T	R	A	D	E		E	N	D

2

P	E	A		P	R	O			D	A	T	E
O	W	E		O	U	R		F	E	L	O	N
P	E	R	S	O	N	A		A	W	O	K	E
		A	I	R		T	A	N		H	E	M
P	U	T	T		C	O	B		M	A	N	Y
E	K	E		E	R	R	A	T	A			
P	E	S	T	L	E		S	A	N	I	T	Y
		A	M	A	Z	E	D		D	O	E	
S	C	A	M		M	I	D		D	I	E	T
L	I	D		G	Y	P		T	O	O		
A	R	O	M	A		P	A	I	N	T	E	D
S	C	R	U	M		E	V	E		I	R	E
H	A	N	D		R	E	D		C	A	N	

3

R	A	G	S		B	U	L	B		R	B	I
A	L	O	E		A	F	A	R		A	R	M
W	A	D	E		S	O	D	A		M	A	P
		M	R	S			C	A	S	E	S	
A	B	A	S	E		R	E	F				
R	A	N		C	L	O	Y		T	O	S	S
C	R	T		A	V	E			P	O	E	
S	E	E	R		M	A	S	H		A	L	E
		A	R	B		I	S	L	E	S		
A	D	A	G	E		H	E	Y				
B	A	T		B	E	T	A		C	A	B	S
B	I	O		E	V	I	L		E	A	R	L
E	S	P		C	E	L	L		S	H	A	Y

4

C	A	D		S	H	E	D		S	A	F	E
A	L	E		W	A	R	E		E	L	A	N
B	O	A		A	M	E	N		C	A	R	D
S	E	R	U	M		S	A	C				
		R	I	D		P	O	P	E	S		
S	C	A	N		A	L	S	O		A	B	C
O	A	T		T	I	P			C	O	O	
U	F	O		B	A	T	E		R	E	N	T
S	E	P	T	A		C	A	B				
		A	R	T		S	I	B	Y	L		
C	R	A	B		A	V	I	S		E	A	U
B	O	M	B		S	E	R	E		A	P	R
S	T	A	Y		S	T	E	T		U	S	E

Providers

5

```
A B M . . H E M . . S O M A
B R A . . S O R E . . E V E N
C A D . . A G E S . . R A N D
S E E M S . . . A I R . .
. . . A H A . . R A P S
T A L C . L A V A . A L E
A L A . M C I . C O N
B A T . C A M S . T E E D
. S E M I . . . A A H .
. . O A F . . R O S E S
A C E S . A B B E . A N N
C O K E . C O M A . F D A
T O E S . T O W . . E S P
```

6

```
S P A . . R P M . B A A S
E O N . S I R E . A L M A
M O T . A G E S . S E A M
I L I A C . . A T E .
. . P S T . U S E R
A L S O . H A N G . B A R
A I M . E R E . O V A
H M O . A N T A . A N E W
. E G G S . R U M
. A H A . S Y C E S
A B E T . L A T E . A L A
B R A E . A R E S . F A N
C A T S . S B A . E N D
```

7

```
M A G . L O S S . B A A S
A N A . A C H E . A L M A
C A B . S T A R . S E A M
E S S E S . H E M S .
. . M O B . A O R T A
S A R I . E P I C . O U R
U N I T . T U T . S A N E
B E T . B A B E . O D E S
S W E A R . M A D .
. S A C K . R A P E S
M A G S . H A L O . A L A
T H E E . A L E S . C A N
V A T S . M E T E . E N D
```

8

```
O F F . . D A D . D A Y
D E A D . P I N E . A L E
D E A R . F E T E . B A A
. . A R C S . P A S S .
D R A M A . E L S E .
I O N . G A L A . O R B
M A N T E L . S E N I O R
. M A O . M E S A . F R O
. T S A R . S A T E D
. B A S E . A M E N .
E A U . P E S O . A B B E
S A N . T O E D . S U R E
P S T . A N D . . S A C
```

Providers

9

```
A N A S   R E P   C R A G
C O P E   A K A   A B L E
T R O D   M E N   F I A T
      A M P   A T E
S T A T E S   C O S M O S
O A R E D   T E E   O P T
F I E   F A A   D I E
A N N   C O B   D I A N A
S T A T O R   C O O L E D
      A L E   A N D
C R A B   M C I   I C E S
B O M B   A I R   D A N K
S T A Y   N O N   E D D Y
```

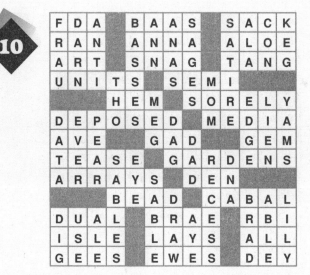

10

```
F D A   B A A S   S A C K
R A N   A N N A   A L O E
A R T   S N A G   T A N G
U N I T S   S E M I
      H E M   S O R E L Y
D E P O S E D   M E D I A
A V E   G A D   G E M
T E A S E   G A R D E N S
A R R A Y S   D E N
      B E A D   C A B A L
D U A L   B R A E   R B I
I S L E   L A Y S   A L L
G E E S   E W E S   D E Y
```

11

```
T H O U   C O B   B A A S
H A I R   A V E   A L M A
O G L E   T A T   S E A M
      A H A   A T E
U S E   A R C   A S S E S
P T A   S A H I B   E E C
S A G   C A D   E R E
E L L   O T T E R   D I N
T E E T H   S O U   S E T
      A M P   L E E
B I B B   U F O   A B B E
A R A B   T U G   C A I N
N A R Y   T R Y   H A N D
```

12

```
A L A S   E E L   C A D
T A L C   A Y E   A M A N
E W E R   S E T   R E L Y
      I C E S   C O S E C
S W A M I   C A B
A I R   A R B O R   M R S
C R T   O R B   E A T
K E Y   A W A S H   S P A
      C B S   M E A T Y
E T H I C   E G O S
S H A D   F D A   S A F E
P A L E   B I B   E A R N
N O R   I T S   S H O D
```

Providers

13

```
U R G E   M E T     T A T
G O A L   E R A S   A L A
H O L M   L E N T   I M P
  T A S T E   A T L A S
    R E B A T E
M A S S Y   E M E R A L D
P I P E   B R A   S H O E
G R A N D E E   M E A T Y
    S I T T E R
T A K E S     A S H E N
S B A   C H U G   O B O E
A L L   S A F E   C O P Y
R Y E     N O R   K N E E
```

14

```
A J A R   A R B   C H O W
C O M A   B O A   H A L O
T E A M   B B C   U N D O
    R U E   K O B
E T H O S   E L F   M I D
E R O D E   N O T   O V A
R O T   R A G     T I N
I L L   R E C   M O T E T
E L Y   A F T   A R O S E
    R Y E   F D A
M A M A   R O E   T A F T
E P I C   E A T   E V E R
D O L E   E R E   D E W Y
```

15

```
R A P     R A F T   M C I
A L E   O U T D O   A R M
G O A   P L E A T   M A P
S E T T E E     N A B S
  E R R   T A N
M A N N A   R E N E W A L
O V A   T R I T E   A M Y
N E G R O I D   M I D A S
  A R B   R O M
T H U G     U N P A C K
H A N   R A I S E   B O A
O L D   E L V E S   E L L
U F O   P A Y S   T E E
```

Shape Changers

1

DEN
NEEDY
KNEED
NODDED
DEFEND
DENUDED
WIDENED
DEFENDED
INDENTED
DEPENDENT
UNDERDONE
ENGENDERED

2

NET
EATEN
TENSE
ENTREE
TENANT
PENNANT
ANTENNA
TENEMENT
INTERNET
ATTENTION
ATTENDANT
ANTECEDENT

3

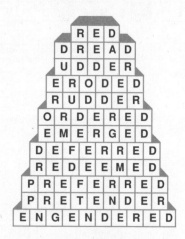

RED
DREAD
UDDER
ERODED
RUDDER
ORDERED
EMERGED
DEFERRED
REDEEMED
PREFERRED
PRETENDER
ENGENDERED

4

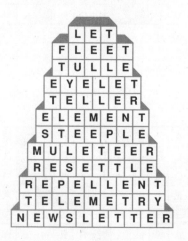

LET
FLEET
TULLE
EYELET
TELLER
ELEMENT
STEEPLE
MULETEER
RESETTLE
REPELLENT
TELEMETRY
NEWSLETTER

5

EAR
ARENA
AWARE
ERRATA
ERASER
SEAFARER
REAPPEAR
REARRANGE
REHEARSAL
PARAPHRASE

Shape Changers

```
      T I N
    N I N T H
    T I N N Y
  I N T U I T
  N I T W I T
T U I T I O N
T R I N I T Y
I N I Q U I T Y
I N S P I R I T
I N T E N T I O N
N U T R I T I O N
C O N T A I N I N G
```

```
      T I E
    T I T L E
    T I T H E
  P E T I T E
  T I T T E R
I T E M I Z E
P I E T I E S
T E S T I E S T
E N T I T I E S
E T I Q U E T T E
R E T E N T I V E
E T E R N I T I E S
```

```
      E A T
    E L A T E
    T E A S E
  A E R A T E
  E S T A T E
T A F F E T A
S T A T U T E
A N T E A T E R
A E S T H E T E
A T T E N U A T E
T E A C H A B L E
S T A T U E T T E S
```

```
      S E A
    E R A S E
    E A S E L
  T E A S E S
  E S S A Y S
L E A S H E S
S E E S A W S
N A U S E A T E
E Y E G L A S S
A W A R E N E S S
A B S E N T E E S
A P O S T A S I E S
```

```
      A G E
    A L G A E
    A G A P E
  G A R A G E
  G A G G L E
A V E R A G E
L E A K A G E
A P P A N A G E
L A N G U A G E
A G G R A V A T E
A G G R E G A T E
A M A L G A M A T E
```

Shared Pairs

1

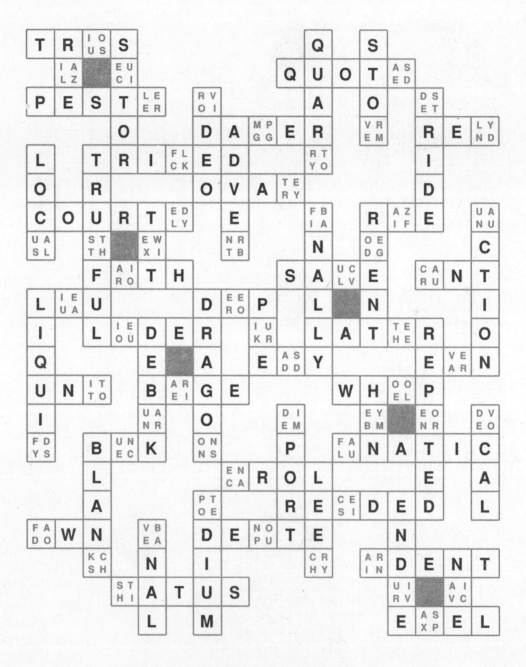

Shared Pairs

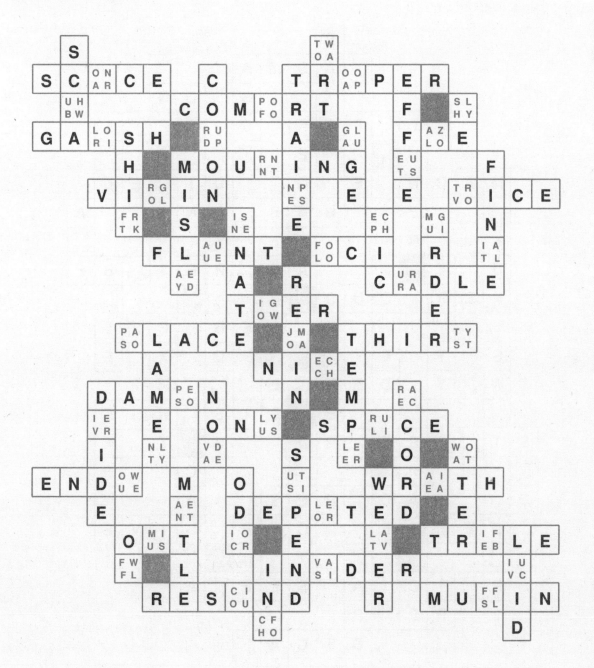

2

Shared Pairs

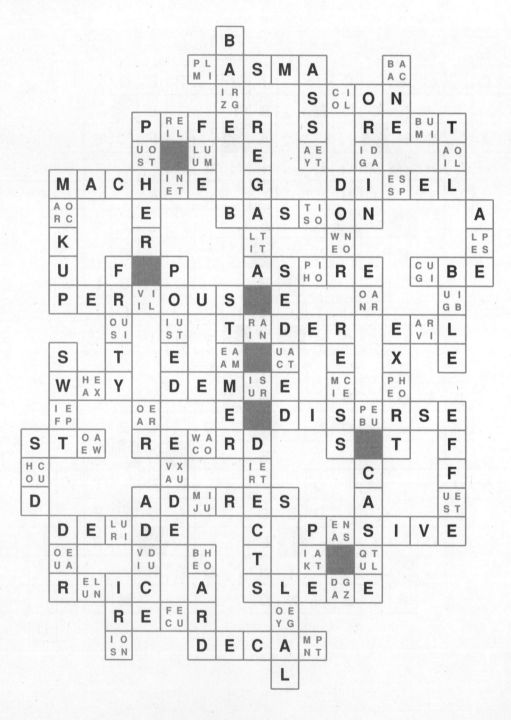

Shared Pairs

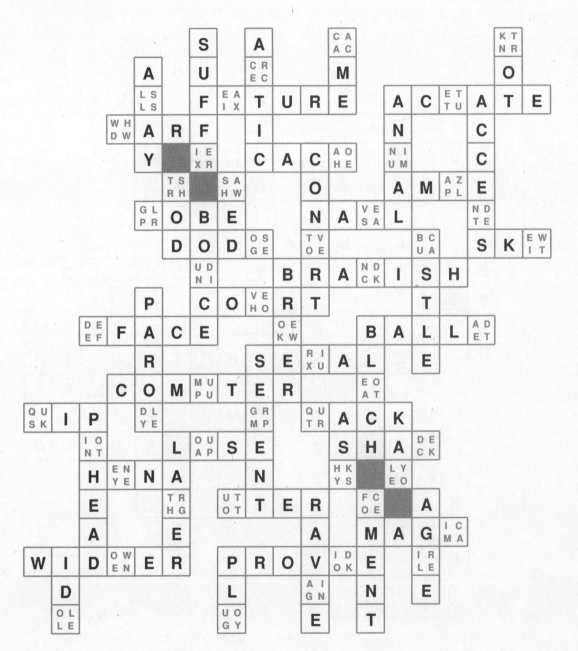

Shared Pairs

Shared Pairs

6

Shared Pairs

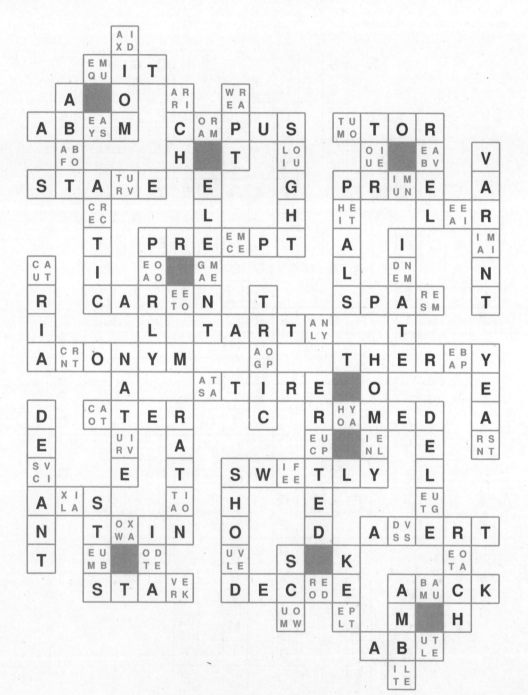

Words Within Words

1 ABROGATE

abet
agar
ager
area
bare
bate
bear
beat
beta
boar
boat
bore
brag
brat
ergo
garb
gate
gear
goat
gore
grab
ogre
rage
rate
robe
rote
tare
taro
tear
toea
toga
tore
abate
abort
agate
agora
aorta
argot
barge
begot
ergot
gater
gator

grate
great
orate
tabor
boater
borate
aerobat

2 ACRIMONY

airy
amir
army
ayin
ciao
cion
coin
coma
cony
corm
corn
cram
cyan
icon
iron
lyar
main
many
mica
moan
morn
myna
narc
nary
norm
orca
racy
rain
rani
rimy
roam
roan
yarn
acorn

cairn
carny
carom
coria
corny
crony
irony
macro
manic
manor
mayor
micra
micro
minor
moray
rainy
rayon
roman
crayon
macron
manioc
micron
acronym

3 ADUMBRATE

abed
abet
abut
area
arum
aura
bade
bard
bare
bate
baud
bead
beam
bear
beat
beau
berm
beta

brad
brat
bred
dame
dare
dart
data
date
daub
dear
debt
drab
dram
drub
drum
duet
dumb
made
mare
mart
mate
mead
meat
mute
rate
read
ream
rube
rude
rued
tabu
tame
tare
team
tear
term
tram
true
tuba
tube
urea
abate
abeam
amber

ameba
armed
baaed
beard
beaut
bread
bream
brute
buret
debar
debut
demur
derma
drama
dream
rebut
rumba
trade
tread
tuber
umber
umbra
abrade
bateau
maraud
mature
trauma
amateur
drumbeat

4 ALLEVIATE

alee
alit
evil
ilea
late
lava
lave
leva
lilt
live
tail
tala

Words Within Words

tale
tali
tall
teal
tell
tile
till
vale
veal
veil
vela
vial
vile
vita
alive
avail
elate
elite
ileal
leave
level
valet
villa
vital

ALLOGRAPH **5**
agar
alga
gala
gall
gaol
goal
hall
halo
harp
opal
oral
pall
para
poll
roll
agora
aloha

alpha
graph
largo
polar
gallop
halloa
pallor

AMBIGUOUS **6**
bias
iamb
magi
miso
obis
sago
smog
smug
sumo
agism
amigo
bogus
gumbo
imago
magus
sigma
biogas

ANTIPATHY **7**
anti
ayin
hint
pain
pant
path
pint
piny
pita
pith
pity
than
that

thin
tint
tiny
inapt
natty
nitty
paint
panty
patin
patty
taint
titan
apathy
attain
patina

APOCRYPHAL **8**
ahoy
arch
capo
carp
chap
char
chop
clap
clay
clop
cloy
coal
cola
copy
crop
halo
harp
holy
hypo
loch
opal
oral
orca
papa
para
play

plop
ploy
pray
prop
racy
aloha
alpha
apply
carol
copra
coral
haply
happy
harpy
hoary
larch
loach
pacha
papal
parch
phyla
playa
poach
polar
polyp
porch
roach
royal
carhop
carpal
choral
papacy
parlay
payola
poplar
approach

ARROGATE **9**
agar
area
ergo
gate
gear

goat
gore
ogre
rage
rare
rate
rear
roar
rote
tare
tear
toga
tore
torr
agate
agora
aorta
argot
ergot
gator
grate
great
orate
roger
errata
garret
garter
garrote

AUSPICIOUS **10**
capo
ciao
coup
cusp
cuss
opus
pass
pica
puss
soap
soup
apsis
aspic

Words Within Words

oasis
pious
spacious

12

CIRCUITOUS
cost
curt
iris
oust
riot
rout
rust
sort
sour
stir
suit
tiro
tori
tour
trio
uric
court
croci
crust
curio
curst
ictus
occur
roust
scour
scout
stoic
torsi
circus
citric
coitus
critic
crocus
rictus
rustic
stucco
succor
suitor
circuit
curious

11

CHRONOLOGY
chon
clog
cloy
cony
cool
coon
corn
goon
gory
gyro
holy
horn
loch
loco
logo
logy
long
loon
lorn
only
orgy
colon
color
crony
croon
glory
honor
lynch
colony
oology
horology
oncology

13

COMPUNCTION
cion
coin
coon
coop
coot
coup
icon
into
mint
mono
noon
moot
muon
noon
noun
omit
onto
pint
pion
poco
pout
punt
unit
unto
upon
comic
conic
count
cumin
input
mount
onion
opium
optic
picot
pinto
piton
point
tonic
topic
tunic
union

copout
coupon
motion
noncom
notion
nuncio
octopi
option
potion
coconut
occiput
unction

14

CONDUCIVE
cedi
cion
code
coed
coin
cone
cove
cued
dice
dine
dive
done
dove
dune
icon
nevi
nice
node
odic
once
oven
undo
vein
vend
vice
vide
vine
void

coven
dunce
envoi
indue
ounce
video
voice
induce
nevoid
novice
conduce
unvoiced

15

CONGRESS
cero
cone
core
corn
ergo
eros
gore
nose
ogre
once
rose
song
sore
cress
crone
cross
gorse
gross
scone
score
scorn
snore
censor
conger
sensor
engross

Words Within Words

16 CONSPICUOUS
cion
coin
coon
coop
coup
cusp
cuss
icon
onus
opus
pion
poco
pons
puss
snip
soon
soup
spin
spun
upon
conic
incus
pious
scion
scoop
sinus
snoop
sonic
spoon
sunup
coupon
cousin
poison
copious
pocosin
sinuous
couscous
conscious

dais
nosy
said
sand
soda
adios
anion
annoy
daisy
danio
noisy
sandy
synod
adonis

18 EFFICACIOUS
cafe
case
ceca
ciao
coca
coif
cuff
face
fief
fife
fuse
safe
sofa
cause
focus
sauce
scoff
scuff
accuse
fiasco
office
suffice

20 EPHEMERAL
ahem
alee
aper
earl
epee
hale
hare
harm

eros
gore
grog
ogre
reis
rise
rose
ruse
seer
sere
sire
sore
sour
suer
sure
urge
user
gorge
gorse
gouge
guise
osier
rogue
rouge
rouse
segue
serge
siege
surge
grouse
orgies
soiree
soggier

harp
heal
heap
hear
heel
helm
help
heme
hemp
here
lame
lamp
leap
leer
male
mare
marl
meal
mere
pale
palm
pare
peal
pear
peel
peer
perm
plea
pram
ramp
rape
real
ream
reap
reel
rhea
aleph
ample
harem
laree
leper
maple
melee
pearl

realm
repel
ampere
empale
hamper
repeal

21 EQUIVOCATE
auto
cave
ciao
cite
coat
cote
cove
cute
iota
quit
taco
toea
vatu
veto
vice
vita
vote
acute
civet
coati
covet
evict
ovate
quiet
quite
quoit
quota
quote
toque
vatic
voice
acquit
active
avocet

17 DIONYSIAN
anon
ayin

19 EGREGIOUS
egis
ergo

Words Within Words

equate
octave

EXACERBATE

22

abet
acre
area
bare
bate
bear
beat
beer
beet
beta
brat
care
cart
crab
race
rate
tare
taxa
tear
tree
abate
acerb
beret
brace
bract
carat
caret
cater
crate
eater
erect
exact
exert
extra
react
recta
taxer
trace
xebec

aerate
berate
create
rebate
cabaret
excreta
excrete
acerbate
execrate

FACTIOUS

23

auto
cast
ciao
coat
coif
cost
fact
fast
fiat
fist
foci
iota
oust
scat
sift
sofa
soft
stoa
suit
taco
tofu
tufa
ascot
coast
coati
focus
foist
ictus
scout
stoic
fiasco

FEASIBLE

24

able
alee
bail
bale
base
beef
bias
bile
ease
else
fail
feel
file
flea
flee
ilea
isle
leaf
lief
life
safe
sail
sale
seal
self
slab
aisle
basil
belie
easel
fable
false
lease
sable
bailee
belief

HOMOLOGOUS

25

glum
gosh
gush
logo

loom
lush
mush
ohms
shoo
slog
slug
slum
smog
smug
solo
soul
sumo
ghoul
gloom
mogul
sough
ghouls
slough

IGNOMINIOUS

26

goon
mini
miso
mono
moon
muon
noon
noun
onus
sign
sing
smog
smug
snug
song
soon
sumo
sung
minus
mongo
onion
union

isogon
mining
minion
musing
nosing
unison
mousing
noising
noising
noosing
ominous
unionism

LOGOGRIPH

27

girl
gogo
grip
grog
hoop
logo
loop
olio
polo
pooh
pool
poor
prig
roil
igloo
polio
gigolo
prolog

LOQUACIOUS

28

also
caul
ciao
coal
coil
cola
cool
loci

Words Within Words

loco
luau
olio
sail
silo
soil
solo
soul
quail
quasi
usual
quails
social

29 OPPROBRIUM

birr
boom
boor
brim
brio
bump
burp
burr
moor
pimp
pomp
poop
poor
pour
prim
prom
prop
pump
purr
romp
rump
broom
burro
opium
primp
prior
rumor

30 PEREMPTORY

eery
meet
mere
mete
mope
more
mote
peep
peer
perm
pert
poem
poet
pomp
pope
pore
port
prey
prom
prop
pyre
repp
romp
rope
rote
teem
term
tome
tore
torr
tory
tree
trey
troy
type
typo
tyre
tyro
yore
emery
emote
empty
merry

meter
mopey
peter
proem
retry
roper
tempo
terry
toper
tromp
trope
emoter
meteor
mopper
moppet
perter
peyote
poetry
porter
pretor
preyer
prompt
proper
remote
report
temper
tremor
emperor
preempt
property
pyrometer
preemptory

31 SOPHOMORIC

chip
chop
coop
corm
crop
hims
hoop
miso
moor

poco
pooh
poor
posh
prim
prom
rich
romp
shim
ship
shoo
chimp
chirp
choir
chomp
corps
crimp
crisp
micro
mooch
ohmic
oomph
pooch
porch
prism
scoop
scrip
spoor
chrism
mopish
scrimp
shrimp
smirch
smooch
isomorph

32 TEMPORIZE

emir
emit
item
meet
mere
mete

mire
mite
mope
more
mote
omit
peer
perm
pert
pier
poem
poet
pore
port
prim
prom
rime
riot
ripe
rite
romp
rope
rote
teem
term
tier
time
tire
tiro
tome
tore
tori
tree
trim
trio
trip
zero
emote
merit
meter
miter
peter
prime
prize

proem
remit
tempo
tripe
tromp
trope
empire
import
meteor
permit
premie
remote
temper
emptier
epitome

Crosswords - Easy

1

```
C A L E B   L E I S   E C H O
A R E N A   I L L Y   A L E C
K I N G S A L M O N   R A N T
E A T   T R I O   S P L I C E
      B E E T   E G R E T
S A R A   S H O W I E R
N O I R   C O C K E Y E D
U N T O   T A H O E   Y O K O
B E A N P O L E   T U E S
    O U T G R E W   E R S E
A L O F T     N O R A
D O U B T S   E Z R A   A L B
L U T E   L A D Y F I N G E R
E I R E   A D A M   N E R V E
R E E F   G A M E   S T A I D
```

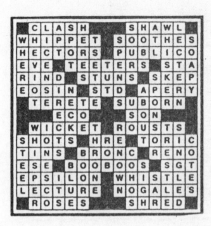

2

```
  C L A S H     S H A W L
W H I P P E T   S O O T H E S
H E C T O R S   P U B L I C O
E V E   T E E T E R S   S T A
R I N D   S T U N S   S K E P
E O S I N   S T D   A P E R Y
  T E R E T E   S U B O R N
    E C O     S O N
  W I C K E T   R O U S T S
S H O T S   H R E   T O R I C
T I N S   B R O N C   R E N O
E S E   B O O B O O S   S G T
E P S I L O N   W H I S T L E
L E C T U R E   N O G A L E S
  R O S E S     S H R E D
```

3

```
S H E M   E N A C T   P A T E
H O S T   D E F O E   A P A R
O U T E R S P A C E   T O R N
D R I V E   A R O M A T I Z E
    M E T T L E   T I N A S
C O A R S E   W E S T   T N T
D O T E   E T E R N A L
T H E S U N A L S O R I S E S
      T R I L L E R   N E L L
B O B   B E L T   E V E N L Y
A R E C A   O G R E S S
H E M I N G W A Y   S P I E D
A G O N   N A R R A T A B L E
M O A N   A D M A N   C L A M
A N N A   T E S L A   E E L Y
```

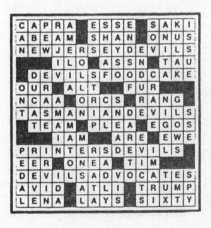

4

```
C A P R A   E S S E   S A K I
A B E A M   S H A N   O N U S
N E W J E R S E Y D E V I L S
    I L O   A S S N   T A U
  D E V I L S F O O D C A K E
O U R   A L T   F U R
N C A A   O R C S   R A N G
T A S M A N I A N D E V I L S
  T E A M   P L E A   E G O S
    I A M   A R E   E W E
P R I N T E R S D E V I L S
E E R   O N E A   T I M
D E V I L S A D V O C A T E S
A V I D   A T L I   T R U M P
L E N A   L A Y S   S I X T Y
```

5

```
S P I C A   C H O W   S H E M
A R G O S   A A R E   T O T O
L O O M S   F R E E Z E O U T
E S T E E M E D   O N D I T
    I R A S   A M M O
S H A N T Y   S W A B   E T A
E A S T   S H A R I   V O N
T I P O F T H E I C E B E R G
U K E   A B O R T   A N T E
P U N   R A T E   M A N T E L
    E R R S   C A R D
A S O L O   O U T R A G E D
C O L D W A T E R   E N O L A
T U L E   I R I S   S N E L L
S P A R   M A L E   T A S S E
```

6

```
C O M O   A L F A   E M S
O N E R   S L U R S   R I T A
T I L T   P O C A H O N T A S
T O G   L A N K Y   R E E L S
A N I M A T E   B A S S E T
  B A N E   B A I T
C A S T E   S E P T E M B E R
A L O T   B I G O T   E E L Y
B E N E F I T E D   B A S I E
    A B E T   S A L T
A T O L L S   M A N S A R D
L A V E S   B R A N D   C O E
B R A V E H E A R T   A T O M
S A T E   M A F I A   S O S O
  S E E   O T T O   A R T S
```

Crosswords - Easy

7

```
P A S S   A R A M   C A B S
A X I O M   L O S E   A G R A
Z E L D A   B O E R   N A I L
    A N N A K A R E N I N A
A L A   T O N Y   I R O N Y
P E N A L T Y   C L A N
P O N G E E   B O Y S   S R A
A N E T   D O N   E T A L
L E X   S T Y X   S E L E N E
    M O R E   S U L K I E R
    P L A T O   S H E A   N E T
T H E G O O D E A R T H
R O A N   P A I R   E E R I E
A N N E   E R N E   D A I S Y
P E S T   R E E D   D O M E
```

8

```
P A C A   G L Y P H   T A P S
I D O L   R A D I O   W R A P
L A N E   E S S E N   A I N U
A N T   A B E   D A N D E R
F O R E V E R Y O U N G
    A V A   O M R I   P S I
H A V E I T   U N A   A R A L
E V E R L A S T I N G L O V E
W O N T   N T H   G A G G E D
N N E   A G E E   F O R
    E T E R N A L F L A M E
R A P I E R   R U E   M O D
A M I D   I N C U R   A M I E
F E T E   N I O B E   B E R M
T S A R   E L G A R   A R E A
```

9

```
S A N A   E G A D S   S E L L
E R I S   R A M I E   P L E A
T I C K E R T A P E   L A N D
A S H   W O E S   D A I N T Y
T E E T E R S   F L I T
    I R S   F L I M S I E R
S C A M S   B R A N   E D D A
T O B E   S L I N G   C O I N
A L E C   P E E K   D O L E D
G E T A H E A D   M O N
    P O E T   L A N D I N G
C H A S E D   S O S O   T O O
P E R U   W A T C H T O W E R
O R A L   A W A K E   D A L E
S A B E   Y E S E S   A S S N
```

10

```
T O M S   S T A L L   A S T A
E T U I   I O N I A   S L O W
A T O N   S I T O N   P A R E
L O N G I S L A N D   E N I D
    L A Y S   S E N D
H E L E N   H A L T   E B B
A L A S   C R E D I T   R E A
G I N   F L O R I D A   O S S
A D D   D E N O T E   S U E T
R E L   I V A N   C E S T A
    O N C E   A G R A
M A C E   L A N D L U B B E R
A U K S   A L A M O   E A V E
T R E T   N O N E S   E R I E
T A D S   D E A N S   S E L L
```

11

```
D A M E   F A K I R   H O S E
O K A Y   E L I T E   A G T S
D I K E   L E T S H E R R I P
O N E   R I C E   E L L E R Y
    T H A N K   S A L E
G A R A G E   S C R A M B L E
A M A Z E   C H E S S   U A R
L U C Y   P H O N E   D R U M
A S K   P R A T E   L E N D A
S E S S I O N S   G E N R E S
    L E T T   B A N T U
S O L A C E   A L G A   B O P
S H A K E S A L E G   A B L E
T I M E   T R I A L   F E E S
S O B S   S T A K E   T R O T
```

12

```
S P A S   S T R I P   S A N D
P U S H   T R I C E   I L A Y
A R I A   R U L E R   N O M E
T E A M M A T E   S E A T E D
    P A T H   A U N T
P A G O D A S   M A D R A S
O L E O   H I D E A W A Y
T I E   S T A I N E D   A V E
S E S S I O N S   B R O W
N E E D E D   C A R E E R S
    D E N Y   O R A L
A R M A D A   F O R M L E S S
M O A T   I M A G E   H A L O
A D Z E   L A M A S   O V A L
H E E D   S C E N T   P E P O
```

Crosswords - Easy

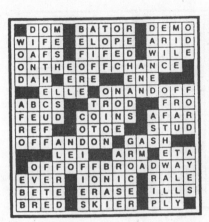

13

```
D E L I S   T R I G     G P O
A G O R A   A U T O S   R E V
L A B O R O F L O V E   E R A
E L O N G A T E   E N T A I L
    H E S S   T R A I T
M U T A N T   C O N T E S T S
I D O N T   C A N O E   L I E
M A I D   T A P E R   S A M E
I L L   E R R E D   F A V O R
C L E A N E R S   M I L E R S
    T I D E S   T O N I
M A R M O T   S A R A N A C S
O V I   W O R K I N G G I R L
V I E   S P A I N   L E R O I
E D S   S E N T   E R E C T
```

14

```
  D O M   B A T O R   D E M O
W I F E   E L O P E   A R I D
O A F S   F I F E D   W I L E
O N T H E O F F C H A N C E
D A H   E R E   E N E
  E L L E   O N A N D O F F
A B C S   T R O D   F R O
F E U D   C O I N S   A F A R
R E F   O T O E   S T U D
O F F A N D O N   G A S H
  L E I   A R M   E T A
  O F F O F F B R O A D W A Y
E V E R   I O N I C   R A L E
B E T E   E R A S E   I L L S
B R E D   S K I E R   P L Y
```

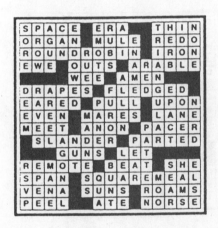

15

```
S T I R   A B B Y   S T O R K
T Y R E   D O R A   A E R I E
E P I C   A N I M A T E D L Y
M E D E   M U D   R E D O E S
S E E D S   S A L A D
  S E T A   L O B   A M P S
E T C   A L I V E   O V E R A
T H E B R I D E W O R E R E D
T I N E S   L I E N S   R Y E
A N T E   D E L   T O R Y
    S E R F S   N E W E L
A S S U M E   A P E   G I L A
M E T R O P O L I S   E D E N
A G E N T   B L E T   N O N E
H O R S E   I S L E   T W A S
```

16

```
S P A C E   E R A     T H I N
O R G A N   M U L E   R E D O
R O U N D R O B I N   I R O N
E W E   O U T S   A R A B L E
    W E E   A M E N
D R A P E S   F L E D G E D
E A R E D   P U L L   U P O N
E V E N   M A R E S   L A N E
M E E T   A N O N   P A C E R
  S L A N D E R   P A R T E D
    G U N S   L E T
R E M O T E   B E A T   S H E
S P A N   S Q U A R E M E A L
V E N A   S U N S   R O A M S
P E E L   A T E   N O R S E
```

17

```
1P A G 2E D  6Y E L 8P  10G O A L
14A G A V E  15O L E O  16I S L E
17C R E E L  18O B O L  19G L A D
20A L L E G H A N Y 22M O O N
     23T O O   24M A L
25F L Y M E T O T H E M O O N
33R E A R S  34R A R A  35N I P
37A A H S  38P L U G S  40T E T E
41U S O  42T R O T  43M E T R O
44H O W H I G H T H E M O O N
  48H I S   49H A L
50M O O N O V E R M I 54A M I
57B A L L  58N I L E  59S P A R E
61A R I L  62E L L A  63S O L A R
64D E N Y  65R E E D  66A D L E R
```

18

```
H A R P   B E R N E   B A L T
O R E L   A N I O N   A W A Y
L A D Y A N D T H E T R A M P
E G O   A N O A     A G R E E
    B R E W   C A R E E R S
R A C I E R   H E F T S
I C O N   M E A R A   A P E
T H E S U N A L S O R I S E S
Z E D   P U R E E   N E A T
    A R D E N   E S T A T E
M O T T O E S   O S L O
A N I T A   A U T O   F A D
R E T U R N O F T H E J E D I
I R A N   A C A R E   O U Z O
E S N E   B A R E R   E D E R
```

Crosswords - Easy

19

```
R U H R   S T A G     B O B
O S I E R   P O R E   T A N A
A N G L E   I N C R E A S E S
M A H O G A N Y   B I K E R S
    W A R T S   M I R E
H E A D E R   P O L E S T A R
I V Y   T I A R A S   T E N O
D O M E S   G E T   P O L I O
E K E D   T I S S U E   E S T
S E N A T O R S   S L A V E S
      C A R L   H E I D I
E N S I L E   N A R C O S E S
L I T T E R B A G   A N I L E
A D A Y   O A H U   N I O B E
L E T   S A S E   S N A P
```

20

```
M A T C H   A M E S   A J A R
A L O H A   P A S T   B A T E
J A M E S J O Y C E   S C A N
    R T A   S A N   T O L E
T I J U A N A   P O T A B L E
A R A B   E R S E   H I J
T A N S   D C I   M E N A C E
U N I   J O H N J A Y   V A T
M I S C U E   G I S   D I S H
    J O G   G E N T   I T T O
S P O N S O R   N E M E S E S
C U P S   B E A   R O D
E R L E   J E N N Y J O N E S
N E I N   E C T O   O W E N S
T E N T   T E S T   S N E E R
```

21

```
B A R O N   A C E D   T B A R
A L A M O   C A S H   R U S E
N I N E S   T U N A   A R K S
J A I L H O U S E R O C K
O R N E   A P E   M U T E S
      T D S   B A T I S T A
A P C   I T A L Y   O L I N
B E R E T   D O T   E N A C T
E R I N   D W E L L   W K S
T O M T O M S   O K A
  T E R R Y   R O C   V I A L
  W E B O F E V I D E N C E
C H A P   P A V E   A N T R A
V I V O   I C E R   L U R E S
I M E T   C E L T   Y E A S T
```

22

```
B O N D   P E C O S   U T A H
A R E A   E X A L T   N I L E
J A W B R E A K E R   F L E A
A L S   O N C E   A M U L E T
    C O A S T   S T A R
S C A L D   S T E R L I N G
O A S E S   T H U G S   N E E
U P T O   S H I N Y   I V A N
S E E   A P A R T   L O I R E
A R R O G A N T   A N G S T
    N E C K   S A Y S O
R E C E D E   G A B E   R A W
A V O W   B A L D E R D A S H
M I C A   A D E A L   E T T A
P L A Y   R E N T E   N E A T
```

23

```
R A P T   M O S T   U R G E D
O L L A   A L E E   N A O M I
A L U M   S I L L   W H O M P
R O M A N C O L L A R   S A L
S T E R E O   S C A L E
      E T A L   O P E N E R
M U T E D   S E A R   T E L E
A S I A   C H A I N   U C L A
M E E T   H E R D   A S K E D
A S S U R E   N E E R
    O P E R A   M A S E R S
F A N   W I N D S O R K N O T
A R E T E   D U E T   I D L Y
S T O O D   E P E E   L U L L
T E N T S   S E N D   L E S E
```

24

```
    C R A N K   R A F T S
  S H A R E D   E R R A T A
T O E N A I L   W E A R A N D
E R A   B L A T A N T   R O I
A T T S   S N O R T   E T O N
S E E K S   G O D   P A U S E
E D D I E S       L I S P E R
      L D S   A M T
T A B L E T   P A M P E R
A D L E R   G A T   S A L L Y
L O U T   C A R E S   N E E D
O R B   S H I M M E R   A V E
N E B U L A E   P R E S S E R
  R E T O R T   L I C H E N
  R E E D Y   E N T E R
```

Crosswords - Medium

1

```
D I R T   C A T S   S H O T
U S E R   U R B A N   T O R E
E L I A   N A C R E   A P E X
S E N D O F F S   A R R E S T
      E M I T   S K I T
S P R I N T   C H E S S M A N
I R A N I   W H E R E   O N E
R A G S   C O A L S   C O N E
E T E   C A R O L   L U R I D
D E S C E N D S   J E R S E Y
      A N T S   C O A T
S A L U T E   S H I P A H O Y
A L O G   E L T O N   I O N S
I T C H   N E A R S   N O M E
L O O T   S A G E   S T E R
```

2

```
H I S S   B I D E D   B A T S
A N T E   A L I V E   O L E O
I T A L   B A S I C   T A R N
L O R D L Y   C L O T H I N G
      O A T H   D O E
R O O M M A T E   E R R O R S
I N T   B L U R S   E R I K
S I T S   K N I T S   D A V E
K N E W   T E A C H   T A W
S E R E N E   S T R U D E L S
      E A R   E A S E
C R I T T E R S   P H A S E S
A I D E   C H E A P   L U L L
S T E S   T E N S E   E R L E
T E S T   S A T E D   R E A D
```

3

```
L A T H   M O T I F   U T A H
O G E E   I L O V E   N O R A
F U R Y   S E R I N   M U M S
T E N D E R   N E C T A R S
      A B U T   D E A N
N A V Y B L U E   S O N A R
O R E   S E N D S   S E D E R
D I R K   E G O   D O L E
E A V E S   R A B B I   R I D
S E E P S   R E A D I N G S
      P I T T   R U E S
M U S T A R D   B A L S A M
S A R A   P E R I L   A L M A
H U N K   L E A V E   N O E S
E L S E   E D G E S   D E S K
```

4

```
B A R N   E S T E S   C L O D
E R I E   G L O A T   L O G E
T A T A   G O R S E   A A R E
E B E R T   P A T T E R N E D
      M O E   H E S S E
R A C I E S T   R O S T E R S
E W E S   S I E N N A   M A E
L A S S O   R T E   Y E A R N
I S T   S T E E R S   P I E D
C H A T T E L   S I M I L E S
      H I R E R   P U G
R E H E A R S E D   D R E A M
A D A M   A S N E R   A L O E
T A R E   C L E A N   P I N A
A M P S   E Y E R S   H E E D
```

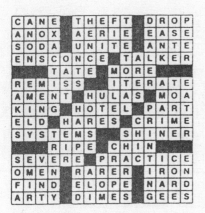

5

```
C A N E   T H E F T   D R O P
A N O X   A E R I E   E A S E
S O D A   U N I T E   A N T E
E N S C O N C E   T A L K E R
      T A T E   M O R E
R E M I S S   I T E R A T E
A M E N T   H U L A S   M O A
K I N G   H O T E L   P A R T
E L D   H A R E S   C R I M E
S Y S T E M S   S H I N E R
      R I P E   C H I N
S E V E R E   P R A C T I C E
O M E N   R A R E R   I R O N
F I N D   E L O P E   N A R D
A R T Y   D I M E S   G E E S
```

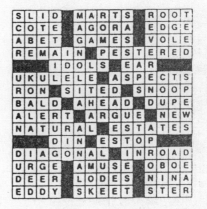

6

```
S L I D   M A R T S   R O O T
C O T E   A G O R A   E D G E
A B E T   G A M E S   V O L E
R E M A I N   P E S T E R E D
      I D O L S   E A R
U K U L E L E   A S P E C T S
R O N   S I T E D   S N O O P
B A L D   A H E A D   D U P E
A L E R T   A R G U E   N E W
N A T U R A L   E S T A T E S
      D I N   E S T O P
D I A G O N A L   I N R O A D
U R G E   A M U S E   O B O E
D E E R   L O D E S   N I N A
E D D Y   S K E E T   S T E R
```

Crosswords - Medium

7

```
MESS  SAMBA  GRAM
ALAW  ADIOS  LOBE
DALE  LODES  IDES
ELEANOR  RUEDELA
    TOME   AWE
ACCEDE  WAGERERS
SHORE  FARES  VAT
HANS  DANES  LENA
END  DOLLS  BONER
STOWAWAY  LENSES
   ANN   DARE
ATTRACT  OUTSIDE
COIN  AHAND  OREL
ERNE  SAREE  MEAL
SEED  TIRED  EDNA
```

8

```
HILT  NESTS  SOLE
ODOR  EATEN  PLAT
SODA  CRANE  REIN
ELEVATE  TAPIOCA
   EGAD   KIN
ANGLER  SMELTING
CARES  SCARE  ROE
TIER  PLODS  DOVE
EVE  ALINE  PINES
DETONATE  HASSLE
   COT   PORT
MEMENTO  AMIABLE
ORAL  EMOTE  NOEL
SILO  RIDER  CATS
SNIT  STENS  ERSE
```

9

```
TARS  CHARS  CHAP
ALEE  HELEN  LANE
BONN  AROSE  ARTE
SEDATION  EASTER
   TIS   GERMS
REVERE  DESERTS
ANISE  AGER  SHOE
ITS  DEFENSE  IKE
SETA  ATTS  WANED
ERASURE  LEMONY
   ANDRE   ERA
ADORER  DRESSERS
PERU  UNDER  SPAT
ELAL  MAINE  EIRE
RILE  SPEED  SCAM
```

10

```
SWAP  SHEDS  SAND
LAMA  CADET  TRIO
EVIL  ALICE  PILE
DESI  MOTORCADE
   MAPS   LOU
ACROSS  SPILLED
MOONS  STAND  LOP
PLOY  BEING  ALOE
STS  EARLS  AGENT
STARLET  SHINES
RIM  COAT
CAMCORDER  PLAT
TORO  READE  RODE
OMAR  ANTES  OVEN
EELY  LEAST  PEND
```

11

```
PEALS  DUD  DIANA
ARROW  UKE  ANGER
CANOE  CAM  STOAT
STONEMASON  OGRE
   TETE   OWN
FACED  BREADED
DETONATOR  ETUDE
ALIT  LURED  INGE
DOLTS  BARITONES
ANTOINE  VANES
   NNE  STAB
AMES  AUTONOMOUS
TENET  ROD  ROUSE
OSIER  SRA  ENTER
PADDY  AMY  TASSE
```

12

```
SPIN  RAPS  RAMP
TARO  EMILE  OPIE
ALAN  CAPER  MESA
GENESIS  DEPARTS
   ITS   CAN
ORATE  POTS  SPA
CLOVE  CARETAKER
HIVE  COPED  RATE
OVERTAKES  TOTES
PER  ONER  LONER
   END   CAL
BRAVELY  RUDDERS
LIME  EATER  AREA
OPEN  SLATE  DIAL
WENT  EDEN  ACRE
```

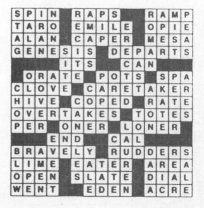

Crosswords - Medium

13

```
D A D O   C A L F   P R A T E
O R A N   A B I E   R U L E D
O G R E   P O M E   E N D E D
R U N A R O U N D   S T O N Y
S E S T E T     S O A O
      N E R D   P O S T E R
A P O R T   E A R N   E A V E
M E N U   P A R E E   E R I N
I R A N   A D E N   A D E L E
D I N N E R   D O T E
    E A S T   A R A B I C
A B O R T   R U N N Y M E D E
M O R S E   O P E N   A R I L
I N C U R   O T O E   S L O T
S N A P S   P S N P   S E T S
```

14

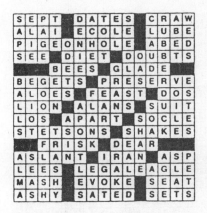

```
S E P T   D A T E S   C R A W
A L A I   E C O L E   L U B E
P I G E O N H O L E   A B E D
S E E   D I E T   D O U B T S
      B E E S   G L A D E
B E G E T S   P R E S E R V E
A L O E S   F E A S T   D O S
L I O N   A L A N S   S U I T
L O S   A P A R T   S O C L E
S T E T S O N S   S H A K E S
    F R I S K   D E A R
A S L A N T   I R A N   A S P
L E E S   L E G A L E A G L E
M A S H   E V O K E   S E A T
A S H Y   S A T E D   S E T S
```

15

```
S A L A   A L D A   I C E D
T O E S   M O I R E   N O L O
O N T H E B R A I N   O R S O
P E A   A L E S   T A N K E R
    O V E N   A R T E
C L O N E S   F R E E S I A
H E R O   P L I E   B R I M
A M A N   C L U E S   L A R A
T O T E   H U N S   O N E R
N E S T E G G   A V O I D S
    C E E S   F R E D
G O P H E R   L I N T   M A C
O G L E   I N O N E S H A I R
O R E S   O A S E S   A I D E
F E A T   T E S S   S L A W
```

16
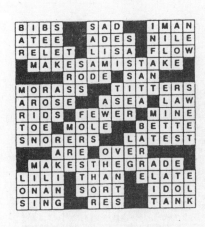

```
B I B S     S A D   I M A N
A T E E   A D E S   N I L E
R E L E T   L I S A   F L O W
M A K E S A M I S T A K E
      R O D E   S A N
M O R A S S   T I T T E R S
A R O S E   A S E A   L A W
R I D S   F E W E R   M I N E
T O E   M O L E   B E T T E
S N O R E R S   L A T E S T
    A R E   O V E R
M A K E S T H E G R A D E
L I L I   T H A N   E L A T E
O N A N   S O R T   I D O L
S I N G   R E S   T A N K
```

17

```
P I P E   D A M P   R A P I D
A V O N   E L I A   E L I T E
R A N G   C O S T   T A L O N
E N D U R A N C E   A R E N T
    L U N E   S L I M
B U F F E T   U N S E A T
O T I S   H A S T E   M A R
R I B   S H E L T E R   O R E
I C E   C O N E Y   S T O A
S A R A H S   P A T E N T
    T O E S   M E N U
E R A T O   C R E D I T O R S
P U P I L   R A R A   T R U E
I S E R E   A N I L   E D I T
C E D E D   P I T S   R O N S
```

18

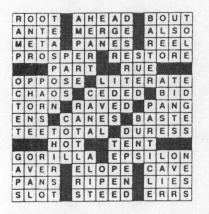

```
R O O T   A H E A D   B O U T
A N T E   M E R G E   A L S O
M E T A   P A N E S   R E E L
P R O S P E R   R E S T O R E
      P A R T   R U E
O P P O S E   L I T E R A T E
C H A O S   C E D E D   B I D
T O R N   R A V E D   P A N G
E N S   C A N E S   B A S T E
T E E T O T A L   D U R E S S
      H O T   T E N T
G O R I L L A   E P S I L O N
A V E R   E L O P E   C A V E
P A N S   R I P E N   L I E S
S L O T   S T E E D   E R R S
```

Crosswords - Difficult

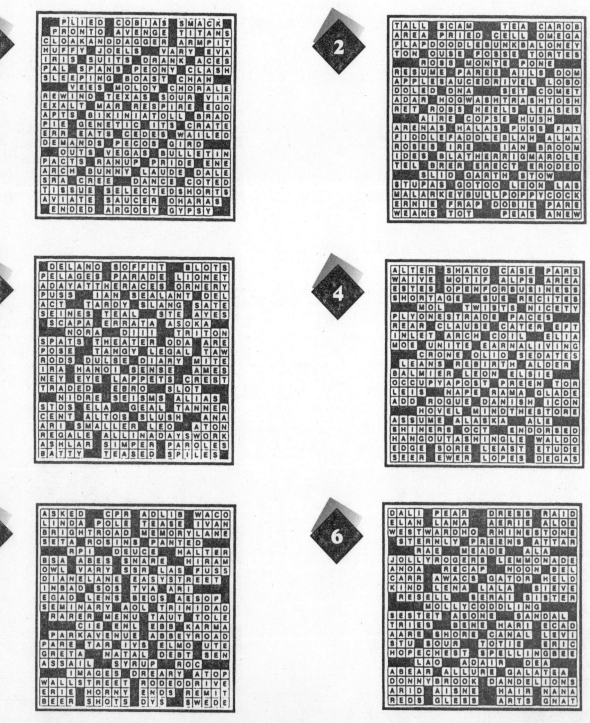

Crosswords - Difficult

7

```
LAMAS PAGAN SEEK FALA
OVATE ALENE ETRE IRON
GERMANYGRABSRHINELAND
ERE MODEM AVON ALLEY
RADAR MIXES PRE
BALONEY NINES BENDERS
ANEW SAND EON LAE
GONEWITHTHEWINDDEBUTS
EDD ROMEO TRADE MODES
LESSENED NEONS SPIEL
ASIN DARTS LOIS
DELTA FROME MAUREENS
ARTEL MIAMI SEINE LAP
ROOSEVELTINALANDSLIDE
INN ARE AGON ADEN
DESPOIL PUTUP CULVERT
AWL PAREE CANOE
ABODE MIND MARIS HOP
BRADDOCKOJTPOINTSBAER
EARL LIEU BERRA ERNIE
LESE DIRT STOOL SADLY
```

8

```
CHEF SOMES POLAR FARM
RARE PROVE IRENE IDEE
AVID EARED RIVAL FORE
SECONDLANGUAGES STRUT
SNARE STENCIL ATHENS
ASSISI AYN ANYA
ENS TED DAB PRY MEAN
ROOF RETELL ORT TERRE
SARI AAR LEGREE INLAW
THIRDPLACE RIF INDEBT
SUE COG OBI NAM
ABATES TRE SIXTHSENSE
GRIST COPSES ERA NOOK
RIDES ARS YESSES TOLE
AGAR DRS EDE ETC NOD
GARY PAL COSELL
CREEPY GREETER AORTA
RABAT FOURTHDIMENSION
IRON LIANA RESEW SANG
CENT OCTET ERODE ETAL
KEYS TASSE ESNES SALE
```

9

```
HOST POSH CAREW SOBER
ACTA CAPO AWASH TROVE
REAM STLAWRENCESEAWAY
ALTER AREAS ATOLL
SOU ODESSA OPTOMETRY
STELSEWHERE SEETO HUE
EINE CREED SCULL
TITAN SPICE FIDEL
YVESSTLAURENT ELIA
LORE RAFTS DANGER ALG
ERS EATEN HORAE RIO
RYE ABHRAM AIRES PIER
ASHE MOUNTSTHELENS
SKIRT OSSIE VALSE
CASKS ATONE OPEN
UNI TERRA STVALENTINE
DESOLATES RESENT SOX
NORIA STUNT STOVE
STPAULSCATHEDRAL OBIT
IRANI ALGAE EASE MACE
BANDS NEATO ELAN BRER
```

10

```
MASSA MAB CCC SEPALS
TACTIC ARAPAHO APOGEE
ESCORT STEELER CAROMS
STEP OSCARWINNER TROT
LESS RIO ILA SANE
ARSIS STEINBECK GUEST
GUM SEVILLE BUD
MARNIE RABAT UNAPT
UVEA MAVIN COROT NORM
RIAL OBIES KNELT TIO
MAGS REX ADE CLEO
UTE ALECS SOTER LUST
REND BENET WHARF ACTE
STILL SAMOA LURKED
VIE TAILORS YMA
MOPED CARDINALS ABASH
ITER POL UTA AQHA
LOOS OGLALACHIEF ROIL
LORIES OLYMPIC INTUNE
ELIOTS WIMPOLE ROOTER
SEANCE SEE SOS ENNIS
```

11

```
MACRO SAIL STIR LURES
ASHEN UCLA AIDE AGILE
THEBEVERLYHILLBILLIES
SETASIDE SONDE RAISES
HEE FLUTE BAKE
CAMEOS GOOSE SEDERUNT
APART PLOWEDUNDER RAW
BUYS BAAL NOES OBIE
ORB BARNSWALLOW BRAVE
TEETERED AVOID HOANED
ROTOR BLAST TOXIC
GERMAN BELIE COMESOFF
RAYES RURALROUTES WAR
ERRS BORE PREY ABBY
ELF COUNTRIFIED THOLE
REDBONES ELAND PRAYER
EONS STILE ORA
CASTLE STEAL IRONSIDE
THEHATFIELDSANDMCCOYS
RAVES ARIL ISEE EATEN
STELA DENS NEER STARE
```

12

```
SGT JOWLS LEADA ACES
LEO ETHERS ACTOR TAFT
ONO THENANDTHERE ACRE
BOLSTERS ORION ROSTER
ASPIRE TWAS TEATIME
ORES FRIGHT HARE
CAFES TRIES RAIDS TAW
ANTE QUEER SIBBY SAGA
BAH CURED DACHA ATTIC
STEPHEN ALICK NONETOO
TRUST NITRO DROVE
CORINTH DATER TIDERIP
ALACK ENTRY TEHEE EGO
SIDE STARS ARTAL ADOS
TOE ELIHU GREAT SPARE
ARID EDEMAS CAIN
STORAGE ERST SALADS
HEARTH FONDA SPRINTER
RAKE TWISTANDTURN OLE
USES LOTTE DEARIE RMS
BENT YESED BYTES NAT
```

Crosswords - Difficult

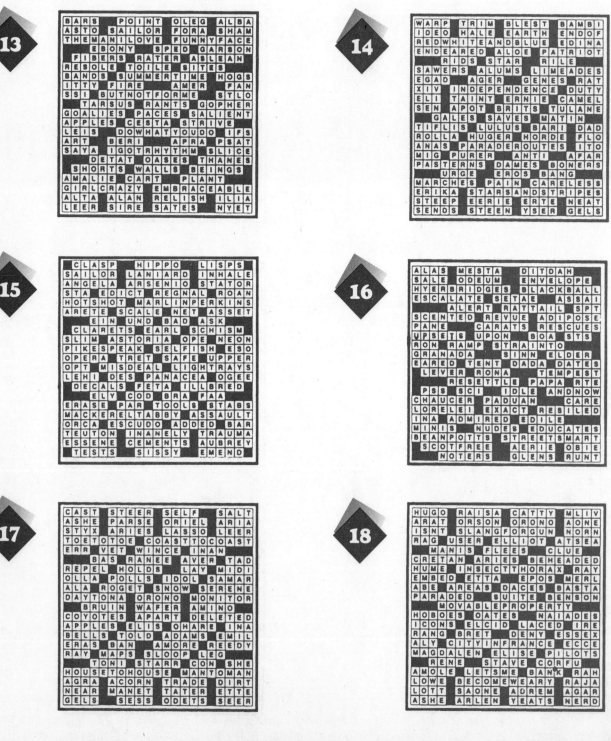

Crosswords - Difficult

Diagramlesses

19

```
PADS CHOP  TREATY SALT
ALOT RENO  EARTHA ANEW
STOA ALEX  KNUTEROCKNE
TORNADOS STEPS  PRATE
   DOLT QUIET GLEE
SPLINE SUETS BOUNDERS
CRANE BLADE OUTRE MAI
AITS IRADE ONTHEROCKS
MME ERIN BRATS   CEES
SPROCKETS RAGE EATERY
   NOES PEALE SINE
APPEND RATS ROCKETTES
BERG DINAH ZOOT   AMA
BREAKROCKS SHORN ABES
ELS NAVES DOONE ALOES
SEAROVER TEASE STARRY
   EWER SABRE SNOB
ABEAM TUNAS CLEMATIS
SOFTENROCKS ALIA MAXI
ANTA ENTREE YANK ARIL
NESS EASERS EDGY NEAT
```

1

```
    T A N   A T E
  P O R E   P A N   M T V
  T A C E T   O D D   C O I N
  A D S   A U G     I N T O
    B R E D       I A N
O T C   G E E   B B C
P E R   G R E   G A L A
T A T T O O   R E T A R D
  R O T O   B M W   T A O
  A Y N   F R O   M P G
C O B   T O L D
O P A L   C E O   O F F
P U C E   E L K   C A B A L
  S K I   L E E   P O S Y
    M O D   T E T
```

2

```
A N N A   R A G   A B E D
D A U B   O L E   B A K E
S Y N E   D I N   C H E W
  T A P E   E R A S
  C I O   S A M
C R A T E   N A B O B
N A B     E A U
N Y M P H   R E E F S
  F A A   S I R
  A C M E   A G E S
S T A B   O C T   O R B S
B A R B   N E E   L O R E
A N T E   S O D   S E A T
```

3

```
  G N P   P R O
  H A I R   L A W
  A B B E   A G E S
B E T S   H E N   A H A
Y E A   C I A   H E M
E L L   L I E U   I R A
  C A C A O   H U B
  P A D   H I S
  D E M   H A T E D
A D O   T A U T   A D S
W A S   E K E   B I O
E W E   L E A   E S P Y
  S A L E   L A S S
  S E A   A T O P
  H O D   M E D
```

Diagramlesses

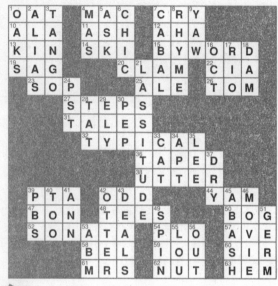

Grid 4:
```
O A T   M A C   C R Y
A L A   A S H   A H A
K I N   S K I   B Y W O R D
S A G   C L A M   C I A
    S O P   A L E   T O M
    S T E P S
    T A L E S
    T Y P I C A L
    T A P E D
    U T T E R
P T A   O D D     Y A M
B O N   T E E S   B O G
S O N A T A   P L O   A V E
    B E L   I O U   S I R
    M R S   N U T   H E M
```

Grid 5:
```
D U O
O F F     M A T   D A Y
T O T S   E V E   D O L E
    A C U M E N   I C E S
    D A N E   S A C
V I D E O     R E B U S
A S H   D R A T   A N T
T H E Y   N I X   D E A R
E R E   B A B E   V I A
S E N O R   A L E R T
    D A D   T A N S
U S E D   A W A K E N
R A Y S   T A B   E A C H
N N E   A R C   D A W
            S L Y
```

Grid 6:
```
F R A
L A P   A F T   F W D
O P T S   P R O M   C H A R
    A R R O Y O   I C I L Y
    U F O   M I A   T E E
    P E T   O N E
M R S   A L A N   M P G
M A O   M E N   A I R
A K A   M A I D   N E E
S E R E N E     B A R
    R A T S   S O T
S C O O P   C A B I N E T
H U T S   A R I D   D A M P
Y E T   M I X   F O E
            T E N
```

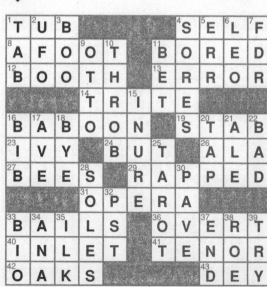

Grid 7:
```
T U B       S E L F
A F O O T   B O R E D
B O O T H   E R R O R
      T R I T E
B A B O O N   S T A B
I V Y   B U T   A L A
B E E S   R A P P E D
    O P E R A
B A I L S   O V E R T
I N L E T   T E N O R
O A K S     D E Y
```

Diagramlesses

8

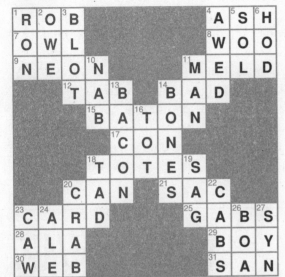

```
 R O B       A S H
 O W L       W O O
 N E O N   M E L D
   T A B   B A D
   B A T O N
     C O N
     T O T E S
   C A N   S A C
 C A R D   G A B S
 A L A     B O Y
 W E B     S A N
```

9

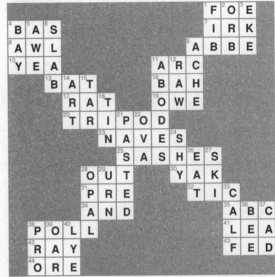

```
                 F O E
 B A S           I R K
 A W L         A B B E
 Y E A     A R C
   B A T     B A H
   R A T   O W E
   T R I P O D
     N A V E S
       S A S H E S
     O U T   Y A K
     P R E   T I C
     A N D     A B C
 P O L L       L E A
 R A Y         F E D
 O R E
```

10

```
         N F L
 T E A   B R E E D S
 A R M   C O O K I E
 B R I G   E E C
 B O A   E R E   C U D
 H O N   M A R   W A S
 P S T   P A L A T E
       S A T
     S E E D E D   A F T
     B A D   R I B   M E N
   M A T   S P A   B L T
 P O I     N O L O
 E N C A M P     D E N
 W E E V I L     D R Y
       E L Y
```